Flashes Forever

Flashes Forever

A History

of the

Greenville High School Flaming Flashes

Greenville, Texas
1928-2015

Mary J. Vance

© 2015 Mary Jane Vance
All Rights Reserved.

Flashes Forever

Dedication

It is a great honor to dedicate this book to

Lori L. Butler
Director
The Flaming Flashes

Miss Butler has reached out and touched the lives of so many young girls through the years. A close, tight-knit group, The Flaming Flashes have flourished under her leadership. As a member, one learns leadership, integrity, respect, and so much more. She is a prime example of the attributes of being a Flaming Flash.

> We are the Flashes, the Flashes are we.
> We never lose our kick ability.
> We have the smiles that outshine the rest,
> And everyday at work and play the Flashes are the best.
> Oh, yes, we're proud of our honor, proud of our fame.
> Proud of our glory and loyal to our name.
> The name of the Flashes will always stand…
> Will stand for truth and right
> Flaming Flashes…you're all right.
> WHOO!

We love you,

Kacie N. Vance, Colonel
The Flaming Flashes
2013-2014

Greenville High School, Wesley Street, ca. 1930.

GHS Gymnasium, King Street.

Author's Note

Many individuals, past and present, have written about the early history of The Flaming Flashes of Greenville High School in Greenville, Texas. The proud heritage of being the first high school precision dance and drill team in the nation was initiated when Gussie Nell Davis, a native of Farmersville, Texas, began her first year of teaching physical education at Greenville High School in 1928. Miss Davis saw the need for activities involving high school girls and created a pep squad which later evolved as a drum and bugle corps. While there were some female drum and bugle corps who performed at football games in the early 1930s, Miss Davis' Flashes were the first in the nation to include dancing and twirling drills. The rest, as they say, is history...a cherished history which must be preserved for posterity.

We offer this history as a token of appreciation for the leadership of Lori L. Butler, Director of The Flaming Flashes, as she celebrates twenty-five years of service as their mentor, and pray that someone else will pick up the baton to continue recording the future accomplishments of such a prestigious organization.

All historical data are accurate as reported. Names of individuals and dates are correct as taken from written records researched for this compilation of facts and memorabilia. The contributions by various individuals are recorded as submitted/edited and are deeply appreciated. All records were not available.

Mary J. Vance
Author of
Mary of the Angels
Darkness to Light

Directors

Flashes

1928-1939	Gussie Nell Davis
1939 Fall	Frances Flournoy (Fifth-Year Flash) (Student Director—Two yrs. as Head Drum Major)
1940 Spring-1943	Eugenia Johnston
1943-1944	Dorothy McQuary
1944-1946	Rosabel Williams (1946-Warren)
1946-1948	Juanita "Bill" Daniel
1948-1953	Rosemary Middlebrook
1953-1954	Sandy Allbright
1954-1960	Margaret Schulze
1960-1961	Mary Jane Vance
1961-1963	Lesby Daniels Rhodes
1963-1964	Janet Bryant
1964 Fall	Gay Kinnamon
1965 Spring-1966	Patricia Danaher
1966-1968	Mary Jane Vance
1968-1972	Linda Brantley
1972-1975	Carol McDonald
1975-1984	Pam Clayton
1984-1985	Betty Ballard
1985 Summer	Mary Patterson & Sarah Jane Wright (Volunteers)
1985-1990	Shannon Karr
1990-	Lori L. Butler

Band

1931-1933	Marvin Bush
1933-1959	Ed Bernard
1959-1962	Eldon Janzen
1962-1964	Bob Ingram
1964-1976	Bob Cartwright
1976-1979	Leonard (Lenny) Walker
1979-1985	Bill Goodson
1985-1986	James Coffman
1986-1998	Larry Miears
1998-Fall 2006	Tony Kullmer
Spring 2007	Bill Goodson
2007-2012	Kyle Treadwell
2012-2013	Aubrey Williams
2013-	Joel Weisberg

Acknowledgements

My deepest appreciation goes to the following:

- Friends, family, and professional contacts (to name each of you would create another chapter), who provided information and resources through phone calls, correspondence, or emails; and, for their encouragement and support;
- Mrs. Cinda Boshart, GHS Librarian, and Kaylee Molina (and others), who provided access and assistance in making copies of selected pages of available copies of the GHS Yearbook, *The Lion,* in order to obtain important information for this history;
- Mrs. Judy Woods, who loaned copies of newspaper clippings, letters, and other documents pertaining to the Flashes;
- Dr. Mike Adkisson, for invaluable photos and memories;
- Mrs. Mae Merrick Pickens and Mrs. Billie Pickens, for sharing their yearbooks and memories of the Flashes (1938-1942);
- Ms. Vivian Freeman, Past President of the Silver Leos Writers Guild, for her steadfast support, and professional services; and,
- Kacie N. Vance, our granddaughter (2013-14 Colonel of The Flaming Flashes), who inspired me, through her dedication and endurance when faced with extreme challenges, to write this book. Once a Flash…always a Flash. Flashes Forever.

Foreword

"Friday Night Football" is an American tradition across this country, not just in Texas! Does football exist anywhere else? You bet! "Friday Night Football" is not just about the game. High school games without drill teams, bands, and cheerleaders are not very exciting for half the population. Programs emerged alongside the sport in the twentieth century. One program in particular, the drill team, has deep roots in Greenville, Texas.

In the early 1930s a Greenville teacher, Gussie Nell Davis, began an all-girl pep squad that grew into a drum and bugle corps. In October 1932, her "girls" used sparklers, firecrackers, and Roman candles to deliver a "flashing" halftime performance. GHS Head Coach Henry Frnka was impressed! He said his team was the "thunder" and Gussie Nell's "girls" were the lightning… "the flash that followed." Frnka brought the Texas State Championship home in 1933. Using Coach Frnka's remarks, "The Flaming Flashes" became the first high school precision drill/dance team in the nation in 1934. Miss Davis left Greenville in 1939 to start a similar group, "The Kilgore Rangerettes," at Kilgore, Texas.

The Flashes developed a loyal following, along with a rich set of traditions, and are more than a precision drill/dance team. Military style discipline and precision dance routines, featuring their famous high kicks, are an integral part of the program. Dedication and commitment are required to become officers… positions held only by seniors.

Greenville has several generations of Flaming Flashes. Why this high level of support? As a public school educator for 43 years, I feel the adults know, and the students learn, this program changes lives! Students deliver a product with every performance at community, state, and national events. A compelling display of skill and timing is the result of discipline, commitment, cooperation, and practice… skills demanded by our society.

What a joy for generations to watch their young prodigies grow through familiar traditions with consistencies maintained by directors from Gussie Nell Davis to current director, Lori Butler. How rewarding to see our young women develop leadership and performance skills they use and can transfer to other situations throughout their lifetimes.

Donald Jefferies, M.A.
Greenville I.S.D. Superintendent

Lori L. Butler

A Tribute

Lori L. Butler, daughter of Larry and Sandra Talley Butler, began her dance career at age two in Denison, Texas, at Denison Dance Academy. They moved to Abbott, Texas, in 1968, and Lori entered Mr. Twitty's Kindergarten in the city of West. The tragic loss of her father in July 1970 precipitated their move to Greenville. Continuing her dance education with Benita Ramzel, she attended the Greenville schools. Lori's sister, Lachelle Butler (Johnson), set the example, and Lori became a Flaming Flash in 1980, and, in her sister's footsteps, served as a Flaming Flash Major. Upon graduation from GHS, she attended North Texas State University, where she joined the Zeta Tau Alpha sorority and served as a "little sister" to Lambda Chi Alpha. Miss Butler earned a Bachelor of Science degree in Early Childhood and later received K-12 teaching certification from Stephen F. Austin University. Her teaching experience includes TEAMS Math at GHS (1988-89) and home economics at Royse City High School (1989-90), before being called to serve as Director of The Flaming Flashes in July 1990…fulfilling her dreams.

Miss Butler, proud aunt of Jordan Wesley and Jacey Lachelle Johnson, is the product of loving father, Larry L. Butler, a caring stepfather, Stanley M. Marak (both deceased), a loving mother, sister, and brother-in-law, and twenty-five years of caring for her "girls."

Lori L. Butler, a major influence in the lives of current and former members of The Flaming Flashes over the past twenty-five years, continues to promote the pride and traditions of the first high school precision drill/dance team in Texas through her leadership. We congratulate Miss Butler on her Silver Anniversary as Director of The Flaming Flashes at Greenville High School and wish her continued success.

Heath Jarvis, Principal
Greenville High School

Gussie Nell Davis

Our history begins when fate brought Robert Augustus Davis from Stone Mountain, Georgia, and Mattie Lavinia Callaway of Union, Arkansas, together to be wed on December 31, 1888. They settled in the countryside near Farmersville, Texas, a small farm community in Collin County. Within two years, they were blessed with a daughter, Vera, born in 1890. When their only child, Vera, was sixteen, they learned another child was on the way.

Mattie, then age 36, and Robert (age 43), wished for a boy...a namesake for Robert, when their second girl made her appearance on November 4, 1906. Perhaps Mattie thought to name the baby, Roberta Augusta...such a long name for a tiny baby. She decided to take her husband's middle name, Augustus, adapt it to fit their new baby, and named her Gussie Nell. The family had their hands full with the care of a new baby and all the farm chores. They were pleased that Vera was old enough to help with the care of Gussie Nell. Their lives would never be the same.

Being sixteen years older, Vera married and left home before Gussie Nell graduated from high school. Gussie Nell was the "apple of her father's eye" and would dance around the room, when her mother played folk songs on the piano in their parlor. Mattie frowned upon Gussie Nell's "cavorting," as she called it, and wanted her daughter to be "ladylike." She even offered to pay her a nickel if she could be still for five minutes. Gussie Nell never earned that nickel. To curb that energy, Gussie Nell was groomed for a career as a concert pianist. After all, they were in the heart of the "bible belt," and a young lady must never dance in public. Gussie Nell was too young to know and just did what came naturally.

Upon graduation from Farmersville High School, Gussie Nell moved to Denton, Texas, and entered The College of Industrial Arts, now Texas Woman's University, to continue her studies toward becoming a concert pianist...although she yearned to be a dancer on the stage.

An active person, Gussie Nell fell in love with her physical education classes, especially those where she could move to music. A strong-willed young woman, Gussie Nell decided her own future and chose the field of physical education instead of music. Following her graduation from college in 1923, she moved to Los Angeles, California, to work towards her master's degree at the University of Southern California, but her sister, Vera, who married

William M. Dicken, was busy taking care of her young son, William Robert (born in 1920), and daughter, Betty Jane (born in 1924).

During the summer of 1928, Vera learned the administration of the Greenville Schools needed a female physical education teacher at Greenville High School. She saw an opportunity to draw Gussie Nell back to Texas, and wrote to Gussie Nell telling her how much they missed her. Vera mentioned the teaching position in nearby Greenville and urged Gussie Nell to return. She could be paid for teaching and complete her graduate work later. The offer was tempting, so Gussie Nell made plans to return to Texas.

Gussie Nell Davis

Gussie Nell began teaching physical education to girls at Greenville High School in the fall of 1928. Music and dancing still filled her soul. She missed the bright lights, social life, and music she left behind in Los Angeles and yearned to share her dancing ability with the world.

"The Charleston" was the national dance craze, and Walt Disney just released the first of many Mickey Mouse films. The peppy music of "Yes, We Have No Bananas," "I Want to Be Happy," and Jelly Roll Martin's jazz echoed through her head causing her to dance around when she was alone.

During the first football game of 1928, she watched as the young girls stood around patting their feet while the local municipal band played for the opening ceremonies and during the halftime break. They needed to dance! Gussie Nell knew what she had to do and set the wheels in motion for the first all-girl pep squad for Greenville High School with twelve brave girls.

A meeting was held for the girls and their parents to explain the purpose and needs of the group. Within a month, the Greenville Pep Squad emerged wearing white skirts, just at or above the knees, and red and white checked blouses. White sweaters, emblazoned with a large red letter "G" and three smaller red letters "P...E (within the G)...P" spaced across the bust line, replaced the blouses during cold weather the next year and were their uniforms for about five years. Most of the girls wore their hair "bobbed" just around or below their ears, in the style of that period.

The GHS Pep Squad performed using head, hand, and marching drills as the local community band played during the halftime period. Gussie Nell felt the girls needed more. Some Texas high schools had drum and bugle corps, and, after considerable study, Gussie Nell added this dimension to halftime shows. Drums, bugles, marching, and precision dance made them the first high school group in the nation to perform in this fashion.

In 1929, with the help of local businessmen, Gussie Nell managed to acquire some drums of various sizes and some bugles. She used her knowledge of music and the help of local musicians to teach the girls how to play those instruments. Membership grew and the pep squad became the GHS Drum and Bugle Corps. They received cheers at the dedication of the new county courthouse and at their first halftime performance at the Fair Park Stadium (renamed the Cotton Bowl in 1936). Performances at the Cotton Bowl continued from 1929 until 1942, according to Lori L. Butler, current director.

By 1930, Gussie Nell noticed a member of the municipal band twirling a baton and made inquiries. The batons cost about ten dollars each. With little money in her budget, she had some wooden batons made, some say from broomsticks, and taught some of the girls, the drum majors, to twirl the batons while doing dance steps as the rest played bugles and drums.

Gussie Nell taught her "girls" how to march, twirl, play drums, bugles, and perform drills as the municipal band played marching music during the halftime period. During physical education classes, she taught "movement to music" using folk songs and marches. The word "dancing" was not used. Any resistance was met with the fact that women were now allowed to move to music in public since Sonja Heine, in figure skating, did so in the Olympics for the first time...winning the Olympic gold medal. Amelia Earhart, the first woman to fly across the Atlantic, was another example of the changing times.

Ed Bernard, GHS Band Director

Gussie Nell had heard about Sam Houston High School's "Black Battalion." They were the first all-girl drum and bugle corps created in 1927, but, she would create an even better organization in 1929...the first precision dance and drill team in the nation!

The popular music of the day kept bouncing through her head and moving her feet. "Crazy Rhythm," "Makin' Whoopee," "You're the Cream in My Coffee," caused her feet to dance. She still yearned to dance on a stage.

On October 28, 1929, "Black Friday" caused the collapse of the New York Stock Exchange. United States securities lost over $26 billion. Panic ensued. A world economic crisis rocked the country. The Earth, however, kept on turning, and so did Gussie Nell and her GHS Drum and Bugle Corps...with bugles, batons, drums, and twirling/marching dance steps. The world had suffered a crisis, but the halftime show at Greenville High School lifted everyone's spirits...even if the football team did not win.

In 1931, the GHS Band was organized under the direction of Marvin Bush, local band director for the municipal band. Ed Bernard was hired as Mr. Bush's assistant. The halftime show grew and the football team kept winning.

Summer of 1932 was exciting for Greenville. Local and national headlines proclaimed the news that GHS graduate and student at USC, Edgar Ablowich, had won the Olympic gold medal in the 1600-meter relay!

Fall brought more news! On October 15, 1932, Jean Conger described the halftime show in her GHS column, "Peppy Points," noting the halftime stunt by Gussie Nell's "girls" was "sensational" with their use of sparklers, firecrackers, and Roman candles on the football field. The crowd went wild! Head Coach Henry Frnka was truly impressed. He said his winning team was the "thunder" and her "girls" were the "lightning flashes that followed."

GREENVILLE HIGH BAND

Director: Marvin Bush   Assistant Director: Ed Bernard
Student Director: Robert Isdale   Band Sponsor: Betty Kilmer

Trumpet:	Isdale	Chapman	Beasley	Denny
	Nabors	Ramsey	Elder	Horn
Clarinets:	Young	Tolbert	Buchanan	Parker
	Greenhalgh	Kennedy	Crosby	Price
Saxophones:	Daniels	McLain	Shavey	
	Adkinson	Bunch		
Trombones:	Lockhart	Looney	Kilmer	
	Hooten	Rabb	Ray	
Bass:	Rorex	McWhirter		
Drums:	Edwards	McEwin	Horn, Jr.	

"With the team until the last toot!"

MANAGEMENT STAFF

Faculty Manager: R. K. Roberts
Football Manager: Chester Brown
Football Manager: Billy Varley

FOOT BALL COUNSELORS

Dr. Ed Taylor   Joe Bergin
M. V. Braselton   R. K. Roberts
J. I, Holdersness   Henry E. Franka

Dedicated to the coach, team, student body, and faculty, pages from the 1932-33 *Yell Book* are shown above. [*Author's Note:* Student editors prepared the *Yell Books*, and some names were misspelled. For example, Henry E. Franka, listed above, should read: Henry E. Frnka.] In 1933, Frnka (pronounced frenka) coached the Greenville Lions to win the Texas

State Championship, during which he used the "fumblerooski," a ploy he invented, for the first time. [Courtesy of Mae Merrick Pickens]

An outstanding musician, Ed Bernard was handed the baton in the summer of 1933 as director of the newly established Greenville High School Band. Mr. Bernard and Miss Gussie Nell Davis worked together to provide the community an exciting show at football games, parades, pep rallies, and concerts. Their uniforms looked similar since the all-male band wore white pants and white shirts. Later, a red cape and military hat were added for effect.

Dr. Mike Adkisson, local physician, noted:
My older sister, Mary Wise Adkisson, was a member of the Pep Squad in 1933 and a Charter Member of The Flaming Flashes in 1934. Gussie Nell was often at social gatherings with my parents, Wise and Lenna Adkisson, who attended most of the GHS games. Gussie Nell had a "significant other" named Penn England. They were close friends of Dr. and Mrs. Dickens, a local radiologist, who lived in a leaky roofed wood-frame house on Walnut Street, a block south of my family's home. Dr. Dickens kept unusual pets...two 4-foot alligators that roamed freely from their shallow rock-lined pond in his backyard!

Gussie Nell Davis (left) and Penn England (back left) with Wise Adkisson Family.

Both organizations flourished. In 1933, the band donned new all-military uniforms to match their military hats and now looked quite different from the pep squad. Gussie Nell tried different approaches to help spark their appearance. Her "girls" needed new uniforms.

During spring 1934, Miss Davis met with parents to convince them of the needs of the group. Since the GHS Band had new military uniforms, patterns were selected so new uniforms could be made, either by their mothers, a relative, or a seamstress. The new design for the forty-two girls and three officers from the ninth, tenth, and eleventh grades, who were invited (no try-outs) to join the group,

Mary Wise Adkisson

> # FLAMING FLASHES
> # CHARTER MEMBERS
>
> ### Drum Majors
>
> Head Drum Major: Jean Fagala
> Assistant Drum Major: Nancy Jo Huffaker
> Assistant Drum Major: Claudine Lancaster
>
> ### Members
>
> | | | |
> |---|---|---|
> | Mary Wise Adkisson | Frances Holleman | Kathryn Sharpley |
> | Ella Beth Andrews | Estelle Johnson | Mary Elizabeth Shelton |
> | Connie Bowen | Jo Ann Jones | Gean Simpson |
> | Dorothy Brown | Wanda Lou McCarley | Sara Frances Sorrells |
> | Dixie June Bunch | Motsye McGaughey | Mary Helen Stevenson |
> | Frances Clements | Pauline McNabb | Marguerite Thomas |
> | Lenora Duck | Louise Medlin | Dorothy Ward |
> | Joyce Dyer | Ouisa Molen | Billy Clyde Warren |
> | Jean Edge | Juanita Orr | Earline Waters |
> | Martha Jane Gross | Jean Price | Evelyn White |
> | Lucille Hackleman | Dorothy Mae Reinger | Mary Sue Williams |
> | Willene Hendrix | Evangeline Riley | Mary Elizabeth Wise |
> | Berniece Henson | Mary Emma Russey | Mary Louise Wolfe |
> | | Kathryn Sadler | |

consisted of red wool flannel single-breasted military jackets with three vertical box pleats in the back that extended from shoulder blades to the waist and was belted only at the back. Gold military-style buttons marched down the front of the blazer and on each sleeve. The white wool flannel (mid-calf) skirt had a five-fold pleat in each side seam that extended about twelve inches toward the waist to allow for movement. Skirts were required to be equidistant from the floor. For the first time, white jodhpur (riding) boots were also selected. Red military-style caps with white bills were worn "cocked" over the right eye and sported white "pony tail" feathered plumes. White gloves, white cotton blouses, and a white satin ascot, embroidered with two Edwardian "Fs", completed the uniforms.

Uniforms for the officers were somewhat different. The two Senior Majorettes wore all-white uniforms styled like those worn by members except their military caps were white with red bills and their ascots were red with two Edwardian "Fs" embroidered in white. The Head Majorette's military-style single-breasted white jacket was heavily adorned with three horizontal rows of red military filigree braid. Two Edwardian "Fs" were embroidered on the left shoulder portion of the jacket. The wide red belt with a large gold buckle accented the waist. Attached to the belt was a one-inch red strap that extended from the left front of the belt to the left side at the back. A tall (at least twelve inches) drum major-style red hat,

Billie Jo Sprinkle (Moore)

complete with wide white feathered plumes extending from the white bill to about three inches beyond the top of the hat, was held securely by a red chin-strap to complete her outfit. Their hand-made wooden batons were replaced with shiny silver drum major batons.

Discussion during this meeting led to their new name, "The Flaming Flashes." Gussie Nell recalled Coach Frnka's remarks, and, in honor of his recent Texas State Football Championship, decided to incorporate his comments of the football team being the "thunder" and her girls as "the lightning flashes that followed."

Sheb Willmon, a Dallas sportswriter, wrote his entire column about the performance of The Flaming Flashes following the Greenville-Dallas Tech football game in 1934. His original purpose in attending this game was to see whether or not the Greenville Lions, who had just won the state championship the previous year, could continue their winning streak. Many of the GHS Lions' star players had graduated and Coach Frnka was working with a "new crop." At the end of the first half of the game, Willmon was more impressed with the halftime show. He described the Flashes as "Greenville's snappily at-

tired drum and bugle corps...led by three beautiful drum majors..." and noted how they "...pranced out like a show horse on parade." Mr. Willmon was very impressed with their perfect marching ability while playing their drums and bugles. The GHS Band and Flashes combined forces for their "grand finale," which included moving smartly to the strains of "Peruna." (The "Peruna Strut" was a quickstep maneuver, with bodies arched, to the tune "She'll Be Comin' 'Round the Mountain" as the GHS Band and Flaming Flashes left the football field.) Flaming Flash Majorettes also did the "Peruna Strut" while marching/leading in parades. Norman Steppe, MCA official, could be heard saying, "Those kids have more showmanship than any similar outfit I ever saw!" Willmon agreed and noted the following in his column:

> Greenville may or may not have as good a football team this year but for stomped down advertising for a little city that gives out and does things, you can't begin to tie that band and drum and bugle corps. Texas high schools can look to Hunt County for musical inspiration. They've a bumper crop up there.
>
> —*Greenville Herald Banner*
> Reprinted March 7, 1971

Coach Henry Frnka could see the "handwriting on the wall." He left GHS in the summer of 1935 to work as assistant coach at Vanderbilt University and stayed there until 1939. He was hired in 1940 as assistant at Temple University and was there only one year. 1941 saw him move to Tulsa, Oklahoma, to be head coach at The University of Tulsa, where he remained until 1945. During that period, his son, who was playing football at Will Rogers High School in Tulsa, suffered a brain injury and was rushed to the hospital. Surgery was performed to remove the blood clot, but Henry Frnka, Jr., age 17, did not survive. Coach Frnka left Tulsa for Tulane University in 1946, where he served as their head coach before retiring in 1951.

Meanwhile, at GHS, the Flaming Flashes continued to thrive. Officers for 1935-1936 were:

> Head Drum Major .... Gean Simpson
> Senior Drum Major .... Berniece Henson
> Junior Drum Major .... Martha Scott

Even though the country was dealing with economic struggles during The Depression, Gussie Nell continued to look for ways to spotlight the Flashes. The rumba emerged as "the fashionable" dance with the popular "Begin the Beguine." She incorporated the Latin rhythms into routines.

1936-1937 was a tremendous year for the GHS Band and Flaming Flashes. The *Yell Book*, 1936-37, emailed to this author by Gill McKay, former student and son of Melba Rawlings, who carried the school flag that year, yielded much information. Flash Officers were:

> Head Drum Major .... Martha Scott
> Senior Drum Major .... Ruth Horn
> Junior Drum Major .... Ruth Berry

Three senior Flashes (one blonde, one redhead, one brunette) were selected to serve in newly created positions as flag bearers, and were:

> United States Flag Bearer..........Elayne Sanford (Blonde)
> Texas Flag Bearer.....................Mary Ann Collins (Brunette)
> School Flag Bearer....................Melba Rawlings (Redhead)

Selecting a blonde, brunette, and redhead as flag bearers became tradition. Members of the Flaming Flashes and their instruments included:

Drums	Sarah Black	Ruth Gilleon	Garnell Smith
	Gladys Bray	Juanita Ray	Jo Ann Palmer
	Cordell Thompson	Carolyn Mallory	Frances Flournoy
	Jean Hildreth		Evelyn Moudy
Bass Bugles	Billie Lois Adams	Mary Lee Black	
	Helen Spencer	Dorothy Bishop	
Cymbals	Glenna May Arnold	Ruth Foshee	
Bugles	Creta Latta	Theda Nell Rogers	Martha Perrin
	Jo Ann Jones	Billy Burk	Camille Foster
	Creta Rogers	Mary L. Brazelton	Margaret Robbins
	Annie Sprinkle	Ethel Treadway	Helen Reece
	Louise Watson	Voy Bell Smith	Merle Babb
	Dixie Bunch	Martha Jane Gross	Virginia Scott
	Frances Saunders	Mary McHam	Olive Moseley
	Lucille Templeton	Billie McHenry	Gala Dutton
	Jeanne Turner	Dorothy Brown	Theresa Bell
	Anna Creswell	Runelle Jared	Gloria Rosenbluth

The first managers for the Flashes were Leo Hackney* and Joe Manning. Leo and Joe owned a convertible. Leo joked that having "transportation" helped them be near all those beautiful girls!

[*Author's Note: A leader in Greenville after twenty-seven years of distinguished service in the U.S. Navy, including serving as captain of the ship that escorted General Douglas MacArthur in his return to The Philippines during WWII, Leo Hackney's proudest achievement was being the father of Susan and Sharon Hackney, members of the Flashes.]

Milton Moffett, Head Coach, and Elva Baker, Assistant, led the Lions. Team members included: Henry Haney and B. Roy (co-captains); Summerlin and C. Phillips (quarterbacks); Roy, Travis, and McClain (halfbacks); M. Phillips and D. Terry (fullbacks); Mason, Walker, Drake, and Waddle (ends); Bickley, Coomer, Mickler, and Moss (tackles); Leftwich and Hawkins (centers); and, Haney, Shipp, Lain, and Jaco (guards).

Ed Bernard, Director, was assisted by Hendrix Merrill, Student Director. Joe Fugitt served as Drum Major and Anna Grace Smith sponsored the band.

Mary Sue Williams, Charter Flash (1934) was named Band Sweetheart for 1936-1937, according to her daughter, Sue Ann Alexander Harting.

Cornets and Trumpets	Joe Germany	H. W. Maier	
	Warren McBride	Murray Pickens	
Clarinet	Ray Hanchey	Billie Merrill	D. A. Steele
	George Jacks	Jessie Allen Wallace	Sammy Flournoy
	Houston Peek	Byron Hayter	
Trombones	Charles Berry	Roy Blakemore	
	Dick Morris	Haden Drake	
Baritone	Albert Spradling	Oscar Jones	Fab Powell
	Joe Fugitt	Lewis Ray	Joe. G. Roach, Jr
Bass	James Blakemore	James Handley	Rusty Rorex
Drums	J. T. Bell	Billy Narramore	
Alto Horns	Eldon Jones	Billie O. Reeves	

[*Author's Note:* Students prepared *Yell Book*s. Some names may be incorrect.]

Texas was celebrating its Centennial in a grand manner with the opening of the 1936 Centennial Exposition in Dallas. An invitation to be a part of the opening ceremonies was received and plans to attend were begun. The GHS Band and Flashes accepted the invitation to be a part of the Texas Centennial Celebration at Fair Park in Dallas, Texas, and their performance, which incorporated the history of Texas under six flags, was heralded as a success. All who attended were amazed with the changes completed at Fair Park in less than a year for the Texas Centennial Exposition. Dozens of buildings were constructed or remodeled. Art deco designs and sculptures graced the new landscaping. It was like a different world. Many students had their first experience with air-conditioning...a fairly new concept. Some had their first taste of the new snack, Fritos.

Spurred by the GHS Band and Flashes successful season, Miss Davis decided to create a floorshow to raise funds for the GHS Band and Flashes. Gussie Nell, working with Mr. Bernard, called a meeting of parents and planned a performance that would develop into an annual event.

The first floorshow, "Greenville High School Band Varieties," was presented in spring of 1937. The GHS gym, transformed into a "modern night club," was beautifully decorated. Card tables encircled the gym floor with an open performance center highlighted by a spotlight. Seating was sold by reservation only. Parents and the public quickly snapped up tickets...four per table. With no more tables available, tickets were sold at ten cents each for a seat in the bleachers. No tickets were sold at the door. The band, located on a platform at one end, played music as guests arrived. Acts were performed by members of the band or Flashes in the open area of the gym floor under the spotlight. According to Rosabel Williams Warren, member of the Flashes (1937-1940) and Flash Director from 1944 to 1946:

> *Acts were performed by Flashes and Band members, and the only costumes were variations of the regular uniforms...one time, we would leave off our blazers and caps; another time, we would alter the uniform in some such simple way. The acts were performed (1) by the entire squad and (2) by*

individuals who happened to have some talent. During the acts, the gym was darkened everywhere except for a spotlight on the performing area. Between acts the Flashes moved among the tables wearing trays suspended from their necks selling cokes and popcorn. The climax of the floorshow was the presentation of new members. We decided to try to start a tradition in the way this was done. Each graduating member met the new member, who was taking her place, in the center of the spotlight and handed the new member her cap and her instrument. The occasion for many tears of both joy and sadness, this ritual was continued for several years.

The first floorshow was overwhelmingly successful with 1,100 in attendance. Proceeds from the floorshow were used to buy award sweaters for graduating band and Flash members. White coat sweaters with "Flashes" embroidered across a large white "G" outlined in red were selected. Sweaters for band members were similar, except they were red and emblazoned with a white lyre. Service stripes on the sleeves designated the number of years of service for both groups. These award sweaters, presented during "chapel exercises" (baccalaureate) to graduating members of the GHS Band and Flashes are as listed in the May 13, 1937 edition of the Greenville (Texas) *Banner*:

GHS Band Members

Joe Fugitt	Jesse Wallace	Houston Peek
Anna Grace Smith	Oscar Jones	Ray Hanchey
Hendrix Merrill (Student Director)	Joe Germany	Charles Berry
	James Blakemore	J. L. LyBrand
Herbert McGaughey	James Handley	

Flaming Flash Members

Martha Scott	Myrle Babb	Virginia Scott
Ruth Horn	Martha Jane Gross	Jo Anna Jones
Theda Nell Rogers	Dorothy Brown	Glenna Mae Arnold
Runell Jared	Martha Perrin	Ruth Fooshee
Dixie June Bunch	Mary Louise Braselton	Joyce Dyer
Billie McHenry	Vay Belle Smith	Garnell Smith
Teresa Bell		

Flag Bearers

Mary Ann Collins	Melba Rawlings	Elaine Sanford

As the Depression Years slid by, rumblings of war in Europe and Asia made the headlines in 1937-1938. Saving the mood of many was the film, *Snow White and the Seven Dwarfs* (Disney). Who could be depressed watching those little men whistle while they worked? Disney's fantasies lulled the nation into the wonderful world of make-believe.

Nancy Quattlebaum was in a gym class taught by Gussie Nell in 1937-38 and recalled that Miss Davis was,

...very strict. You had good posture if you went to school with her. She made you line up like soldiers and march like the army. She was very good at what she did. The Flashes were so good because of her discipline and precision. She was very outgoing. She was a small lady, especially next to me at 5'9" tall.
[Source: Carmen Vance, Physical Therapist]

Mae Merrick Pickens recalled the excitement of her first year in the Flashes. Mae, in the tenth grade, was selected to play a bugle. (Students from grades 9, 10, and 11 were invited to serve in the Flashes. There was no twelfth grade.) She kept an eye on a trumpet player in the GHS Band, an eleventh-grader, named Murray Pickens. She knew then that Murray, besides being an excellent trumpeter, would play an even larger role in her future.

The Flashes moved forward with new music and a new set of officers.

1937-1938 Officers

Head Drum Major	Ruth Berry
Assistant Drum Major	Frances Flournoy
Assistant Drum Major	Carolyn Mallory
Assistant Drum Major	Ethel Treadway

Flag Bearers

United States Flag	Creta Mae Rodgers

(Information on other flag bearers was not available.)

World tensions continued to grow as the Japanese invaded China and established a puppet government in Nanking. In Europe, Hitler named himself as War Minister, and Italy invaded Albania. The Duke of Windsor abdicated the throne, married Mrs. Wallis Simpson, and left England. The world was trembling. Songwriters tried to lift spirits with songs like "Flat Foot Floogie with a Floy Floy," "A Tiskit, A Tasket," and "Jeepers Creepers." War songs filled the airwaves in England. The reality of another world war was not realized until "God Bless America" filled the airwaves in 1939.

The GHS Band and Flashes included more patriotic music and military routines during their halftime shows. The focus was on the war "Over There."

No one could envision what was about to happen or predict the changes that would occur in the next two years, as the Flashes and Miss Davis made plans for 1938-1939. Chosen as leaders were:

Head Drum Major	Frances Flournoy
Assistant Drum Major	Jean Turner
Assistant Drum Major	Billie Jean Molen
United States Flag	Margaret Dyer (Blonde)
Texas Flag	Anna Katherine Elder (Brunette)
School Flag	Camille Foster (Red Head)

The GHS Band, under the direction of Ed Bernard, listed the following in *The Lion,* the GHS annual yearbook:

    Drum Major .... Nick England
    Band Sweetheart .... Nancy Jones
    Student Directors .... Dick Morris, Russell Rorex

An eleventh grader, Mae Merrick (Pickens)—second row, fifth from left— was assigned the honor of playing the snare drum...only a select few were chosen.

1938-39 Flaming Flashes

Frances Flournoy

The 1939-1940 year brought many changes as Germany invaded Poland. Britain and France declared war on Germany on September 3. The U.S. economy was making its slow recovery after The Depression when Gussie Nell Davis was called to use her expertise with precision dance and drill team instruction to build a similar organization at Kilgore Junior College...the now world famous Kilgore Rangerettes. *Gone With the Wind* hit the silver screen and Gussie Nell hit the road for Kilgore. The Flashes were stunned.

Miss Davis left before the end of the 1939 school term. Routines for the football season had not been planned. Frances Flournoy, an amazing student and current Head Drum Major, who had served in the Flashes since 1935-36, and who had served as Assistant Drum Major in 1937-38, plus as Head Drum Major the year prior, took the baton in her hands and, with Mr. Ed's guidance, led the Flashes through their paces during the fall semester. A multi-talented young lady and a natural leader, she was well trained and led with confidence through this transition period. Not only were there changes in the headlines...there were changes in the hemlines. The skirts of Flash officers' uniforms, once worn two inches below the knees, were now set at about three inches above the knees!

Mae Merrick Pickens (Flashes 1937-1939) recalled that Frances Flournoy, Head Drum Major, guided the new Flashes during the last month of school and through fall of 1939. Frances prepared them for halftime routines until a new director could be hired. "Mr. Ed" served as director of both the band and Flashes. [Source: Mae Merrick Pickens and Billie Pickens, 2015] A photo, provided by Wynn Warren Sikes, daughter of Rosabel Williams Warren, shows Head Drum Major, Frances Flournoy, flanked by two of the three Assistant Drum Majors, Anna Patton Clark and Rosabel Williams. The third, Geane Birdsong, was not pictured.

Leading the Flaming Flashes for 1939-40 were:

    Head Drum Major .... Frances Flournoy (Fifth Year)
                                                Head Drum Major (1938-39)
                                                Assistant Drum Major (1937-38)
                                                Played Drum (1935-37)
    Assistant Drum Major .... Geane Birdsong
    Assistant Drum Major .... Anna Patton Clark
    Assistant Drum Major .... Rosabel Williams
    American Flag Bearer............. Betty Wylie (Brunette)
    Texas Flag Bearer .... Helen Banks (Blonde)
    School Flag Bearer................. Billie Jo Bray (Red Head)
    Flash Managers....................... Tom R. Poole, Billy Hoff, Tom Inabinette

Nick England continued his prancing and twirling routine in his second year as Head Drum Major for the GHS Band and Elganna Handley was selected as Band Sweetheart. Roy Warren served as Student Director.

Ed Bernard made most of the decisions regarding performances of the Flaming Flashes during the 1939 football season. He put his musical talents to work and wrote both music and lyrics for the GHS School Song, "We Hail from GHS" which is still in use. The 1940-1941 annual was dedicated to "Mr. Ed" in recognition of his service.

Anna Patton Clark, Frances Flournoy, and Rosabel Williams

Eugenia Johnston

In 1940, with the resignation of Chamberlin, Winston Churchill became Britain's Prime Minister. The Home Guard was formed in Britain as Germany invaded Holland, Belgium, and Luxembourg. Churchill hit the airwaves with his famous "blood, toil, tears, and sweat" speech. The "war to end all wars" became a distant memory as the realities of World War II ravaged the land. Congress passed the Selective Service Act to mobilize the military. "The Last Time I Saw Paris" became a popular song with its nostalgic lyrics as many European composers moved to the United States to escape the war in Europe.

Miss Eugenia Johnston was hired to lead the Flashes in the spring of 1940. She worked with "Mr. Ed" to incorporate several patriotic songs and routines for halftime performances. No significant changes were made to their uniforms, which were the pride of every girl who had the honor of being a Flash. They continued to play their shiny bugles and keep their precision perfect to the beat of their drums. Selected as leaders of the 1940-1941 Flashes were the following drum majors and flag bearers:

Eugenia Johnston

Head Drum Major	Pattilou Germany
Assistant Drum Major	Rosemary Wylie
Assistant Drum Major	Marie Merrill
US Flag	Joy Carden (Blonde)
Texas Flag	Barbara McCartney (Brunette)
School Flag	Virginia Phillips (Redhead)
Flash Managers	Tom Inabinette, Edward Gross

The GHS Band, directed by "Mr. Ed" and two student directors, Allen Stephenson and Morris Kearney, was led by Thomas Sinclair, Drum Major, with Band Sweetheart, Lea Rose Moffett, at his side.

The war "across the pond" intensified with the sinking of the *Bismark*. In April 1941,

US Congressman Sam Rayburn notified Hunt County officials that the airport project, discussed earlier with City officials and the Civil Aeronautics Administration (CAA), would be part of a $5 million Army Air Force Training Base for about 4,000 personnel and 300 airplanes.

War appeared to be eminent. German and Italian assets were "frozen" in the United States, as Germany invaded Russia and the Ukraine. Joseph C. Grew, our ambassador to Japan, warned President Roosevelt of the possibility of an attack from Japan. Sadly, our country was caught "with our pants down" when Japan attacked Pearl Harbor on December 7, 1941. President Franklin D. Roosevelt denounced this "day of infamy" and declared war against Japan.

"Praise the Lord and Pass the Ammunition" was popular on the Hit Parade in 1942, alongside "Paper Doll," and "White Christmas."

Citizens rallied to support the war effort and activities at GHS reflected those efforts. Miss Johnston and "Mr. Ed" worked to boost the public's spirits, as young men were called to serve their country. Position titles of "Senior and Junior Assistants" were added for 1941-42. Named were:

Head Drum Major	Marie Merrill
Senior Assistant	Anna Jean Acker
Junior Assistant	Elizabeth Ann Yeager
Stars and Stripes	Christine Barkley
Lone Star State	Doris Salter
GHS Flag	Edna Lois Culberson
Managers	Billy Lee Davis, Mary Jane Horton Glendale Hawkins

Leading the GHS Band was Drum Major Davis Scott with Band Sweetheart, Dorothy Mason, at his side. Student Director was J. O. Hayter.

The GHS Band and Flashes marched to patriotic music at parades, Victory Bond rallies, and to see the young men off to war as they boarded busses or trains in downtown Greenville.

On June 26, 1942, Majors Field, named for Lt. Truett Majors, first pilot from Hunt County killed in action during WWII, opened and became fully operational on January 5, 1943. Anxious citizens trained to be Civilian Air Observers (CAO). The public was informed about "blackouts, air raids, and rationing." Victory Gardens were planted to supplement the food supply and ration cards were issued. In April 1942, Lt. Col. Jimmy Doolittle led a group of sixteen B-25s on a bombing raid to Japan. The pilot of the sixth plane to leave the USS Hornet was Dean Hallmark, GHS graduate. The bombs were dropped, but his plane crashed in the ocean. He was captured and executed by the Japanese. The Greenville VFW was named in his honor.

The navigator of the eighth plane was Nolan Herndon, another Greenville native. His plane landed in Russia after the mission and the crew was held by the Russians until they escaped months later.

[*Author's Note*: The (Greenville) *Herald Banner,* Thursday, April 16, 2015 (pp. A1-A2) noted that Dean Hallmark and Nolan Herndon had recently been posthumously awarded the Congressional Gold Medal for their part as Gen. Doolittle's Raiders in their raid on Tokyo, Japan.]

Another native of Hunt County, who enlisted at the Greenville post office in 1942, became the most decorated soldier of WWII...earning every possible medal before age 21. He became an actor, poet, songwriter, and a revered veteran. Audie Leon Murphy, 1924-1971, was killed in a private plane crash. The Audie Murphy/American Cotton Museum in Greenville honors his memory and that of Claire Chennault of the Flying Tigers, Dean Hallmark, and Nolan Herndon of the Doolittle Raiders...to name a few. The Hall of Heroes honors some of the many who served our country, with several giving the ultimate sacrifice that we may continue to live in freedom. The AM/ACM also features a display on the early history of The Flaming Flashes as the first high school precision dance/drill team in the United States of America.

The Flaming Flashes lead the send off for WWII recruits on Washington Street, 1942. (Municipal Auditorium on left and Junior High School in background).

As time and the war marched on, so did the GHS Band and Flaming Flashes. Leading the GHS Band as Drum Major in 1942-43 was Harris Morgan and Band Sweetheart, Joan Robbins. The Flaming Flashes were:

Head Drum Major	Elizabeth Ann (Lizzie) Yeager
Senior Assistant	Pat Davis
Junior Assistant	Martha Jo Reiger
US Flag	Jeannie Forrester
Texas Flag	Dorothy Saunders
GHS Flag	Robbie Brashear

J. H. Flewharty, teacher at GHS, was named as GHS principal. When "Little Moron" jokes emerged in 1943, he began a tradition. As emcee of the floorshow, he opened with "Why did the Little Moron cut a hole in the rug?" and answered, "To see the floorshow!" The tradition continued.

Dorothy McQuary

More changes were on the horizon. Hitler's "scorched earth" policy horrified the world. General Dwight D. Eisenhower took command of Allied armies in North Africa. British and American troops joined forces to fight the enemy. U.S. planes destroyed a 22-ship Japanese convoy in the Battle of the Bismark Sea. America's hopes for an end to war were beginning to rise. Popular songs of the year, "I'll Be Seeing You," "Comin' in on a Wing and a Prayer," and "Oh, What a Beautiful Mornin'," floated across the airwaves and into the hearts of Americans.

The war kept marching on, as did the beat of the drums and the bugles of The Flaming Flashes in 1943-44, under a new director, Dorothy McQuary, who changed "Assistant" titles to "Majorette." Serving for the Flashes were:

Head Drum Major	Martha Jo Reiger
Senior Majorette	Joy Little
Junior Majorette	Patsy Baldwin
US Flag	Jackie Key
Texas Flag	Bettye Graves
School Flag	Dorothy Smith

Joseph (Tony) Price held the position of Drum Major for the GHS Band, and Martha Majors was selected as Band Sweetheart. Dan Reid served as Assistant Director to Mr. Bernard.

Everyone pitched in to make the best of a bad situation. The young men of Hunt County kept stepping up to join the military services... even those too young to serve came forward. Many women also joined the military services to do their part in the war effort. Countless women went to work to fill jobs left vacant by the shortage of men in factories and defense plants. "Rosie the Riveter" posters were seen in every town to encourage women to join the work force. Many local women enlisted as Women Air Force Service Pilots (WASPS) and were trained in Greenville at Majors Field. Members of the Mexican Air Force (*Escuadron* 201) also came to Greenville to train as pilots.

Those who could afford to go to the movies gazed in awe at the many battle scenes shown in the newsreels. While many saw these as "America Winning the War," few really understood the realities of being in battle. The media understood and presented a favorable report. The most popular film of 1943 was *Casablanca,* which won the Academy Award for best movie. "As Time Goes By" could be heard almost daily over the airwaves.

During the Band and Flash Floorshow, Mr. Ed Bernard was honored for his tenth year of service as Band Director and received a standing ovation from appreciative students, parents, and school and community leaders. A quiet man, "Mr. Ed" said nothing more than, "Thank you." Dr. Mike Adkisson, local physician, was a freshman in the GHS Band in 1943. He recalled the following:

> *Greenville won the football district title and we played Highland Park in a Bi-District game in Dallas. It was a cold and rainy day. The game ended in a tie, with Highland Park winning on penetrations. Star of the Highland Park team was Doak Walker.*

Rosabel Williams

World War II dragged on for yet another year. Americans were holding on to the hope that Allied victories in Europe and the Pacific were bringing this war to an end. D-Day, June 6, 1944, became a day to be remembered in the hearts of many American families and in the history of this country. The sacrifices were tremendous. Crowds attending movie theaters sobbed as they saw some of the casualties and cheered when the enemy was blasted. Many felt the war would end soon, but the end was yet to come.

Rosabel Williams, a member of the Flashes from 1937 to 1940, was hired in 1944-1945 to be the new director for this precision dance and drill team. She knew what needed to be done. Gussie Nell Davis had taught her well and Miss Williams put her training and knowledge of Flash traditions to good use. The Majors and Flag Bearers selected were:

Rosabel Williams

Head Drum Major	Patsy Baldwin
Senior Majorette	Nora Jeanne Summers
Junior Majorette	June Scott
US Flag Bearer	Theda Nalls
Texas Flag Bearer	Jean Young
School Flag Bearer	Lucille Love

Members

Minnette Hayter	Rita Britt	Phyllis Hendrix	Ruby Price
Elaine Little	Frances Beall	Mary Nell Jones	Ruth Price
Elizabeth Adkisson	Addie Mae Brun	Beulah Jane LeRosen	Betty Pearson
Gloria Roberts	Margaret Brigman	Jean Lewis	Nelda Joy Pickens
Mary Ruth Collins	Janie Banner	Joe Ann McDaniel	Doris Riley
Bettye Ann Myre	Nancy Butler	Marily McWhirter	Doris Roberts
Beverly Fox	Claudine Cook	Reba McPherson	Vera Lee Standford
Sue Lain Hughes	Gladys Ann Cooper	Bennie Lee McGuire	Doris Smith
Frances Dooley	Jean Cody	Mary Nancy Mockford	Betty Swindell
Nona Lee Murray	Mary Crabb	Margaret Owens	Dorothy Van Dyke
Charlyne Yetts	Wanda Faye Clancy	Jimmie Dee Peyton	
Patsy Wolfe	Betty Dean	Sarah Payne	
Nancy Acker	Mary Faulkner	Peggy Pullen	

Head Drum Major was George Murdaugh, the Band Sweetheart was Rita McMeans. Band Members included:

Mike Adkisson	Phil Fugitt	Billy Reynolds	Mark Stapleton
Edgar Biggs	William Goen	Ernest Riddle	Charles Stuth
Edwin Bradley	Allen Harrison	Billy Robinson	James Trapp
Sam Brooks	Bennett Head	Charles Robinson	John Milton Tucker
Benny Bell	D. G. Hudson	Billy Rushing	James Wacasey
Gordon Bryson	Donald Kerr	Joe Rutherford	William Wise
Louis Clark	Cecil Lake	David Shirey	Murray Wilson
Louis Guy Creel	Charles Mayo	Gary Scott	James Webb
Danny Darby	Louis Patillo	Irving Skibell	Bobby Owens
Dale Darby	R. L. Perser	Durwood Speed	Jack Owens
James Duncan	Robert Reed	Max Spikes	John Sanders
Ben Marion Davis			W. O. Smithers

Mr. Bernard had big plans to start a beginning band for students in the lower grades.

The mood of the country had improved in 1944-1945. The Allied forces were winning the war in both the European and Pacific theaters, but the casualties continued to mount. Gold Star emblems appeared in many windows in very city, town, and community. Each Gold Star represented a casualty of war to that family. The death of President Franklin D. Roosevelt in 1945 rocked the world. Harry S. Truman, Vice-President, was named his successor.

Chaos seemed to reign as Americans picked up the pieces. The popular songs reflected the mood of the people and the airwaves were filled with "Sentimental Journey" and "Accentuate the Positive." The "Big Band Era" was in full swing and so were members of the GHS Band and The Flaming Flashes. The audience was ready for a celebration with the announcement of V-E Day on May 8. Upbeat music and happy notes filled the decorated gymnasium for the annual floorshow. Costumes were made of whatever was available, but spirits were high. The goal was inspiration and entertainment…and it was successful. Once again, the "Little Moron" joke began the show, and a standing ovation ended it.

"Japan Surrenders!" was the headline in August 1945. Atomic bombs dropped on Hiroshima on August 6th and Nagasaki on August 9th caused the Japanese to rethink their stance on winning the war. President Truman felt the dropping of those bombs would help save the loss of American troops as the Japanese were determined to continue their fight.

[*Author's Note:* This author and her family were aboard a repatriation ship, The USS Uruguay, from July 24 to August 13, 1945, running dark in enemy waters in the Pacific Ocean as both atom bombs were dropped. One day after arrival in San Francisco, the worst riot in that city's history occurred with the announcement of Japan's surrender.]

Miss Williams and Mr. Bernard continued to keep the music and the marching going at GHS for the 1945-1946 year, along with Drum Major George Murdaugh, who was serving his second year in that position. Leaders of The Flaming Flashes selected by Miss Williams and Miss Bill Daniel, her new assistant, were:

Head Drum Major	June Scott
Senior Majorette	Beverly Fox
Junior Majorette	Mary Lou Otts
US Flag	Nancy Acker (Blonde)
Texas Flag	Betty Swindell (Brunette)
School Flag	Sue Lain Hughes (Red Head)

Cymbals	Minette Hayter	Peggy Pullen	
Bass Drums	Gladys Mockford	Kathlyn Spurlock	
Snare Drums	Beth Morgan	Martha Sue Benson	Nona Murray
	Ruth Scott	Betty Porter	Theresa Goen
	Sally Buchanan	Camille Scott	Charlene Yett
		Margaret Courtney	

Flashes

Pattilou McIen	Marilyn McWhirter	Rae Fullington	Margaret Owens
Lynn Trimble	Mary Faulkner	Florence Smith	Betty Kees
Ruth Price	Margaret Brigman	Betty Pearson	Frances Youngblood
Ruby Price	Elaine Little	Peggy Phillips	Alice Turner
Marilyn Atchison	Nancy King	Jimmie Dee Peyton	Marcella Delandy
Wanda Fae Clancy	Mary Atwell	Janice Leftwich	Mary Rabb
Lugenia Gibbs	Mickey Hunt	Helen Smith	Daphne Harvey
Margaret Felmet	Nancy Butler	Beulah Follis	(Substitute)
Mary Sprinkle	Beulah Jane LaRosen	Sarah Payne	

Miss Williams assured that all Flashes had passing grades before she chose new members and officers. She continued to work closely with Mr. Bernard, Band Director, who trained all the Flashes who played bugles.

New uniforms, three new flags, newly designed jackets for members and officers made the crowds take notice on the field and during parades. The GHS Band and Flaming Flashes performed at the Tyler Rose Festival, the Cotton Bowl, and at the Parade of Lights at the Texas State Fair. The highlight of the year was winning the First Place Award at the First Annual Highland Music Festival at Highland Park in Dallas where they competed against such prestigious high school groups as: Crozier Tech, Sunset, and Woodrow Wilson, Dallas; Palestine, McKinney, Waxahachie, Central High School in Oklahoma City; and, the famous "Bengal Guards" of Orange, Texas. The Flashes received a standing ovation during presentation of the award by Raymond Fletcher, head of the education department of Highland Park High School, to June Womack, representing the Flashes. The "icing on the cake" was Miss Williams' marriage to Roy L. Warren, Jr. on September 10, 1946!

Dr. Mike Adkisson, local physician, who served in the GHS Band during the time Rosabel Williams was Flash Director, remembers her as being artistic, innovative and talented at teaching the Flashes who comprised his class, especially working with the three majorettes who fronted the band and were the only baton twirlers. Dr. Adkisson stated:

"Mr. Ed" taught the drum and bugle members to play their instruments. When I was chosen to be drum major of the band in the spring of 1946, I thought there was no competition for the position. I was a close friend of George Murdaugh, the outgoing Drum Major. George was "Mr. Everything" at GHS, including president of the student body for two years. I had been lead clarinet beginning my junior year, and held the position of "concert master" of the band. But I was surprised a couple of weeks before the appointment when another band member (Jack Owens, bass drums) threw his hat into the ring. I had prepared very little prior to this, and I was suddenly aware that I needed to work on use of the baton and signals for the band. I never acquired a skill in baton twirling (nor did I wish to), thinking I'd use a military style. The last GHS drum major who was a "twirler" and "prancer" was Harris Morgan (1942-43). A tryout was held after school one day with each candidate leading the band as we marched on the field adjacent to the band hall, and on Crockett Street at the side of the building. Jack went first, was skilled with baton use, was taller, and (I thought) performed better. I was relieved to be chosen. The Flashes' Drum Major, Mary Lou Otts, was my "steady" girlfriend the last two years of school. I cannot recall a previous history of Drum Majors as a "pair" before or since.

Mr. Ed Bernard was band director in Greenville since the early 1930s. His musical experience was from performing in circus bands. I don't believe he had a college degree. He was a quiet, stern, and accomplished musician and director. He taught the playing of every instrument—from reeds, to percussion, to brass, but very little in the realm of music theory. Students from his bands that entered college proved to be outstanding performers at that level. In the late 1930s, the Texas A&M Aggieland Orchestra was a premier dance band that played statewide gigs, and about one-third of that band were former GHS players. Other notables were Murray Pickens, who took private trumpet lessons from Mr. Ed and later played trumpet in the Majors Field Orchestra that broadcast a thirty-minute Air Corps tribute nationally from the Municipal Auditorium every Tuesday night. William Holden was the emcee and participated (from New York) in a fifteen-minute dramatization of heroic acts involving airplanes in WWII. The band was transferred to New York to replace the Glenn Miller Orchestra when Glenn Miller was sent to England. Tillman Smithey was another talented trumpeter who was a featured player in the SMU Band in the 1940s. Marshall Head, a younger student, went on to have a career in music. During the 60s, 70s, and 80s, he was the first call reed player in Dallas…playing in the orchestra pit for all the shows at The Fair Park Music Hall, as well as playing in Dallas high society dance bands.

Juanita "Bill" Daniel

The movie titles seemed to reflect the mood of the nation as our troops returned home to rebuild their lives. *The Best Years of Our Lives* and *Great Expectations* filled the silver screen in 1946 and were followed by two lively songs: "Zip-a-dee-doo-dah" and "Shoo-Fly Pie and Apple Pan Dowdy."

Miss Bill Daniel, assistant to Miss Williams for the past two years, became their new director in 1946-47. Selected to lead were:

> Head Drum Major .... Mary Lou Otts
> Senior Majorette .... Beth Morgan
> Junior Majorette .... Shirley Riley
> US Flag Bearer .... Theresa Goen (Blonde)
> Texas Flag .... Lynn Trimble (Brunette)
> School Flag .... Mary Sprinkle (Red Head)

Drums	Betty Porter	Patsy Dooley	Marcella Delaney
	Barbara Winans	Ruth Scott	Leah Nell Clayton
	Sally Buchanan	Aline Patterson	Margaret Courtney
	Janet Bush	Camille Scott	Betty Pearce
Cymbals	Rae Fullington	Marilyn Atchison	
Bugles	Bobbie Jean Green	Beulah Deskins	Burnell Blount
	Betty Lake	Betty Cornelius	Martha Lewis
	Martha Davenport	Gylene Edwards	Ella Harwell
	Catherine Chambers	Peggy Wheatley	Frances Cotton
	Martha Felmet	Barbara Davis	Helen Smith
	Jane McCoy	Mickey Hunt	Frances Youngblood
	Betty Kennedy	Laura Plaxco	Patsy McKinney
	Patricia Davis	Suzanne Powell	Daphne Harvey
	Jane Jenkins	Linda Gross	Alice Turner
	Mary Atwell	Jimmie Jones	Julia Leftwich
	Lucella Isham	Betty Kees	Lugenia Gibbs
Managers	Charleita Flenniken	Tilman Daniel	

The GHS Band continued under the able direction of "Mr. Ed" and was led by Head Drum Major Mike Adkisson. Marching along his side as Band Sweetheart was Florence Smith. While Florence was a lovely young woman and a friend, Mike was dating Mary Lou Otts, Head Drum Major of the Flashes, and preferred to have her marching by his side. Junior Drum Major, Billy Robertson worked with Student Directors Joe Rutherford and Durwood Speed to assure Mr. Bernard's instructions were followed.

Members of the GHS Band were: Mike Adkisson, Edwin Bradley, Gordon Bryson, Ben Butler, Oliver Chandler, Louis Clark, Billy Ray Collum, Raymond Chumley, Jerry Pat Crumpton, Dale Darby, Ben Marion Davis, Laney Duck, James Duncan, Roy Edwards, George Green, Thomas Felmet, Phil Fugitt, Melva Joe Hamilton, Allen Boyd Harrison, Bennett Head, D. G. Hudson, Lonnie Jones, Cecil Lake, Sammy Leinert, David McCollum, Charles Mayo, Irvin Morgan, Jack Owens, Norman Prather, Louis Patillo, Robert Reed, Billy Robertson, Charles Robertson, Billy Rushing, Joe Rutherford, David Sagen, Durwood Speed, Max Spikes, Charles Stuth, G. T. Scott, David Shirey, James Trapp, John Milton Tucker, James Wacasey, James Webb, Murray Wilson, William Wise, and Ray Whetsell. Band Managers Ben Butler, Dowell Mathews, and George Green worked together to move equipment, load, and unload the school busses.

Dr. Mike Adkisson, serving as Head Drum Major in 1946-47, recalled:
> *A few weeks before the floorshow, fire created extensive damage to the gymnasium requiring the show to be held at the Municipal Auditorium. Performances by the Flashes had to be limited.*

The Band and Flash Floor Show, held in the Municipal Auditorium due to fire damage to the gym, was emceed by Superintendent H. H. Chambers. The floor show was opened with the traditional "Little Moron" joke, and the audience gave a resounding cheer.

Following the opening number, with the Band and Flashes marching down the aisles to, "Thunderer March," Max Spikes and Durwood Speed played a coronet duet to "Al and Pal." The crowd clapped to the music as the Flashes marched down the aisles, across the front of the stage, and back up the aisles doing a precision drill to "Sound Off" played by the GHS Band. Charles Pickens and Helen Moudy charmed attendees by singing "Night and Day" followed by a whistling solo to "My Blue Heaven" by William Wise. Mary Helen Goad played an accordion solo, "Tea for Two," and received a large ovation. After the band played "Jalousie," the new Flashes were presented. The crowd returned to their seats as the second half began with the band's rendition of "Colonel Bogey's March." Dancing to "Limehouse Blues," were Bobby Ashley and Helen Moudy, followed by a saxophone solo by Charles Morris playing "An Earl." Geraldine Irons, Gloria Swindell, and Helen Mary Goad, accompanied by Mrs. Donald Course, sang "Guilty." Gary Scott played a solo, "Blue Skies," followed by Mike Adkisson's clarinet solo, "Gaiety Polka." The Flashes wowed the crowd with their routine to "Parade of the Wooden Soldiers." Joe Rutherford drew applause with his horn solo "When Day Is Done." Following "Little Rhapsody in Blue," the band upped the tempo for the rousing finale and both groups performed as the crowd cheered.

Despite a fire in the gymnasium, the GHS Band and Flashes showed the crowd that, "The show must go on!"

The 1947 royal wedding of Princess Elizabeth to Phillip Mountbatten, Duke of Edinburgh, made world headlines and dominated the airwaves. The popular songs "Almost Like Being in Love" and "I'll Dance at Your Wedding" seemed appropriate. "Flying Saucers" were reported in the United States as the "New Look" dominated female fashions. Jackie Robinson became the first Black to sign a contract with a major baseball club.

In 1948, Ghandi's assassination and the creation of the Jewish state (with Weizman as President and Ben-Gurion as Premier) made headlines. The USSR stopped all road and rail traffic between Berlin and the West. It seems the world was about to enter a war of a different kind.

The GHS Band and Flashes continued lifting spirits at community and school events. The 1947-1948 school year saw the title of "Head Drum Major" of the Flashes changed to "Head Majorette." Leaders were:

    Head Majorette.................................Shirley Riley
                              (sister of Doris Riley Smith)
    Senior Majorette ....Betty Jean Kennedy
    Junior Majorette...............................Bobbie Lou Scott
    US Flag...Suezane Powell (Brunette)
    Texas Flag..Julie Leftwich (Blonde)
    School Flag ....Barbara Davis (Red Head)

Members

Amiteen Arey	Helen Mary Goad	Martha O'Hara
Mary Lee Aven	Maurine Hall	Joyce Ray
Joan Beckham	Virginia Hall	Wanda Rogers
Lou Ann Bell	Gloria Hill	Bobby Lou Scott
Alta Blackwell	Jimmie Hulsey	Jackie Spigner
Mary Ann Boyd	Jenny Irons	Janelle Stapleton
Benny Brown	Joyce Jones	Gloria Swindell
Elaine Connally	Lou Ann Lloyd	Barbara West
Doris Combs	Laurie Lockhart	Betty White
Robbie Duncan	Lou Jean Mahaffey	Virginia Wilson
Dorothy Dulaney	Ruth McDonald	Patsy Young

Head Drum Major for the GHS Band was Billy Robertson with Bobbie Jean Green, Band Sweetheart, marching alongside. Another successful floorshow helped the Band and Flash Parents Club to provide better award jackets to graduating members. New band equipment was also purchased along with replacement uniforms for the coming year.

Rosemary Middlebrook

September of 1948 brought changes with a new superintendent, J. A. Anderson, at Greenville ISD and a new director of The Flaming Flashes, Miss Rosemary Middlebrook. Headlines and airwaves were dominated by debates, speeches, and campaign promises with the presidential election racing toward the November election. All Harry Truman wanted was to be elected as president, since he had succeeded FDR upon his death in 1945. On a popular note, "All I Want for Christmas Is My Two Front Teeth," made its way to the top of the Hit Parade. Prince Charles, the Prince of Wales, was born and Babe Ruth, baseball Home Run King, died.

Miss Middlebrook inherited a well-trained group of Flashes in 1948-49 and was pleased that "Mr. Ed," a seasoned veteran of halftime and floorshow performances, was there to guide her through the paces. Flash Leaders were:

Rosemary Middlebrook

Head Majorette	Bobby Lou Scott
Senior Majorette	Gloria Swindell
Junior Majorette	Dionne Moore
American Flag Bearer	Lou Jean Mahaffey
Texas Flag Bearer	Lou Ann Bell
School Flag Bearer	Joan Beckham
Managers	Sue Taylor, Buddy Baldwin

Flash Members

Amiteen Arey	Helen Fowler	Lillian Harvey	Martha Jane Pugh
Alta Blackwell	Martha Boffard	Gloria Hill	Peggy Reynolds
Bennye Brown	Helen Mary Goad	Mary Lou Hoff	Betty Riddle
Iva Lea Carter	Evelyn Goad	Helen Hogue	Wanda Rogers
Claudine Caldwell	Katherine Green	Jerry Irons	Ann Rutherford
Margie Castle	Maurine Hall	Coye Lee Jones	Barbara Seaman
Jewell Cotrell	Bobby Faye Scott	Laurie Lockhart	Lou Warren
Doris Combs	Peggy Scott	Ruth McDonald	Oleta Weaver
Jean Couch	Suzanne Smith	Anna Mary Morris	Betty Wilhite
Dorothy Dulaney	Jackie Springer	Martha O'Hara	Peggy Spradling
Robbie Duncan	Lanell Sumrow	Audrey Pannell	Martha Van Landingham
Anna English	Barbara Tacker	Nasa Pollard	

Leading the GHS Band was Drum Major Allen Boyd Harrison with Band Sweetheart, Jimmie Hulsey, at his side. Melva Hamilton, Student Director, assisted Mr. Bernard and kept the music going when "Mr. Ed" was busy. Ben Butler and Hal Bryant served as Band Managers.

Greenville High School was abuzz with excitement during spring 1949. Hollywood was coming to Greenville! *The Stratton Story,* the amazing story of local baseball legend Monty Stratton, played by James (Jimmy) Stewart with June Allyson as his wife, Ethel, had its world premiere at The Texan Theater in downtown Greenville.

Dionne (Moore) Wade recalled the excitement she felt, as a Junior Majorette in the Flashes, when the GHS Band and Flashes marched in the Monty Stratton Day parade. During the festivities, Dionne was privileged to meet the movie star, June Allyson, who played the role of Monty's wife, Ethel. Dionne was impressed with Miss Allyson's beauty, poise and enthusiasm. People came from all over the United States for this special event.

Stratton, an outstanding professional baseball pitcher for the Chicago White Sox for five years, made the American League All-Star squad. An unfortunate hunting accident caused the amputation of his right leg. Equipped with a wooden leg, he continued to play baseball and won eighteen games. Stratton later served as pitching coach for the White Sox before retiring to Greenville.

Springtime in Greenville is floorshow time. New Superintendent J. A. Anderson learned quickly that the "Little Moron" joke was a vital part of the show, and did not disappoint the crowd. A number of musical renditions by band members and specialty numbers followed the opening. Patsy Young tapped her way into the hearts of the audience with "Is You Is or Is You Ain't My Baby." Tap dancing seemed to be "the rage." The Flashes performed a "Cowboy Tap" to "I'm An Old Cowhand" and received a standing ovation. Presentation of the new Flashes, during intermission, once again was a time for tears of joy and sadness.

President Harry S. Truman was inaugurated in January of 1949, and had to deal with "hot potato" issues throughout 1949-1950. China fell under Communist rule and Mao-Tse-tung took control. Israel was admitted to the United Nations and its capital was moved from

Tel Aviv to Jerusalem. The United Nations warned of war in Korea. Gene Autrey's song "Rudolph, the Red-Nosed Reindeer" and the music from the movie *South Pacific* helped to soothe the public as they turned a deaf ear to more talk of war.

Activities at GHS kept moving with the times. Another year of making music and marching was in order, so Mr. Bernard and Miss Middlebrook planned accordingly and leaders, presented during the spring floorshow, stepped into their roles. As always, the GHS Band and Flaming Flashes had a plan and a mission for 1949-1950. Leaders named were:

Head Majorette	Dionne Moore
Senior Majorette	Lillian Harvey
Junior Majorette	Ina Rue Mooney
American Flag Bearer	Iva Lee Carter
Texas Flag Bearer	Claudine Caldwell
School Flag Bearer	Helen Hogue
Flash Managers	Betty Baggett, Bobby Connell

Flashes

Barbara Brown	Erika Heidman	Peggy Reynolds	Peggy Spradling
Marilyn Carter	Evelyn Hilmer	Betty Riddle	Suzanne Starling
Helen Converse	Belda Hughey	Billie Joyce Ross	Earlene Stevens
Jewell Cantrell	Janie Kilgore	Ann Rutherford	Frances Stinson
Norma Davenport	Betsy Kincade	Peggy Scott	Ava Nell Taylor
Greta Deweese	Coye Lee Jones	Wanda Scott	Doris Tipton
Helen Dickson	Doris Lewis	Barbara Seaman	Mary Virginia Turner
Joan Dorman	Jacklin Long	Suzanne Smith	Joan Wright
Pat Dye	Audrey Pannell	Jane Seaman	Martha VanLandingham
Lonnie England	Zelma Partridge	Delores Slaughter	Charlotte Wood
Mary Ann Frazier	Nasa Pollard	Lanell Sumrow	Mary Lynn Waldin
Curtis Ann Gibbs	Martha Jane Pugh	Dixie Smith	

The GHS Band had a different "look" this year. Females were selected to be members of the band for the first time and joined the males in making "Music, Music, Music"...the popular song that year. Wanda Branch, Rama Henry, Frances Higgins, Ruth Humphrys, and Idris Traylor were listed as members of the GHS Band in the floorshow program. Tommy Felmet served as Head Drum Major and Margie Castle was Band Sweetheart. Buddy Young, Dwight Pickens, and Reeves Perry were managers.

Dionne Moore Wade wrote:

> *One of the most profound memories of being Drum Major of The Flaming Flashes...was when we performed at halftime at the Cotton Bowl to mark a special recognition of Allan Shivers, Governor of Texas. I still am amazed at the feeling of immense size of the stadium when we, and the band, marched out of the south end entrance onto the field. The feeling was*

just short of terror. [*Author's Note:* Governors Allan Shivers and Rick Perry are the only two lieutenant governors, to date, to become governor through succession and are the only two to serve four times as Governors of Texas.]

Mr. Harry Flewharty, Principal, opened the GHS Band and Flash Floorshow with his usual "Little Moron" joke on March 16 and 17, 1950. Dionne Moore performed a solo number to "A Pretty Girl Is Like A Melody," followed by Marshall Head playing a saxophone solo. Joan West tapped her way across the gym floor to "Ain't We Got Fun." "Clowning Around" was performed by Riley Walker, followed by Lillian Harvey and Iva Lee Carter dancing the "Mexican Hat Dance." "Rhythmoods" by the band led to a precision drill routine by the Flashes just before intermission. After the presentation of new members, the crowd was delighted by the Flashes' dancing to the music of "Stardust."

Peggie Spradling Darby recalled a particular floorshow costume:

In the spring of 1950 Flash director, Rosemary Middlebrook, selected a costume with shorts for one of the floor show numbers. After making the decision for the Flashes to wear shorts she began to worry about her decision, because the Flashes had never appeared in a short costume before. Miss Middlebrook almost worried herself sick about the reaction of those attending the floor show. All of her worry was in vain, as the audience loved the number and thought the costume was great.

The headlines in 1950 spouted North Korea's thrust across the 38th parallel into South Korea. Military conflict ensued. The general public could watch the news and programs unfold on their black and white television screens, while the affluent watched in "color." Some people now had "live" entertainment in their homes…but, this is Texas, and that means football games and halftime performances.

Miss Middlebrook and Mr. Ed planned another year of exciting activities for the GHS Band and Flashes. Leaders for 1950-51 were:

Head Majorette	Ina Rue Mooney
Senior Majorette	Mary Lynn Walden
Junior Majorette	Ramona Dunlap
US Flag	Pat Dye
Texas Flag	Zelda Hughey
School Flag	Erika Heidmann
Flash Managers	Frances T. Thomason, Willene Duncan

Flash Members

Mary Ann Alexander	Glenna Duff	Zelma Partridge	Jackie Shaw
Mary Helen Bland	Lonnie England	Nancy Patella	Ava Nell Taylor
Barbara Brown	Mary Ann Frazier	Billy Ray	Doris Tipton
Marilyn Carter	Billie Clyde Freeman	Carmen Smith	Mary Virginia Turner
Joyce Canup	Freia Friddle	Dixie Smith	Sofia Torres
Norma Combs	Louise Harris	Barbara Stanford	Joan Wright
Helen Converse	Betsy Kincade	Suzanne Starling	Charlotte Wood
Nita Dees	Davy Jane Lynch	Wanda Scott	Billie Joyce Ross
Norma Devenport	Doris Lewis	Jane Seaman	Rue Nell McMillan
Greta Deweese	Jacklin Long	Earline Stevens	
Helen Dickson	Peggy Moore	Frances Stinson	

Leading the GHS Band was Drum Major Marshall Head and Joan Dorman, Band Sweetheart. Bobby Ingram and Wayne Boyd served as Student Directors. Reeves Perry and Benny Gaddis were Band Managers.

Another "first" was the addition of a twirling line for the GHS Band. Lee Ann Feagan served as Head Twirler for twirlers Laverne Headrick, Frances Sigler, Joan Newby, Ann Bramlett, and Shirley Youngblood.

GHS Principal Harry Flewharty, a fixture as emcee of the floorshow, made sure the "Little Moron" joke opened the show, followed by a cornet quartet, "The Trumpeters," played by Wayne Boyd, Jerry Coker, Phillip Love and James McKinney. "Ship Ahoy," a routine by the Flashes, followed the Charleston, a dance solo by Joan West. Ina Rue Mooney, Mary Lynn Walden, Ramona Dunlap, Pat Dye, Erika Heidman, and Zelda Hughey performed as if they were skating on ice to "Skaters Waltz." The last routine by the Flashes was a lovely hula dance. Another successful floorshow helped to raise funds for replacement items and honor jackets for graduates of both groups.

In 1951-1952, King George of England died, and his daughter, Queen Elizabeth II, succeeded him. Prime Minister Churchill announced that Britain had produced an atomic bomb and President Truman released the news of hydrogen bomb tests in the Pacific. "Wheel of Fortune," "Jambalaya," and "Your Cheatin' Heart" were at the top of the music charts. *High Noon*, starring Gary Cooper and Grace Kelly, plus *The Greatest Show on Earth* were the top movies on the silver screen.

Ramona Dunlap (Wright)'s childhood dream came true in 1951-52:

> *As a young girl, my parents would take my little brother and me to the GHS football games. I would watch the Band and Flashes march up*

Ramona Dunlap (Wright)

and down the field and imagined myself as someday wearing the big hat as Head Majorette. Being a part of the GHS Flaming Flashes is one of my most memorable life experiences.

Not only did Ramona realize her childhood dream, but also her graduating class moved from the old high school in 1951, and became the first to graduate from the new high school on Texas Street in 1952. Band and Flash leaders were:

Head Majorette	Ramona Dunlap
Senior Majorette	Nancy Patella
Junior Majorette	Ollene Carpenter
American Flag Bearer	Carmen Smith
Texas Flag Bearer	Joyce Canup
School Flag Bearer	Rue Nell McMillon
Student Flash Director	Jackie Shaw (a new position)
Flash Managers	Carleen Turner, Riley Walker

Joyce Canup, Carmen Smith, Rue Nell McMillon (1951-1952)

Flash members listed in the annual floorshow program were:

Betty Kate Anderson	Shirley Dixon	Betty Jacks	Allie Mae Stevens
Mary Helen Bland	Barbara Erwin	Bessie Mae Landrum	Virginia Sykes
Pat Boyce	Anita Fletcher	Davy Jane Lynch	Sofia Torres
Bennie Bowen	Billie Clyde Freeman	Mary Lynn Marion	Betty Tune
Gloria Brown	Carolyn Gauntt	Nancy Nalls	Joann Walker
Dorothy Chandler	Billie Green	Nancy Neal	Linda Sue Wall
Norma Combs	Ruth Green	Ramona Orr	Nancy Kate Warren
Jane Crawford	Norma Hanson	Eva Nell Parmely	Sue Nan Wells
Doris Copeland	Louise Harris	Billye Ray	
Loretta Cunningham	Hope Ann Hawkins	Jackie Shaw	

Carmen Smith (Foti) and Mary Lynn Marion (Patterson)

Mary Lynn Marion (Patterson) recalled playing a drum in the drum and bugle corps. "Funky" boots and skirts below the knees were worn.

For the first time, GHS Cheerleaders were listed in and were a part of the annual floorshow. Head Cheerleaders were Sara Jacobs and Billy Clyde Davis. Junior Cheerleaders were Ann Roberts and Gene Hulsey.

Leading the GHS Band was Drum Major Bobby Bush with Band Sweetheart Barbara Stanford. Head Twirler, Frances Sigler led Melba Lowe, Johnnie Erwin, Jo Ann Newby, Lou Benson, and Laverne Hedrick in twirling routines. Jimmy Ray Hamilton was Student Band Director. Reeves Stuth and Jerry Dees were Band Managers. Principal J. H. Flewharty served as emcee of the floorshow and the "Little Moron" joke christened the gym floor of the new high school on Texas Street. Following the opening number by the GHS Band and Flashes, Wayne Boyd delivered his coronet solo and Joane Walker performed to "Birth of the Blues." The Flashes strutted to "Darktown Strutters" followed by a vocal selection, "Moonlight and Roses," by Wanda Branch, Lou Benson, and Peggy Rice. Jimmy Stuth entertained with a saxophone solo and Ramona Dunlap wowed the crowd with acrobatics. Mary Lynn Marion and Pat Boyce slowed the tempo with a soft shoe routine to "Tea for Two."

GHS Dance Band members Wayne Boyd and Philip Love (trumpets), James Wilson (bass), Johnny Thompson (drums), Wanda Branch (tenor sax), Jimmy Stuth and Morris Long (alto sax), Bobby Bush (clarinet) with Carolyn Sheperd, on the piano, played various selections following the traditional presentation of new members of both groups plus the cheerleaders, during intermission. "Which Way Did They Go?," a routine by the Flashes, was followed by "They Went That-A-Way" performed by the cheerleaders. A precision dance routine by the Flashes to "Winter Wonderland" was followed by the twirlers performing to "Lullaby of Broadway." Another successful floorshow closed with mixed emotions for outgoing and incoming members.

Carmen Smith (Foti) noted that being in the Flashes was always fun, "We made lifelong friends, and it would not have been possible without the band."

Carmen's comments ring true. The GHS Band and The Flaming Flashes are an integral unit. As the lyrics to the song "Love and Marriage" state, "you can't have one without the other."

1952-53 ushered in a new school year and brought the inauguration of Dwight David Eisenhower as President of the United States and Winston Churchill, British Prime Minister, to visit him. Changes also took place in Europe with the crowning of Queen Elizabeth II, and the deaths of Queen Mary of England and Joseph Stalin of the USSR. *From Here to Eternity* won the Academy Award as "Doggie in the Window" hit the music charts.

New Superintendent of Schools Ray Brown quickly learned, through his daughter, Betty, how important the GHS Band and Flaming Flashes were to Greenville. Within a year, Betty would be a member of the Flashes…followed by being Junior Majorette, then Head Majorette. He would be steeped in Flash Tradition. Leaders for 1952-53 included:

Billie Berry (Thompson) and Mary Lynn Marion (Patterson)

Head Majorette	Ollene Carpenter
Senior Majorette	Ruth Green
Junior Majorette	Nancy Rogers
American Flag Bearer	Mary Lynn Marion
Texas Flag Bearer	Billie Jean Green
School Flag Bearer	Nancy Kate Warren
Flash Manager	Betty Stansel

Flaming Flash Members

Delia Asberry	Barbara Erwin	Betty Jacks	Kathy Remington
Beverly Becton	Florence Erwin	Nancy Jenkins	Carolyn Shepherd
Billie Berry	Carolyn Gauntt	Peggy Little	Virginia Sikes
Gloria Brown	Mary Ann Green	Bessie Mae Landrum	Amanda Temple
Doris Copeland	Martha Hoff	Lavera McMillan	Joan Walker
Anita Carter	Norma Hanson	Ludene McWhirter	Linda Sue Wall
Dorothy Chandler	Hope Hawkins	Nancy Neel	Sue Nan Wells
Jane Crawford	Lucy Harwell	Eva Nell Parmely	Ann Williams
Shirley Dixon	Julia Herlocker	Patricia Phillips	Loreta Cunningham
Shirley Dugan	Durelle English	Carol Porter	

Leading the GHS Band was Drum Major Bob Bush with Ramona Orr as Band Sweetheart. Philip Love and Morris Long served as Student Directors. Head Twirler Lou Benson led twirlers Lynda Ball, Martha Cozart, Shirley Boose, and Florinne Carson. Reeves Stuth served as Band Manager.

Ollene Carpenter surprised the Flashes by resigning at the end of football season. She secretly married Bobby Ray during the summer of 1952 and hoped to keep her secret through her senior year. Mother Nature changed her plans. Records of the annual floorshow list only two majorettes, Ruth Green and Nancy Rogers. Everyone knows, "the show must go on" as it did on March 26 and 27 of 1953.

Principal Flewharty unleashed the "Little Moron" joke to open the show. Wayne Boyd played a cornet solo to "Smoke Gets in Your Eyes." Norma Feezor danced to "Doggie in the Window" followed by a delightful Flash routine to "Singing in the Rain." Bobby Bush, Billy Morgan, Gordon Thomas, and John Robert Fraser made music to "Dry Bones" followed by a solo by Ramona Orr. The Flashes and Ronnie Houston shook things up with the "Charleston" followed by Joan Walker's rendition of "Lady of Spain." Presentation of new members led to a second half of Indian Interlude. "Taw Ye Taw" by Mary Lynn Marion, Julia Herlocker, and Nancy Rogers followed Ramona Orr's solo to "Indian Love Call". The "Heap Big Pow Wow" Flash routine closed the Indian theme and the twirlers danced to "Highland Fling." "Liberty Belles" by the Flashes brought the crowd to their feet. The Grand Finale by the entire cast kept them standing and clapping as the show closed. The usual emotions of sadness were doubled as Miss Middlebrook announced her departure. Leaving GHS after five years, she married Max E. Causey and taught P. E. plus directed the Golden Jackets at Garland High School.

Mary Lynn Marion

Julia Herlocker (Gibson Schwartz) and Mary Lynn Marion (Patterson)

Mary Lynn Marion (Patterson) recalled:
> *My senior year, 1953, I was American Flag Bearer. The uniforms took a drastic change. The short skirt was added, plus white Western boots. With Rosemary Middlebrook as our director, I must say these two years were a*

great joy in my life. The icing on the cake was the Band and Flash Floorshow. Wonderful memories were made during this time. P. S. All three of my daughters were Flashes.

Eva Nell Parmely (Collinsworth) added her memories.

We only had bugles my first year. A front row of drummers was added in 1953. Learning to play the drum was an achievement. The floorshow routine where we wore lovely nylon net dresses as the band played "Deep Purple" and raising my right foot to the beginning strains of "Peruna" are two favorites. The crowds in the grandstands would go wild!

Sandy Allbright

Local newspapers, radio, and television stations spread the news that the USSR had exploded a hydrogen bomb. Churchill, Eisenhower and Laniel met in Bermuda to discuss world affairs. Col. Nasser seized power in Egypt and became premier and head of state. Once again, change was in the air... and Greenville was no different.

Mrs. Sandy Allbright reported for duty as the new director of the Flashes for 1953-54. GHS Band and Flash members were already in place and knew what to do, but as a novice to teaching, she was overwhelmed. She decided to eliminate the use of drums and bugles and change routines. Officers and Members were:

Sandy Albright

Head Majorette	Nancy Rogers
Senior Majorette	Martha Hoff
Junior Majorette	Betty Brown
American Flag Bearer	Billye Berry
Texas Flag Bearer	Mary Ann Green
School Flag Bearer	Patricia Phillips
Flash Managers	Dolores Harbuck, Carolyn Wells

Members

Bonnie Apple	Gail Dunlap	Nancy Jenkins	Kathie Remington
Delia Asberry	Barbara Gardner	Peggy Little	Anna Fay Reynolds
Jo Ann Barrett	Becky George	Bonnie Long	Kay Russell
Jean Baumgardner	Anna Green	Ludean McWhirter	Maurice Sawyer
Patsy Brown	Margaret Green	Jo Ann Miller	Carolyn Shepherd
Ida Mae Connatser	Lou Nell Hansard	Sara Miracle	Amanda Temple
Anita Carter	Julia Herlocker	Mary Dee Odell	Ann Williams
Leah Covington	Durelle Inglish	Carole Porter	Mary Kay Wilson

Drum Major Leon Swindell led the band with Band Sweetheart Laverne McMillon. Head Twirler Martha Cozart led Shirley Boose, Florinne Carson, Glenda Henry, Mary Beth

Erwin, and LaJoy Scott in their routines. John Robert Fraser served as Student Director for the band. Reeves Stuth was Band Manager.

Principal J. H. Flewharty and the "Little Moron" joke were fixtures...so another floorshow opened traditionally. The theme was "The Months of the Year." The Band and Flashes opened with January, and February brought the "Battle Hymn of The Republic" by the band and "Let Me Call You Sweetheart" by John Robert Fraser and Barbara Bennett. March featured a ballroom dance to "Girl of My Dreams." April ushered in the "Easter Parade" sung by Patsy Hawthorne, Mona Blocker, and Carolyn Belew. The band played prior to the Flashes' routine to "Bunny Hop." May featured a routine by the Senior Flashes to "Graduation Day." (The first time the Band and Flashes danced together in a floorshow.) Presentation of new members, held during intermission, was followed by "I Love You Truly," a solo by Nancy Jenkins, for the month of June. The twirlers presented a spirited routine to "Stars and Stripes Forever" for July. The cheerleaders were again included in the floorshow with an August "Vacation By the Beautiful Sea," featuring Joan Glassman, Dean Gantt, Bettye Johnston, Paula Patterson, Ann Newell, and Joe Bryant. The Flashes danced to "School Days" for September, and for October, the Flag Bearers and Majorettes danced to "Old Black Magic." (Another "first"...their own number in a floorshow, minus Senior Majorette Martha Hoff, who had left to marry Maxey Stone.) The band played "Thanksgiving Medley" for November followed by "White Christmas" for December. The final routine to end the parade of months was the "Parade of the Wooden Soldiers" by the Flashes...the final performance for seniors.

Floor Show, 1954: Paula Strawn (Jacobs), a new flash, and Anita Carter (Wallace).

Lois Dooley (Myers) wrote:
> *I remember trying out for the Flashes in 1954 and how scared I was, because, I wanted to be selected so badly. I couldn't wait to get home from school the day the names of the ones picked were to be announced on "Lion's Roar" on the radio. The suspense of waiting to hear your name called was unbelievable, but, sure enough, I heard the name "Lois Dooley"*

and I screamed with joy! That was one happy day! I remember all the hard workouts, getting ready for the floorshow and going on all those fun bus trips to out of town football games. I loved the camaraderie we all shared and how we always looked out for each other. Those were the days...I should never forget!

Mrs. Allbright decided to leave after one year, so the search began for another director for the Flashes. Many were sad to see her leave, except one, Jane McMillon (Hankel), who suffered a disappointment under Mrs. Allbright...as noted below:

My dream, since elementary school, was to try out for Junior Majorette and to be the Head Majorette of the Flashes in my senior year. The director, Sandy Allbright, who was only at GHS for a year, changed the structure so there would no longer be a Junior Majorette position moving to Head Majorette. Instead, there was a Head Majorette and two Senior Majorettes. I can't tell you how bitterly disappointed I was to have to wait another year. The emotion that I feel now, at age 76, just thinking about it is proof enough of how important Flashes were to the young ladies of Greenville. Nevertheless, I did try out the next year, and I was selected as Head Majorette for the 1955-56 year by Margaret Schulze.

Margaret Schulze

The era of "Couch Potatoes" was growing as over 29 million homes in the United States now had television... and the numbers kept growing. Americans made up six percent of the world's population but owned 60% of all cars, 58% of all telephones, 45% of all radios, and 34% of all railroads. One thing is guaranteed in life... there will be change.

Exciting changes came to GHS in 1954-55. James (Mutt) and Margaret Schulze were positive faculty additions. Mutt, a tennis star, entered East Texas State Teachers College with a tennis scholarship, but left to serve the U.S. Air Force as pilot in WW II. He was part of the D-Day invasion dropping paratroopers and pulling Horsa gliders into France and took part in the Battle of the Bulge. After WWII, he earned two degrees from East Texas State Teachers College in Commerce (now A&M-Commerce) and was teacher/coach for Commerce ISD. Margaret and Mutt were proud parents of a little girl, Dixie.

Mrs. Schulze was excited about coming to GHS to serve as director of the Flashes, as she had read much about them in the Greenville newspapers. She knew her job would be challenging, especially with a young child at home, but she was ready for this new experience. Instead of having Junior and Senior Majorettes, two Senior Majorettes were named at the prior floorshow. The order of succession had changed. These Flashes were ready for challenges.

Head Majorette	Betty Rae Brown
Senior Majorettes	Bonnie Long, Sara Miracle
American Flag Bearer	Barbara Gardner
Texas Flag Bearer	Jo Ann Barrett
School Flag Bearer	Lynne Williams

Flash Managers were identified as Senior Manager Carolyn Wells and Junior Manager Ann Arant.

Flash Members

Pat Alexander	Janet Flewharty	Betty Love	Anna Faye Reynolds
Bonnie Apple	Sandra Flick	Jane McMillan	Kay Russell
Jean Baumgardner	Dee Gardner	Dodie Mastro	Marice Sawyer
June Benner	Becky George	Jo Ann Miller	Nini Sawyer
Barbara Bennett	Martha Goad	Virginia Morgan	Sue Stinson
Patsy Brown	Anna Green	Francine Morris	Paula Strawn
Lynn Bryant	Margaret Green	Jo Rene Myers	Kay Treadway
Ida Mae Connatser	Barbara Gray	Marilu Neel	Mary Alice Warren
Claudia Carter	Lou Nell Hansard	Sue Newell	Joyce Watson
Lois Dooley	Pat Harbuck	Jane Nix	Mary Williams
Gail Dunlap	Kay Hawkins	Mary Dee O'Dell	Gwendolyn Wilson
Shirley Erwin	Judy Jenkins	Gail Palmer	Mary Kay Wilson
Peggy Felmet	Barbara Little	Alice Nell Powers	

Drum Major Bill Morgan and Pat Bussey, Band Sweetheart, led the band. Student Directors were Douglas Driggers and Bill Hardaway. Head Twirler Mary Beth Erwin led Bonnie Lager, Sarah Denton, and Cecile Sivley in twirling routines. Band Managers were Jerry Clark and John McDaniel.

Spring 1955 was filled with plans for the annual floorshow scheduled for March 24-25. Tryouts for new officers and new members of the band and Flashes were held and selections were made. Current Flash officers contacted those selected to replace them in the coming year by going to their homes during the night and sharing the good news. Senior Flashes did the same for those selected as new Flashes, their "Little Sisters," much to their delight.

Once the music was selected, a schedule arranged, and routines planned for the floorshow, both groups worked diligently to provide another successful show. Ads for programs were sold in January, costumes and decorations were selected before the end of February, and the show was ready by March.

Principal Flewharty had a "vested interest" in this floorshow. Not only was "Mr. Flew" the "emcee of choice" with his delivery of the "Little Moron" joke, his daughter, Janet, was a member of the Flashes and would be performing. He was, indeed, very proud as the band playing marches by John Philip Sousa while the Flashes conducted their sharp precision drill. Bill Morgan, Bill Le Rosen, and Bobby Spradling followed with a cornet trio. "Sympathy" sung by Barbara Ben-

Pat Bussey passes the hat to incoming band sweetheart, Paula Strawn (Jacobs), 1956

nett and Gordon Thomas, allowed the Flashes to get into costumes for their next numbers. After the band played "Spook Session," the twirlers performed to "Tea for Two." A "first" for the program was the Junior Flashes' routine danced to "Arkansas Traveler." The band followed with "When the Saints Go Marching In" sung by Gordon Thomas. Intermission brought the presentation of new members of both groups for the next year. The Flashes opened the second half with a precision routine to "There's Something About A Soldier" followed by a routine by the cheerleaders to "Old Grey Mare." Another "first" was the routine danced by the Senior Flashes to "Shuffle Off to Buffalo." The outgoing majorettes and flag bearers followed by dancing to "Mood Indigo." A clarinet quartet by James Cole, Larry Miller, Denny Herndon, and David Flinn, led to the closing number for the Flashes dancing to "Mambo Marcho." The finale involved both groups as the crowd showed their appreciation with a standing ovation. Credit for lighting for the show was given to Mr. Bob Andrews, who was assisted by Bobby Dicken, Allen Ablowich, and Robert O'Dell. Mr. George Murdaugh, Assistant Principal (and a former leader of the GHS Band), was in charge of the sound.

Jane McMillon (Hankel), who was presented as the Head Majorette during the floorshow, recalled the following:

> *During the summer of 1955, Mrs. Schulze and I drove everyday to TWU at Denton for two weeks to a drill team camp conducted by Gussie Nell Davis and her Rangerette officers. What a thrill that was to get to work with the woman who was an icon at GHS and in the whole town, for that matter.*

Winston Churchill resigned as Prime Minister of Britain, Peron stepped down as President of Argentina, and President Eisenhower suffered a heart attack in 1955. Blacks in Montgomery, Alabama, boycotted segregated city bus lines. "Rock and Roll" music, according to

Greenville High School Flaming Flashes, 1955-1956.
(Courtesy: James Narramore)

some parents, was ruining teenagers. The news media made sure the public was informed. What happened to those "happy days?" The GHS Band and Flashes absorbed the news and moved forward into 1955-56 without missing a step. Moving forward were:

> Head Majorette .... Jane McMillon
> Senior Majorettes .... Barbara Gray
>   Mary Alice Warren
> American Flag Bearer .... Sue Stinson
> Texas Flag Bearer .... Gayle Palmer
> School Flag Bearer .... Nini Sawyer

Managers were Ann Arant and Doris Ross. Dixie Schulze, the daughter of Mutt and Margaret Schulze, was the first mascot. Flash members were:

Pat Alexander	Lois Dooley	Barbara Little	Barbara Row
Billie Kate Anderson	Sue Dorman	Betty Love	Joan Samuel
Beryle Asberry	Charlsie Duncan	Betty Millsap	Janelle Shepherd
Jocelyn Baumgardner	Shirley Erwin	Francine Morris	Carolyn Simmons
Melvina Benesch	Peggy Felmet	Marilou Neel	Jane Sinclair
June Benner	Janet Flewharty	Sue Newell	Suzanne Smith
Barbara Bennett	Sandra Flick	Jane Nix	Carol Ann Stephens
Gwendolyn Bowen	Carolyn Fowler	Pat Norsworthy	Sue Stephens
Lynn Bryant	Martha Goad	Ann Poole	Dee Spradling
Claudia Carter	Pat Harbuck	Alta Pope	Kay Treadway
Patsy Combs	Kay Hawkins	Dow Nelle Porter	Jackie West
Nancy Craig	Carolyn Henson	Alice Nell Powers	Dolores Williamson
Carol Deberry	Melba Hunt	Linda Roark	Leah Rita Stephenson

Drum Major, Ronald Howard, and Band Sweetheart, Paula Strawn, led the GHS Band. Student Director was Gary Paul Johnson and Head Twirler was Mary Beth Erwin. Bonnie Lager, Sarah Deaton, Cecile Sivley, Ann Marshall, and Janet Henson were twirlers. Band Managers were Jimmy Hooten and Jerry Clark.

Time and floorshow preparation wait for no one. Plans were made for another stellar performance for March 22 and 23. Routines and music must be learned, ads must be sold to pay for printing the floorshow program, costumes must be bought or made, tryouts for new membership must be completed, and a practice schedule must be followed so all would fall into place by dress rehearsal. Over two months of dedication and hard work by all is necessary. The show must go on... this time with a new emcee.

Assistant Principal George Murdaugh, a veteran of many floorshows, was chosen, with the stipulation that the "Little Moron" joke be included. The rousing opening to "There's Something About A Home Town Band" had the crowd clapping as Band and Flash members marched around the gym with new multi-colored spotlights providing a kaleidoscope of color swirling through the decorated gym. "Twilight Dreams," a baritone solo by Jerry Thomasson, helped to slow the pace before "Big Horn Boogie," played by the band, set the crowd clapping again. The pace slowed dramatically as Ronald Howard and Jane Mc-

Millon danced the tango to "Jalousie." The Flashes revved up the tempo with their polka routine followed by the twirlers with "Can Can." A brass quartet eased the tempo toward intermission and presentation of new members and officers of both groups. The Flashes waltzed gracefully into the second half to "Waves of The Danube" followed by GHS Dance Band (Adrian Smith, James Copeland, Richard Price, Betty Bennett, Larry Miller, Charles Johnson, George Shepherd, and Ronald Howard) playing popular tunes. "*Chiapañecas*," brought the Flashes back with a Latin beat. Changing the tempo, the flag bearers, majorettes, and band sweetheart danced to "Ballet Egyptian." (A "first" for Flash officers to invite Band Sweetheart, Paula Strawn, to join them.) "Colorama" was played to lead the program to its finale to "Mickey Mouse March," performed by the entire cast. Credit was given to Mr. Bob Andrews and members of the Lighting Committee: Allen Ablowich, Ronnie Ablowich, Jimmy Bowen, Rodney Follis, Wallace Fowler, Gary Johnson, Bobby Jones, and Robert O'Dell. [*Author's Note:* Head Cheerleaders Janice Permenter and Bobby Brigman, plus Juniors Donna Kay Crawford, Laska Hughey, and Jean Hudson did not perform a routine as in past years. New cheerleaders Melva and Belva Rice and Dianne Patterson were presented.]

Jane McMillon (Hankel) recalled:

> *My senior year leading the Flashes was all I ever hoped it would be. I loved working with Mrs. Schulze choreographing routines. I loved teaching the routines to the Flashes and going from the chaos of beginning to learn the routines to the polished performances at football halftimes. That sense of accomplishment for all of us, I still cherish. There are so many memories... the bus rides to away games, the chartered train to the game in Sherman, my mother sitting at her sewing machine making my floorshow costumes, all my Flash sisters, my senior majorette good friends, Mrs. Schulze's young daughter, Dixie, who was the Flash mascot, late night practices for the floorshow, and many more.*
>
> *Once a Flash, always a Flash. Four years ago I started taking line dance lessons with a group of senior women and fell in love with choreographed dancing all over again. A couple of years ago, our teacher, who drove from another town to teach us, decided to give up the class and asked me if I would take it. I was thrilled. For the last two years, I have been teaching line dance twice a week to an extraordinary group of women who have bonded in a way that I have rarely experienced before. We come together to exercise our bodies and our minds but also to support each other in those sad times that happen too often at our age when someone is diagnosed with a serious illness or loses a loved one. We are important to each other. In addition, we donate $1 each per lesson, let it accumulate to $100 and give it to a community charity. Without the experience of Flashes, I would not be involved in teaching line dance, and I would have missed a very special and important experience in my golden years.*
>
> *One of my fondest memories was of the tradition of leaving the foot-*

ball field to "Peruna." After getting back into marching formation, the band would play the first few notes of "She'll Be Comin' 'Round The Mountain," and we would start the footwork. The crowd would roar. What a thrill to prance off the field with the people in the stands yelling and clapping. I do hope that tradition has persisted. Remembering it actually brought tears to my eyes.

1956-57 recorded many changes around the world. Khrushchev, now leader of the USSR, denounced Stalin's policies and Soviet troops marched into Hungary. Nasser was elected President of Egypt, causing the USA and Britain to withdraw financing for building the Aswan Dam. In retaliation, Nasser seized control of the Suez Canal. President Eisenhower was busy being reelected President of the United States with Richard M. Nixon as Vice-President. Martin Luther King continued to make headlines with desegregation issues and emerged as the leader for that cause. Fidel Castro landed in Cuba with an armed force to overthrow the dictator, Batista. The USSR successfully launched Sputnik I and II. World issues had changed drastically.

Elvis Presley was doing "a whole lot of shakin'" with his "Blue Suede Shoes" and "Hound Dog" causing the locals to recall his past appearance in Greenville at the Municipal Auditorium. *Around the World in 80 Days* won the Academy Award for best movie and color television was the purchase of choice for home entertainment.

Mrs. Schulze, welcomed new teacher, Mary Jane Vance, and asked her to serve as cheerleader sponsor, thus relieving her of those responsibilities. Mrs. Vance agreed and also offered her help with the Flashes, since she had taught dance at the university in Commerce. Their friendship grew into a mutual admiration society over the years. The twirlers approached Mrs. Vance and asked for her help with dance routines, which she did.

Football season opened with a huge pep rally in the gym that spilled out into the streets for a downtown parade by the band, Flashes and cheerleaders.

Leading the 1956-57 Flashes were:

Head Majorette	Linda Roark
Senior Majorettes	Jeannell Shepherd
	Jacquelyn West
American Flag Bearer	Patsy Combs
Texas Flag Bearer	Suzanne Smith
School Flag Bearer	Sue Stephens

Dixie Lee Schulze continued as Flash Mascot and Maxine Baxter was Manager.

A "first" for the Flashes was the naming of Carol Carsey, daughter of Mr. and Mrs. Eben Carsey, as Honorary Flash. Although Carol was wheelchair bound, she wore the same Flash uniform, attended the games, and rode in parades.

Flash Members
Carole Carsey, Honorary Flash

Billie Kate Anderson	Charlsie Duncan	Linda Little	Jo Ann Samuel
Beryl Asberry	Nelda Dunn	Frances Ann McNatt	Connie Sandlin
Jocelyn Baumgardner	Wanda Eastup	Betty Lou Milsap	Ann Seller
Melvina Benesch	Charlotte Ferguson	Julia Morris	Linda Sheley
Margaret Cathey	Jean Finney	Pat Norsworthy	Jane Sinclair
Susan Chapman	Carolyn Fowler	Judy Pickens	Judy Steen
Millie Cleveland	Delores Gray	Alta Joy Pope	Carol Ann Stephens
Nancy Craig	Sue Green	Dow Nell Porter	Leah Rita Stephenson
Sandra Daniels	Billie Louise Gregory	Cozbie Reed	Luanne Trentham
Bette Davis	Carole Harbuck	Emily Robbins	Judy Williams
Carol DeBerry	Melba Hunt	Ann Robertson	Delouris Williamson
Charlotte Dickerson	Sarah Ingram	Nola Robinson	
Sue Dorman	Judy James	Barbara Row	

Leading the band were Drum Major Larry Miller and Band Sweetheart Ann Poole. Twirlers were Betty Erwin, Sheila Ferguson, and Dona Smith. Head Twirlers Janet Henson and Ann Marshall left after football season. Student Director was George Shepherd, and John Miller was band manager.

"Around the World with Band and Flashes" was the theme for the March 28 and 29 floorshow. Assistant Principal Murdaugh was the emcee and made sure the "Little Moron" joke was asked as soon as he welcomed a packed gymnasium of attendees. A trombone trio with Jerry Thomason, Jimmy Cummings, and Philip Luttrell kicked off the show followed by "Begin the Beguine" by the band. The majorettes, flag bearers, and band sweetheart danced to "Night Train" and the twirlers followed with "Dancing in the Dark." The band played "Stormy Weather" and the Junior Flashes danced an interesting routine to "Angry." New members of both groups were presented prior to intermission. Returning for the second half, the band and Flashes performed to "Minstrel Daze." Jerry Thom-

Band Sweetheart passes from Paula Strawn (Jacobs) to Ann Poole, 1957

ason, Larry Miller, William Fowler, and Hugh Hancock played "Baby Face" followed by the Senior Flashes' routine to the "Charleston." Judy Williams sang, "Look for the Silver Lining" and a clarinet trio played "Three Blind Mice." Both groups performed "Rhapsody in Blue," which led to the finale... another closing of another show.

While Major John Glenn set a new speed record of 3 hours, 23 minutes and 8.4 seconds between California and New York, a desegregation crisis caused President Eisenhower to send paratroopers to Little Rock, Arkansas, to forestall violence. Britain exploded their first thermonuclear bomb in the central Pacific. Egypt and Syria joined to form the United Arab Republic with Nasser as president. Alaska became the forty-ninth state in 1958. Change was inevitable with the Russians' launch of Sputnik III. High school studies would change to emphasize science... to win the race for space. Vocational courses were cut back and more science courses were added.

"Seventy-Six Trombones" "Purple People Eater," and "Volare" filled the air on radio and television... in "stereophonic" sound for the first time.

In Texas, football is "king," so, no matter what was happening in the world, the Band and Flashes prepared for another football season of halftime presentations and parades. Leading the Flashes in 1957-58 were:

>   Head Majorette ....Susan Chapman
>   Senior Majorettes ....Jean Finney
>   Frances McNatt
>   American Flag Bearer.................Judy Steen
>   Texas Flag Bearer ....Judy James
>   School Flag Bearer.....................Luanne Trentham

Carol Carsey continued as Honorary Flash and Maxine Baxter and Glorianne White were Managers. Members were:

Linda Ashley	Sandra Daniel	Carole Harbuck	Cozbie Reed
Pat Barry	Jean Denton	Diane Hulsey	Emily Robbins
Linda Brochet	Charlotte Dickerson	Linda Johnson	Ann Robertson
Luanne Brooks	Sharon Dolan	Linda Miller	Nola Robinson
Ray Ann Calder	Wanda Eastup	Julia MorrisCarol	Ann Seiler
Jimmy Callaway	Norma Edgar	Dolores Nevill	Linda Sheley
Margaret Cathey	Charlotte Ferguson	Sandra Norman	Rita Sue Smith
Millie Cleveland	Genie Geesey	Donna Cay Norton	Barbara Stegall
Jimmye Coker	Dolores Gray	Mary Mac Parker	Pauline Umbarger
Sharon Collins	Sue Green	Judy Pickrell	Carolyn Vaughn
Sue Crossett	Billie Gregory	Judy Pickens	Sandra Weikel

Serving the band as Drum Major and Student Director was Charles Johnson with Judy Williams as Band Sweetheart. Head Twirler Betty Erwin led twirlers Stella Ferguson, Betty Hutchinson, Gloria Foster, and Martha Sivley through their routines. Jerry White was Band Manager.

Another spring semester ushered in another floorshow with Mr. George Murdaugh as emcee and, of course, the "Little Moron" joke. Following the opening by the band and Flashes, Charles Johnson played a trumpet solo "My Regards." After a band number, the majorettes, flag bearers, and band sweetheart danced to "Birth of the Blues." Robert Chapman and Thad Blocker played "Al and Hal," and Sue Blackshear, Joyce McGee, and Joan Ellis followed with "My Blue Heaven." The Junior Flashes performed to "Siboney" prior to the presentation of new members. The Flashes opened the second half with a moving routine to "Deep Purple" followed by a solo, "Over the Rainbow," by Judy Williams. The twirlers' routine was to "Sugar Blues," and the Senior Flashes countered with a routine to "By Heck." "Merry Widow," played by the band preceded the final number by the Flashes to "Wedding of the Painted Doll." Another year slipped by and another successful floorshow provided many memories that would follow them for the rest of their lives.

Norma Edgar (Reynolds), Class of 1959, recalled:
> *The best part of high school for me was being a Flash from 1957-1959. I loved the football games, the parades, the Band and Flash Floor Show and all the Flashes themselves. Mrs. Schulze was our amazing director. I still have my red Flash jacket. I will always treasure it as part of my high school memories. I think it is amazing that the Flashes are still going strong at Greenville High.*

1958-59 was another year of challenges for the world and Greenville High School. The "Beatnik" movement spread from California throughout America and Europe. The "Beat Generation" brought a different lifestyle, and unemployment was on the rise. NASA (National Aeronautics and Space Administration) was established for the exploration of space and launched the first moon rocket, but it failed to reach the moon. The USSR Lunik reached the moon and Lunik III took photos of the moon. The race was on to see who would be the first to land a man on the moon. Castro became Premier of Cuba. Hawaii became the fiftieth state.

Popular songs floating across the airwaves into homes were "He's Got the Whole World in His Hands," "Tom Dooley," "The Sound of Music," and "High Hopes." As usual, the music reflected the pulse of the nation.

1958-59 was a year full of celebrations. The Flaming Flashes celebrated their Silver Anniversary in 1959 since they were chartered in 1934 under Miss Gussie Nell Davis. Leaders were:

Head Majorette	Jimmye Coker
Senior Majorettes	Mary Mac Parker
	Judy Pickrell
American Flag Bearer	Dolores Nevill
Texas Flag Bearer	Diane Hulsey
School Flag Bearer	Sharon Dolan
Manager	Patricia Waid

Flash Members

Beth Asberry	Donna Chavey	Linda Miller	Sherry Sansing
Linda Ashley	Millie Cleveland	Julia Morris	Ann Seiler
Vicki Baker	Sharon Collins	Elaine Newell	Linda Sheley
Pat Barry	Sue Crossett	Sandra Norman	Rita Sue Smith
Donna Belew	Sandra Daniel	Donna Cay Norton	Gela Steen
Karen Benesch	Carol Jean Denton	Sara Overall	Barbara Stegall
Linda Bennett	Charlotte Dickerson	Jeannie Phipps	Sue Tolbert
Diane Billingslea	Norma Edgar	Judy Pickens	Pauline Umbarger
Kathy Black	Genie Geesey	Rachel Pope	Carolyn Vaughn
Marilyn Blanton	Judy Henson	Julia Price	Carolyn Wall
Linda Brochet	Brenda Hodgson	Cozbie Reed	Beverly Webb
Luanne Brooks	Patty Hollon	Ina Reeves	Sandra Weikel
Ray Ann Calder	Lelloine Horton	Emily Robbins	Nancy White
Jimmy Callaway	Linda Johnson	Ann Robertson	Betty Wilson
Margaret Cathey	Jo Ann Kilgore	Nola Robinson	Linda Yandell

Substitutes

Kelsey Ann Burcham	Judy Holloway	Susan Sinclair
Opal Faye Duvall	Sandra Mullins	Mary Lynn Stiles
Sandra Fletcher	Gay Sampson	Theresa Wright

Floor Show 1959: Renda Graham, Linda Yandell, Judy Huffaker

Drum Major Robert Chapman led the band, and Band Sweetheart was Genie Geesey. James Ownby was Student Director. Head Twirler Betty Hutchinson led twirlers Gloria Parrish, Martha Sively, Sue Blackshear, Gloria Foster, and Carol Ann Erwin. Band Manager was Richard Porter.

"Another Op'nin', Another Show" opened the annual floorshow on March 19 and 20. John Denny, a new emcee, was instructed on the "Legend of the Little Moron" to make sure the show opened as before. *"El Relicaro"* followed a cornet trio by James Poe, Carroll Duvall, and Joan Combs. The twirlers sashayed onto the floor to "Old Cowhand" followed by a bassoon and bass clarinet duo by Robert Chapman and Thad Blocker. The majorettes, flag bearers and band sweetheart performed to "Indian Love Call," and Sue Blackshear, Joyce McGee, and Carol Ann Erwin sang "True Love." The Junior Flashes performed to "Varsovianna" prior to presentation of new members.

The band and Flashes opened the second half with "Country Style" followed by "Tea for Two" by the band and twirlers. A routine by the Senior Flashes to "Children's Marching Song," led to the band's rendition of "Sweet Kentucky Babe." The last routine by the Flashes was to "Anniversary Waltz." Dressed as Southern belles, Flashes and their escorts (who had been taught to waltz by Mrs. Vance) waltzed around under multi-colored spotlights to the delight of the crowd. [*Authors Note:* These young men had never waltzed before.]

Mr. Ed Bernard, had served as Band Director for over twenty-six years and assistant for the first two years that the band existed. A quiet, unassuming man, he decided to retire without calling attention to himself. The word was out and at the close of the floorshow; the crowd honored Mr. Ed with the longest and loudest standing ovation ever given to an individual. A well-deserved "Well Done!" for a talented musician who touched hundreds of lives and inspired many. He had brought the GHS Band from a handful of untrained students to an award-winning marching and dance band unit with over sixty dedicated musicians.

Diane Billingslea, 1958-60

The challenge facing the GISD was finding a new band director to move the band forward. A successful search brought Mr. Eldon Janzen to GHS. A graduate of Medford High School where he played the trombone, he was also a member of the Oklahoma All-State Football team and was offered a scholarship to Oklahoma A&M (Oklahoma State) but chose to accept a $25 music scholarship instead. His teaching career began at his former high school before accepting a position at New Boston, Texas. He earned his master's degree in education from North Texas State University and served as assistant to the director of bands there. GHS had found an outstanding director to pick up the baton at GHS. Mr. Janzen recalled:

The "Flaming Flashes of Greenville" were already "Legend" when I arrived in the fall of 1959 to replace Band Director Ed Bernard, who was retiring after over 27 years at the post. Advance notice from friends who heard I was taking the position were congratulatory but mostly ominous, that I would find it difficult to establish a credible marching concert band in the shadow of a premier drill team established by none other than Gussie Nell Davis who had moved on to direct the nationally famous Kilgore College Rangerettes. Having previously worked alongside her in Cotton Bowl appearances, I knew the "drill" well!

Then Flash Director Margaret Schulze gave me a gracious hearing as we began to work toward fall football performances, and recognized that I would not be content to direct the band that had stood at the sidelines playing for the main event... The Flaming Flashes.

As strains of "The Sound of Music" and "Mack the Knife" filled the airwaves, the sound of band music filled the band hall at GHS. Mr. Janzen and Mrs. Schulze worked through several changes to showcase the band on the football field performing without the Flashes. Mrs. Schulze understood the need for Mr. Janzen to highlight the band's performance, but also knew she would be hearing from parents about the changes. Modifications were made, including the addition of new hats for the Flashes, but not without tension. Leading the Flashes for 1959-60 were:

<pre>
Head Majorette.............................. Beth Asberry
Senior Majorettes........................... Sherry Sansing, Betty Wilson
American Flag Bearer..................... Diana Tarpley
Texas Flag Bearer .... Kathy Black
School Flag Bearer.......................... Nancy White
Flash Managers .... Patricia Waid, Sandra Smith
</pre>

Flash Members

Sally Anderson	Frances Coats	Renda Graham	Elaine Newell
Kay Ayers	Leah Jan Cobbs	Frances Henson	Patti Petterson
Vickie Baker	Carey Collier	Judy Henson	Julia Price
Joyce Barry	Sammie Daniel	Brenda Hodgson	Judy Faye Ragan
Karan Benesch	Saundra Dickerson	Patty Hollon	Gay Sampson
Linda Bennett	Linda Dickey	Judy Holloway	Marleta Shields
Diane Billingslea	Charlene Duncan	Lelloine Horton	Ruth Steger
Vicki Blain	Tina Durrett	Judy Huffaker	Carolyn Wall
Marilyn Blanton	Opal Faye Duvall	Saundra Johnson	Linda Weikel
Jane Bramlett	Patty Finney	Jo Ann Kilgore	Joan Winters
Kelsey Burcham	Sandra Fletcher	Suzanne Kirkman	Linda Yandall
Ann Cantrell	Judy Gambrell	Jerry Lee	
Pat Carter	Linda Glasscock	Sandra Mullins	

Drum Major James Poe led with Band Sweetheart Carolyn Ford...the first one who was not a Flash. Mr. Janzen created new positions naming Lieutenants James Handley, David Bolton, Eldon Doonan, and Bobby Craig to assist Band Captain Bill Eason. Twirlers were Joan Combs, Carol Ann Erwin, Gail Morehead, Janie Nelson, and Aileen Lockhart. Student Director was Thad Blocker, and Manager was Richard Porter. Mr. Janzen noted:

The year continued to go well as I settled into the routine and learned that the main event of each year was "The Band and Flash Floor Show." It was totally amazing that a combined effort of the girls in the drill team, the school faculty, and community volunteers could convert a very ordinary gymnasium into the decorated grandeur comparable to the RKO Music Hall, home of the well-known Rockettes.

Mr. Janzen learned quickly how important the floorshow was to the community. The theme "Holiday," was selected and a new emcee, Mr. J. W. Ward, moved the show forward with the usual "moron" joke. The opening number, "June Is Bustin' Out All Over," was followed by the band playing "Holiday Tune." Renamed the "Stage Band," the former Dance Band delighted the crowd with "Little Brown Jug." The Flashes came on strong with a patriotic routine to "Yankee Doodle Dandy" followed by "Autumn Leaves," a specialty number by the band. The twirlers followed by dancing/twirling to "Spook Session." The Junior Flashes glided over the floor to "The Skaters Waltz" before the presentation of new members.

Opening the second half, "Love and Marriage" was played by the band followed by a second band number, "And Suddenly." The flag bearers and majorettes (Flash Officers) performed to "Mardi Gras." The Stage Band followed with "Southern Style," and the Senior Flashes created some misty eyes with their routine to "Graduation Day." The finale brought to a close another evening of entertainment and mixed emotions for many.

Margaret Schulze with new Flash Officers during her farewell reception, Spring 1960. (l-r) Sally Anderson, Tina Durrett, Renda Graham, Margaret Schulze, Judy Huffaker, Jerry Lee, Patty Finney.

After their six-year tenure at GHS, James (Mutt) Schulze and his wife, Margaret, decided it was time to leave Greenville. An offer for Mr. Schulze to coach tennis at North Texas State University was accepted and the Schulze's left Greenville. Sally Anderson, Tina Durrett, Renda Graham, Judy Huffaker, Jerry Lee, and Patty Finney, new Flash Officers for the coming year, hosted a farewell reception for Mrs. Schulze and her family.

When asked to write a few thoughts about being in the Flashes, Judy Huffaker (McPhail) replied:

> *A short paragraph? I could write an entire book about my experiences as a Flash! I became a new member during the Flashes' Silver Anniversary, and here it is, 50 years later! In those days, new members learned of selection by tuning in at the appointed time to KGVL, the Greenville radio station. The names of new members and new officers were read on the air, so, if you didn't get selected, you could cry in private, which I always thought was a great idea. That was in spring of 1959. My junior year was a blast, with a highlight being a trip to Galveston by bus to march in the Splash Day Parade.*

Frances Henson (Green) added:

> *Looking back at my experiences in the Flaming Flashes brings back wonderful memories. Of course, I remember my initiation into the Flashes and simultaneously finding out I was going to be a Flash. It happened when a group of current Flashes came calling at an hour when most people were asleep! The next big event in my life as a Flash came when Judy Gambrell and I went shopping for that special dress for the presentation at the Floor Show. Our mothers took us to a business in Sulphur Springs to choose our dresses. We had a great time looking at more formal dresses than we had ever seen in one place at one time. As everyone else did, I thought mine was the prettiest dress of all.*

The search was on to find a new director when someone recalled that Mary Jane Vance, who had left GHS two years prior to teach in the elementary grades, had helped Mrs. Schulze with the Flashes, cheerleaders, and twirlers.

Mary Jane Vance

The world watched the live broadcast of the debate between presidential candidates John F. Kennedy (Democrat) and Richard M. Nixon (Republican). Viewers also learned that Prince Andrew, born to Queen Elizabeth II and Prince Phillip, was the first birth to a reigning monarch since 1857.

I was surprised to hear Superintendent Ray Brown's voice when I picked up the phone in early June of 1960. I had just completed my master's degree and two years teaching sixth grade at Lamar Elementary after the two years of teaching Home Economics at GHS. The three Sputniks brought changes to the curriculum and the addition of science course requirements for graduation created cuts to all vocational programs. What could the superintendent possibly want with me?

Mr. Brown asked if I would take the position of Flash Director for the coming year. Since the position involved extra time and much responsibility, I felt I should think it over and return his call. He agreed.

As soon as we said our "goodbyes," I sat down to let this conversation sink in.

I had enjoyed helping Margaret Schulze with the Flashes, but I recalled the long hours of preparation, out-of-town games, try-outs, decision-making, parents meetings, and...the floorshow! What are you thinking? Did I really want this? The answer was "Yes!"

I had survived the Japanese Occupation of the Philippines during World War II as a child and made it through enemy waters on a repatriation ship while atomic bombs were dropped on Hiroshima and Nagasaki...I could do this!

Mary Jane Vance

Once contracts were signed, a meeting was scheduled with GHS Principal Flewharty and officers of the Flashes. Time was of the essence as football season was only six weeks away.

My meeting with Principal Flewharty was brief and cordial, as I had worked at GHS two-years prior, so I knew what to expect, or so I thought. The new officers waiting to meet me in the outer office were:

Head Majorette	Judy Huffaker
Senior Majorettes	Patty Finney
	Jerry Lee
American Flag Bearer	Renda Graham
Texas Flag Bearer	Sally Treadway
School Flag Bearer	Tina Durrett

These delightful young ladies were full of wonderful ideas for the coming year and had already worked on several routines for the season. My first task was to meet with Mr. Eldon Janzen, Band Director, to get a "feel" for our working relationship. I had known and worked with "Mr. Ed" for two years and had an understanding of how the football season presentations were arranged and the format of the floorshow. Tradition was vital, but new ideas and enrichment of the program was also important.

I later met Flash Managers Sandra Smith and Judy Duvall…two very lovely and solid individuals, who made me feel comfortable right away.

A date and time was set to meet with the members that included:

Ann Ablowich	Saundra Dickerson	Frances Henson	Judy Ray
Mary Lou Attison	Linda Dickey	Sandra Johnson	Dwilene Rhodes
Pat Beane	Mary Ann Duncan	Suzanne Kirkman	Becky Sampson
Linda Benesch	Opal Faye Duvall	Nancy Leeper	Marleta Shields
Jane Bramlette	Donna Ernest	Betty McClanahan	Ruth Steger
Janeen Bray	Sandra Fletcher	Shirley McGill	Carol Strader
Ann Cantrell	Judy Gambrel	Cecelia Mehmert	Eileen Thompson
Pat Carter	Mary Ann George	Janice Moser	Kay Turner
Frances Coats	Linda Glasscock	Patti Patterson	Linda Weikel
Leah Jan Cobbs	Linda Hassell	Carolyn Peterson	Dolores Whitney
Kay Cox	Billie Hathaway	Judy Faye Ragan	Jo Anne Winters

Times and dates were set for practice sessions with each of the officers having a "squad" of members with whom they worked on their own before meeting at the gymnasium or on the practice field to evaluate the finished routine. Mr. Janzen had agreed to tape most of the music we were to use during practice sessions.

Leading the GHS Band was Drum Major Vernon Glossup with Mary Lynn Stiles as Band Sweetheart. Band Captain was Jackie Erwin with Daryle Jordan, H. B. Earle, David Crim, and Jim Eason as Lieutenants. Wayne Brewer was Student Director and Richard Porter was Manager.

Several years prior to becoming Flash Director, a one-page set of "rules" for Flashes was put in place and, thankfully, Beth Asberry (Horton Dittrich) and Carey Collier (Flashes 1959-60) found a copy of the "rules" to include.

While a review of the "rules" today might be amusing, they were the existing "rules"

Greenville High School Flashes
Respect For The Uniform

- Have boots shined at all formations.
- Have clean and pressed uniform. (This does not mean that you have to have a clean and press job before each game. It does mean that you should keep your uniform hanging at home and be careful to keep it clean. Have occasional cleaning job when necessary.)
- While in uniform, hair must be combed out. No pin-curls, pony-tails, etc.
- No smoking, rowdiness, loud talking, etc.
- On time in complete uniform for each formation.

Bus Trips

- Flashes must go on one of the two busses designated for the Flashes.
- You must return on the same bus that you went on.
- If you go on a Flash trip you must return with the Flashes.
- There will be no unnecessary boisterousness on the busses.
- Do not yell at persons outside of the bus or attract attention of persons passing in cars.
- Do not throw anything out of the bus. Put sacks and any other refuse in floor.
- Keep arms in the bus.
- When the bus arrives at its destination, get into formation immediately. If there is any extra time you will be dismissed from the stands and told what time to be back in formation.
- Do not open emergency door under any circumstances. Enter and leave from the front door.

Formation

- No gum while in formation. This means class, too.
- At no time can you break formation unless you are instructed to do so. Stay in formation during the first, second, and fourth quarters of a game. You will be dismissed at the half and should be in formation at the beginning of the fourth quarter.
- When you are in formation at games do not allow friends or strangers to join the formation. (This applies to Flagbearers and Majorettes also.)
- Any sign of disagreeable attitude, reluctance to obey instruction or work, may eliminate a member permanently.
- An absence on Friday automatically disqualifies you to perform at that evening's game.

and created some serious issues during football season. My job was to uphold and enforce them. On several occasions, the principal chose to override them, when parents came to him at an "away" game to take their daughter(s) home after the halftime performance, which was all right with me as long as I was notified. At one game, the Flash did not return to the stands at the beginning of the fourth quarter, and I became concerned. I learned from one of the Flashes, that she left with her boyfriend after receiving permission from the principal. Upon our return to Greenville on the school bus, I called her parents even though it was quite late. I wanted to make sure she had arrived home safely. The parents were very upset, as she was not home. They wanted to know why she was allowed to leave and I related the message given to me by one of the Flashes... that the principal had given her permission. I asked that they please call me as soon as she arrived, which they did about an hour later. She told her parents that Mr. Flewharty had given her permission and that they had stopped to eat before coming home. Regardless, "rules" had been broken, and I should have been notified of Mr. Flewharty's decision. Early the next week, Superintendent Ray Brown called a meeting at the administration building. The Flash's parents, Principal Flewharty, and Superintendent Brown were seated around the table with his secretary posted at the far end to take notes. I was asked to explain the situation, which I did, and Mr. Flewharty denied having given permission for the girl to leave the game. He suggested that we "overlook the infraction this time and felt sure it would not happen again." My hands were tied. At that point, all I could do was agree. I decided then that staying another year as Flash Director under those conditions would not be a good idea, but kept it to myself.

During the football season, my husband, Charles, and I became better acquainted with Eldon Janzen and his wife. Charles enjoyed playing tricks on others. He asked Eldon Janzen whether or not he liked chicken, and Eldon replied that he did. We lived in the country and had a few chickens and other livestock, so Charles caught one of our Rhode Island Red roosters, put it into a burlap sack, and delivered it to Eldon and his wife, who lived on Stanford Street, almost across from Jack and Lou Finney's home. Eldon was shocked to find a live rooster being delivered as a gift and did not know what to do with the creature. He recalled the incident...

Charles Vance appeared at my door with a smile, word of welcome, and a LIVE CHICKEN, to be slaughtered, plucked, dissected, fried and served. This girl and her husband, I thought, obviously wanted to be friends.

With the football season, Cotton Bowl Parade, the election of John F. Kennedy as President, and Greenville's Christmas Parade behind us, we worked together to prepare for the annual floorshow. Since the popular songs "Itsy Bitsy Teenie Weenie Yellow Polka Dot Bikini" and "Let's Do the Twist" were not exactly what we would choose for a floorshow, Mr. Janzen and I agreed the theme should be "The Heart of Broadway," and planned to have the theme prominently displayed at one end of the gym and on the printed program for the first time. The show, scheduled for March 23 and 24, would bring the best of Broadway to Hunt County. Decorations and costumes were designed or chosen. Helen Mehmert, a Flash mother and member of the Band and Flash Parents, stayed late to help me with the final touches on the decorations the night before dress rehearsal. Around 10:00 p.m., her spouse,

Janice Moser

Dr. Hank Mehmert, walked in and announced he had reserved a room for the two of us ladies at the local hospital. We got the message. We were tired, and it was late. Final touches would have to wait until the next day.

Bill Rust, announcer for KGVL and football games, was emcee. His commanding voice opened the show with the traditional moron joke, followed by the Overture…"Curtain at Eight." The majorettes, flag bearers, twirlers, and Mr. Rust "set the mood" with presentation of the theme. The band and Flashes performed the opening number to "Oklahoma" followed by highlights from "The Music Man." A medley from "Guys and Dolls," by the Stage Band, followed with a routine by the Flashes to "Over the Rainbow." The twirlers were next with a dance/twirl to "Hallelujah." Gary Choate played a clarinet solo…"Summertime," and the Junior Flashes jazzed up the tempo with their routine to "I Got Rhythm." Presentation of new members concluded the first half of the show.

The rousing music of "Big 'D'" caused the crowd to clap to the beat as the Senior Flashes did their famous high kicks to a precision routine. Slowing the tempo, a brass sextet played "Surrey With the Fringe on Top," followed by the Stage Band's lively medley from "Damn Yankee." The soothing sounds of "Bali Hai" transported the audience to the South Pacific via a routine danced "barefoot" by the majorettes and flag bearers…costumed in floral sarongs and wearing flower leis. The band and twirlers continued with "If I Had My Druthers" and the Flashes picked up the tempo with a fringe-shaking routine to "Charleston." The entire cast marched to "Seventy-Six Trombones" during the finale. Another unforgettable floorshow was now history as congratulations were extended to all who were involved.

Judy Huffaker (McPhail) recalled:
When I served as Head Majorette my senior year, it really was a life-changing experience for me! Truly an honor and a highlight of my life! The football and basketball games, pep rallies, parades, Floor Show, all the practices, the friendships, working with Mrs. Vance and the Band and all my Sister Flashes, it was all the greatest! I still consider it one of the defining times of my life. Being a Flash was an honored tradition, which taught us discipline, loyalty, dance skills and much, much more. Plus, it was loads of fun. May the Flashes Flame forever!

Renda Graham (King), American Flag Bearer, remembers:
> Being a Greenville High School Flaming Flash was certainly the highlight of my high school years. Performing at the GHS football games, the bus trips, the parades, and especially the Band and Flash Floor Shows were so much fun. It was such an honor to be chosen to be the American Flag Bearer during my senior year in 1960-61. My best friends were also officers, and we still share the memories. My two younger sisters also became Flaming Flashes. Mrs. Schulze and Mrs. Vance were not only great directors, but also wonderful role models for all of us.

As Frances Henson (Green) noted:
> The show must go on! We performed in all kinds of weather and under all circumstances. I remember those bus trips to Ennis, Gladewater, Sulphur Springs, Mt. Pleasant, McKinney... always fun and never a dull moment! Who could ever forget that our Officers called themselves "The Magnificents!" That really set our class apart!

Sandra Smith noted:
> Well, as Edith and Archie Bunker would say, "Those Were the Days." What wonderful memories I have as Flash Manager under Mrs. Schulze and Mrs. Mary Jane Vance. Both ladies were beautiful inside and out! The bus trips were out of this world fun to the football games and back. Oh, yea, our trip to Galveston put the icing on our cakes. It did not get any better that that one. Thank you, Mrs. Schulze and Mrs. Vance for your sage advice and life lessons... we love you both!

Janeen Bray (Cunningham) noted:
> In 1960, our sophomore year at GHS, many of us waited with bated breath to see if we had been chosen to one of the "famous" Flaming Flashes. We were well aware that our drill team was the first of its kind ANYWHERE and that many people had heard of the Greenville Flashes. We wanted to be a part of that legendary group... or maybe we just wanted to wear those short skirts and cute boots! After being chosen for the drill team, we became a tight knit group of girls dedicated to perfection. That perfection often came at a price... itchy red gym suits, hair rollers under hats, long bus rides on hard seats, early morning drills, and freezing cold bleacher seats. But the applause! And the parades! And the floorshow costumes!

Carolyn Peterson (Beauchamp) shared her Flash memories:
> I was a proud Flash from 1960-62 and loved every minute of it! You were the director when I became a Flash and Lesby Rhodes followed you. Some of my best memories center around: 1) the road trips to out-of-town games—we had so much fun sharing food and laughs and singing to the top of our voices. What we lacked in harmony, we made up for in volume! 2) those

lovely red gym suits we got to wear for practice; 3) the "esprit de corps"—it didn't matter what little clique you might be a part of in school, we were all friends...we were all Flashes!; 4) marching in the Christmas parade in Dallas and shivering in the cold when we paused but not breaking formation!; 5) traveling to Tennessee for a parade appearance, taking a paddle boat tour, and, probably, keeping other guests from sleeping at the hotel!; 6) all the practice and hard work it took to learn all those routines and how proud I felt marching out to the field at halftime; 7) hand signals in the stands at pep rallies; 9) "Night Train"; and 9) of course, The Floor Show!

As a token of appreciation for their year's work, arrangements were made for the Flash Officers to serve as Ambassadors of the Greenville Chamber of Commerce and deliver the "Key to Lake Tawakoni" to the mayor of New Orleans. Following a breakfast at Jack and Lou Finney's home, Jill Scott (Honorary Flash), Judy Huffaker, Jerry Lee, Patty Finney (Majorettes), Renda Graham, and Tina Durrett (Flag Bearers), traveled to New Orleans where they had an audience with Mayor Pro Tem Victor Schiro and were interviewed live on radio station WNOE. The mayor and his staff hosted brunch at Brennan's and all were presented certificates as "Honorary Citizens" of New Orleans and given a "Key to the City" charm. I made sure they took a tour of the various sights of the city before conducting a tour of southern mansions on their return. These young ladies continue to be my friends and will always be part of my family.

Judy Huffaker hands the hat to incoming Head Majorette, Judy Ray, 1961

Lesby Daniels Rhodes

1961 brought the construction of the Berlin Wall, separating the East from the West. "Freedom Riders," organized to test and force integration in the South, were attacked and beaten in Birmingham. Yuri Gagarin (USSR) orbited the earth in a six-ton satellite. Alan Shepard made the first U.S. space flight. The race to the moon continued as changes took place in GISD.

Wesley N. Martin was named as Superintendent of Schools and hired Lesby Daniels Rhodes as Flash Director. Mrs. Rhodes had a strong background in dance, having been a twirler at East Texas State College in Commerce during her undergraduate years in the early fifties. A vivacious and aggressive individual, she had many ideas for music and routines to incorporate as Director. [*Author's Note:* I pledged Tooanoowe Social Club as a freshman under Lesby and we both lived in Binnion Hall. When she learned I played the piano, she insisted I play —day or night—so she could practice her twirling routines.]

Mrs. Rhodes was in the middle of summer planning sessions when tragedy struck. One of the Flashes, Nancy Leeper, had driven to visit her grandmother in Wood County. She lost her life when a train demolished her small Volkswagen as she crossed the tracks. Jeri Walker (Wynn) recalls:

> *I was away at boarding school in the tenth grade, so didn't get to try out when everyone else in my class did. When I returned to GHS my junior year, all my friends were in their wonderful new lives of the Flashes world. Then in August, before we began our senior year, a terrible tragedy happened when my best friend, Nancy Leeper was killed. Oh, the unbearable loss for all of us. I believe Flash practice had begun. I was helping at Bible school one morning when Mother called and asked me to come home. Lesby Rhodes had called to say Sam and Liz Leeper wanted me to take Nancy's place in the Flashes and wear her uniform. I still remember falling to the floor sobbing and sobbing. Practice was later that day and I remember walking into the gym with guilt, confusion, but also honor. Sam and Liz never missed a game and each Friday night, I put on the "Flash smile" with tears streaming down my face.*

> *I think two new positions were added that year—lieutenant and sergeant. Dolores Whitney was chosen lieutenant and I was named as sergeant. Sam and Liz asked that I have a picture made in Nancy's Flash uniform and kept it on their living room table. As I write this, I can still feel many emotions. I loved being a Flash, but would give anything for a difference in the way it happened.*

Mrs. Rhodes and Mr. Janzen worked out the music for halftime shows and practice began in earnest. The Flashes, divided into squads, were led by:

Head Majorette	Judy Ray
Senior Majorettes	Ann Ablowich
	Janeen Bray
US Flag Bearer	Kay Turner
Texas Flag Bearer	Kay Cox
School Flag Bearer	Celia Mehmert
Lieutenant	Dolores Whitney
Sergeant	Jeri Walker
Managers	Judy Duvall
	Vickie Warren

Flash Members

Peggy Abernathy	Linda Ferguson	Wendelyn Love	Helen Rodgers
Sandra Ames	Mary Anne George	Sheila Lumpkin	Becky Sampson
Mary Lou Attison	Vre Haefliger	Betty McClanahan	Janet Steger
Sandra Bearden	Gala Harwell	Jeanye McDaniel	Suzanne Sansing
Linda Benesch	Linda Hassell	Barbara McGee	Sandy Stone
Pat Benson	Billie Hathaway	Shirley McGill	Carol Strader
Sue Bostick	Jackie Houk	Betty Morris	Eileen Thompson
Cheryl Brown	Judy Howse	Joan Moseley	Peggy Vallancey
Carolyn Drake	Ginger Hudson	Janice Moser	Martha Vittetoe
Mary Ann Duncan	Mary Huggins	Judy Newman	Elaine Wilkerson
Donna Ernest	Pat Hunsaker	Carolyn Peterson	
Kathy Fagan	Nell Lindsey	Dwilene Rhodes	

Drum Major Steve Stephens led the GHS Band and Aileene Lockhart, a twirler, was named Band Sweetheart. David Crim was Band Captain and Gayle Carden, James Voss, James Braswell, and Johnny Morris were Lieutenants. Twirlers were Aileene Lockhart, Judy Pelton, and Judy Henderson. Student Directors were David Crim and James Braswell. Bobby Crow was Manager.

"Proud Heritage" was the theme for the March 22-23 floorshow. Changes were made to the program. Linda Muller and Goodloe Lewis, dance consultants, were utilized to prepare and oversee all the scenes and choreography. John McCasland, dance consultant, was brought in as Assistant Choreographer. The program was divided into scenes depicting The South. News of this "extravaganza" reached a Dallas television station, and they came

Jeri Walker (Wynn)

to film the event during dress rehearsal night. Clips of the Floor Show were aired for the public and a copy of the televised version was given to Mrs. Helen Mehmert (Bauman). [*Author's Note:* This film was given to Miss Lori Butler in 2015 to see if a DVD version could be made from that copy.]

Mr. Bill Rust, emcee, dutifully told the "Little Moron" joke to open the show, then the band played a "Southern Salute" overture. Scene One depicted a street scene in Charleston, S.C. and the entire company performed to "Shall We Dance," "Old Folks at Home," "Carolina in the Morning," "Waitin' on the Robert E. Lee," and "Basin Street Blues." Scene Two featured a Planters' Ball in Savannah, Georgia, with the Junior Flashes dancing to "Alabama Jubilee" followed by the Senior Flashes slowing the tempo with "Georgia On My Mind." New members of the Band and Flashes danced to the center spotlight to be presented while the band played "Merry Widow Waltz."

John McCasland, Choreographer, recalled the following: *Each incoming Flash had to find a partner who would rehearse with us. I can't tell you how long a period the rehearsals lasted, but to get a bunch of guys and girls to learn to waltz so it looked natural took over a period of about six weeks or so. It was a fun thing to do.*

Scene Three, entitled "Gone With The Wind," had Flashes performing to "Are You From Dixie?" followed by "Alabama Bound," "Kentucky Babe," and "Mississippi Mud." The entire cast performed to "Yellow Rose of Texas." Mr. Janzen recalled what happened next…as if it were yesterday.

The feature number was "Battle Hymn of the Republic." The band was playing well. Flash Director Lesby Rhodes had choreographed an entry of gorgeously costumed Flashes. The lighting was focused and dimmed to perfection as the girls emerged from the opposite end of the "hall" moving onto the floor in halting dramatic steps. As the band made a crescendo transition to the main theme of "Battle Hymn," accompanying precision movement in glorious costume, there was not a dry eye in the building. The South was ready to rise again! I recall very little of what concluded the show, but to this day, the "Battle Hymn" is still clear in the memory of every Band and Flash member and their directors.

Scene Four, entitled "Minstrel Night at the Majestic," featured Mr. Bill Parker, as Interlocutor, with Dolores Whitney playing "Mr. Bones" and Jeri Walker as "Mr. Tambo."

Sue Sport presented by Billy Parker, Flash Floor Show, 1962

The three "actors" tossed quips, jokes, and questions around as the Stage Band played "Swingin' on the Swanee." They continued the "banter" between "I'm Forever Blowing Bubbles," performed by the Flashes, and "Ballin' the Jack," done by the flag bearers. The twirlers did a routine to "Chattanooga Choo Choo," followed by "Birth of the Blues," danced by the majorettes. Guest performer for this routine was John McCasland. The Senior Flashes followed with a dance to "Swanee."

The 1962 floor show ended on a high note, but band members were saddened by Mr. Janzen's decision to leave Greenville for a position at Irving ISD, where he later became Director of Music and, in 1970, Director of Bands at the University of Arkansas...leaving there in 1995.

Janeen Bray (Cunningham), Senior Majorette, The Flaming Flashes:
As a senior in 1962, leaving my Flash friends was bittersweet. But the confidence gained, the memories made, and the discipline learned went with me to the next parts of my life. Being a Flash was an honor to be earned and a thrill to be lived, and I loved every minute.

Betty McClanahan (Williams) wrote:
I loved every minute I spent in the Flashes. After tryouts, the knock on the door from Senior Flashes to take me to the breakfast was a thrill. I, like a lot of my friends, was nervous and unsure. It was a big deal. We marched in so many great events. I especially remember going to Memphis. Felt so grown up. I cherish the friends I made and most of all the two directors I had (Mrs. Vance and Mrs. Rhodes).

The school year of 1962-63 was filled with change. The media was kept busy with news of the Cuban Missile Crisis, the death of Eleanor Roosevelt, riots at the University of Mississippi when James Meredith was denied admission because he was Black, and the arrest of Martin Luther King during civil rights riots in Birmingham. Valentina Tereshkova was the first female to complete a three-day flight in space. Gordon Cooper, US astronaut, completed 22 orbits in an Atlas rocket.

While all this news is important, the most pressing problem at GHS was to hire a new band director during the summer of 1962. Before Mr. Janzen left GISD, he recommended Bob Ingram. Mr. Ingram, a graduate of GHS in 1951 and ETSTC, had served as band director at Longview Junior High, East Mountain High School, and Sabine High School. In Greenville, where he had begun his musical career in the sixth grade with a Silvertone metal clarinet he earned by mowing a lady's yard all summer, he was former president and student director of the GHS Band. Bob knew the history of the Flaming Flashes and looked forward to working with his friend and classmate, Lesby Rhodes, a twirler in college during his tenure in the college marching band. He was also a member of the "East Texans," the college dance band, and the ROTC marching band.

1962-63 saw *Lawrence of Arabia* win the Academy Award. Popular songs included "Days of Wine and Roses," "*Danke Schoen*," and "Call Me Irresponsible." The media complained of the "credibility gap" between the truth and official reports of events in Cuba, Vietnam, and Russia. Dr. Michael De Bakey used an artificial heart to control circulation of a patient's blood.

Mrs. Rhodes and Mr. Ingram had football halftimes, pep rallies, parades, and "away" games on their minds. Friends since 1951, the two worked out details rather quickly and had everything ready. Leaders of the Flashes were:

Head Majorette	Ginny Thompson
Senior Majorettes	Gala Harwell
	Elaine Wilkerson
American Flag Bearer	Wendelyn Love
Texas Flag Bearer	Cheryl Brown
School Flag	Ginger Hudson
First Lieutenant	Betty Morris
First Sergeant	Peggy Vallancey
Corporal	Joan Moseley

Managers included Arlene Carter, Jackie Houk, Marty Scott, Susan Venus, and Vickie Warren. Members for 1962-63 included:

Peggy Abernathy	Carolyn Drake	Linda Moser	Suzanne Sansing
Mignon Acker	Sharon Eck	Barbara McGee	Judy Simmons
Sandra Bearden	Paula Feagin	Jean McGuire	Sue Sport
Pat Benson	Sue Glasscock	June McGuire	Janet Steger
Sharon Blanton	Ann Gordy	Judy Newman	Phyllis Stovall
Sue Bostick	Ann Graham	Beverly Otts	Karen Teller
Bonnie Cheves	Elizabeth Henson	Vickie Pennington	Susan Treadway
Phyllis Coker	Judy Howse	Betty Rivera	Martha Vittetoe
Shirley Coker	Mary Huggins	Nancy Reynolds	Ginger Willis
Kristi Cross	Carol Johnston	Anna Rice	Jan Wood
Carole Daum	Mary Patricia Kelly	Helen Rogers	
Sue Dawson	Sheila Lumpkin	Marilyn Rowe	

Three veteran teachers, Miss Elenita Patton, Miss Norine Herndon, and Miss Minnie Lee Smith, named Honorary Flashes, were featured during a pep rally, at the halftime event, in the Floorshow Program, and in the GHS annual.

Uniforms for the Flashes changed dramatically from the formal military style to velvet petal skirts, with matching sleeveless tops with mandarin type collars. The soft dancing boots were changed to cowboy boots and all wore white cowboy hats, with the exception of the Head Majorette, who wore a red one. White gloves and neutral Danskin tights completed the outfit.

Steve Stephens served as Drum Major and Jean Ann Ethridge was Band Sweetheart. Band Captain was Jimmy Johnson with Buddy Carsey, Jim Eason, and Bobby Holmes as Lieutenants. Twirlers were Su Laine Blanton, Nelcine Chapin, Aileene Lockhart, Judy Pelton, Jenny Pullen, and Cathy Smith. David Crim and James Braswell were Student Directors. Manager was Bobby Crow.

Fall 1962 found the Flashes no longer wearing the military uniforms to perform at football games and wore the red velvet sleeveless uniforms with white satin lined pleats. The officers wore all white with the exception of the Colonel who wore a red hat and red boots with her white uniform.

The two directors decided to put a "twist" in the floorshow program by first changing the event to a three-night production on March 28, 29, and 30, 1963. They selected "Cibola" as the theme and changed the format so there would be no formal presentation of new band and Flash members prior to intermission. The new members of each group selected their own dance partners and danced as a group while the band played two numbers, "*Chipañecas*" and "*La Raspa*," just prior to intermission. New members wore the peasant style clothing of Mexico rather than the usual formal wear. Their names were printed in the floorshow program.

Several of the band and Flash members came to evening practice session in early March with news of the tragic plane crash of country music performers Patsy Cline, Cowboy Copas, and Hankshaw Hawkins near Camden, TN. They recalled their trip to Memphis and listening to the song "Crazy" being played during the parade.

Mr. Bill Rust continued as emcee. Assistant Choreographers were Linda Muller

Elizabeth Henson (Green) presented by Ronnie Graham, Flash Floor Show, 1962

and Pat Daniel. Consultants were Honorary Flashes Elenita Patton, Minnie Lee Smith, Norine Herndon, and the Mitchell Grenadiers.

The band opened with "Giant" followed by an American Indian motif as the twirlers performed to "Cherokee." "Sioux Ghost Dance" by the Flashes followed tribal dances by the *Yukapalis* dressed in traditional tribal costumes. A second section, "Parade of Flags," included a Spanish dance by the Senior Flashes and a routine of the French Follies by the Junior Flashes. The "Mexico Magnifico" section featured the new members of both groups, beginning with Kristi Cross and Steve Stephens doing the "Mexican Hat Dance." The new twirlers performed to "Toreador," and the new Flash officers danced to "The Breeze and I." Current corps officers danced to "Bolero," while the Band and Flash Managers performed to "Little Old Men."

After intermission, the majorettes and flag bearers performed to "Greenleaves of Summer": Theme from *The Alamo*. A star spangled spectacular followed with the Flashes and band performing to "Grand Old Flag," "Feudin' and Fightin'," and "Slaughter on 10th Avenue." More numbers featuring both groups were "Good Day," Shakin' the Blues," "School Daze," "Charleston Twist," and "Give My Regards to Broadway."

Elizabeth Henson (Green) and Wendelyn Love (Dixon), 1963

Cheryl Brown (Briggs) had a pocketful of memories.

> *Being in the Flashes was such a great experience. Our director was Lesby Rhodes. In August, we had practices twice a day. I think we practiced more than the football team! Boy, did she give us a workout, but it was worth it.*
>
> *I think the highlight of our junior year was the trip to Memphis, TN, to march in the Cotton Carnival parade. We had also marched in the Cotton Bowl Parade and the Tyler Rose Festival Parade earlier in the year. Our senior year was "Cibola." Both the Thursday and Friday night performances were sold out. Somehow, word spread and a Dallas television station had a cameraman at the Friday night performance and we made television news! Friday night, it was announced there would be an encore performance on Saturday night and it was also sold out.*

One of our uniforms included white cowboys hats. Ginny Thompson, our Head Majorette, wore a red hat. As we were marching off the field after a half-time performance, a child near the sidelines made the comment that she must be the "bid daddy rabbit." Ginny was known the rest of the year as "Big Daddy Rabbit." Ginny went on to become a Kilgore Rangerette and was their "Big Daddy Rabbit" as well.

Gussie Nell Davis held a summer camp on Caddo Lake in East Texas and the incoming officers attended. One of the routines we learned was to the music "The Stripper," an instrumental popular at that time. It was a great routine, but it could have caused a little uproar as a high school performance in that day and age. However, we pulled it off at the homecoming game dressed as little old ladies...returning Flashes. It went over so well that the officers were invited to perform the routine at one or two other events in town

Change is inevitable. Lesby Rhodes decided to leave GHS and move in another direction. Another search was begun to find someone to direct the Flashes for the coming school year...a daunting task during difficult times.

1962-63 Flaming Flashes

Janet Bryant

No one could have begun to predict the events impacting the news. As the football season opened, over 200,000 "Freedom Marchers," arrived in Washington to demand their civil rights on August 23, 1963. The songs of Joan Baez and Bob Dylan fueled the many protesters. By late November the unthinkable happened. President John F. Kennedy was assassinated in Dallas as well wishers stood nearby waving welcoming flags. Time seemed to stand still as viewers watched the solemn ceremony on Air Force One of former Vice President Lyndon Baines Johnson repeating the oath of office with a tearful Jacqueline Kennedy and Lady Bird Johnson as witnesses. Americans watched with sorrow, which later changed to shock, as Jack Ruby shot Lee Harvey Oswald. All other news took a back seat as these events unfolded.

Time, tide, and major events were set aside, but not forgotten, as football season rolled forward and plans were made for the 30th Anniversary celebration for The Flaming Flashes. Challenges faced new Director Janet Bryant. Both directors had work to do and organizations to keep moving forward. Changes, instituted by Mrs. Bryant were to titles. Head Majorette was transitioned to the name "Colonel," Senior Majorettes to "Lieutenant Colonels," and Flag Bearers to "Majors." Leaders were:

- Head Majorette (Colonel) .... Kristi Cross
- Sr. Majorettes (Lt. Colonels) ...... Carol Johnston
  Mary Patricia Kelly
- U.S. Flag Bearer (Major) .... Elizabeth Henson
- Texas Flag Bearer (Major) .... Jan Wood (Fall Semester)
- School Flag Bearer (Major) .... Beverly Otts

Corps Officers were:

- First Lieutenant .... Sharron Blanton
- First Sergeant .... Sharon Eck
- Corporal .... Sue Glasscock

Managers were Arlene Carter, Patti Geesey, Susan Venus, and Kathy Young.

1963-64 Members

Isla Abraham	Jon Dendy	Linda Moser	Sue Sport
Mignon Acker	Paula Feagin	Billye Nicholson	Sherron Stevens
Wanda Adkins	Ann Graham	Camille Pickens	Mary Stinebaugh
Sue Ann Alexander	Susan Hackney	Sandra Pittman	Phyllis Stovall
Phyllis Baxter	Jeannie Henson	Gertrude Plunket	Mary Mac Taggart
Barbara Benton	Pamela Hitchcock	Diane Pratt	Karen Teller
Betty Bransom	Pat Holloway	Jane Ramsey	Susan Treadway
Reba Cathy	Trudy Ford	Anna Rice	Betty Tucker
Cheryl Chavey	Carol Jaco	Betty Rivera	Patsy Vaughn
Rose Crim	Jane Kirkman	Marilyn Rowe	Linda Walker
Sherry Cromer	Harriet McDonald	Judy Simmons	
Carole Daum	Jean McGuire	Nancy Smart	
Sue Dawson	Dwanan McMullen	Kay Sport	

Drum Major Willis Bailey led the GHS Band, and Jenny Pullen, Twirler, was named as Band Sweetheart. Dick Grice served as Band Captain with Vincent Scott, Johnny Morris, and Mike Nichols as Lieutenants. Twirlers were Alicia Burton, Patricia Burton, Nelcine Chapin, Karen Little, Karen McMillon, and Jenny Pullen. Farrell Freeman was Band Manager.

Mrs. Bryant had her hands full trying to select music and routines for a floor-show production. Mr. Ingram had one year's experience under his belt, but he was looking around for another position as band director. Mrs. Bryant, overwhelmed with her responsibilities, was also looking to leave. GHS patrons were expecting a floorshow. Jan Stimson, Choreographer, (Jan Stimson's School of Ballet) was hired to develop routines for "Seasons Swing" scheduled for March 19-21, 1964. Marjorie Ethridge designed the costumes.

Bill Rust, seasoned emcee, welcomed guests to the opening of "Spring" as the overture moved into "Mardi Gras" danced by the Junior Flashes. "Dance of the Hearts" followed with all Flashes performing. "April Showers" brought the twirlers to the floor with their routine followed by "Graduation Day" by the Senior Flashes.

Flash Officers, 1963-1964

Betty Bransom, Susan Hackney, Jane Ramsey, and Melissa Stimson (seated) daughter of Jan Stimson (choreographer).

The "Summer" section featured "Vacation Time" by the Flashes dancing to "By the Sea," and "California, Here I Come." A routine to "Chicago" featured the Flash Officers, before all the Flashes danced to "Chattanooga Choo Choo"…just prior to the formal presentation of new band and Flash members…a tradition was reinstated.

The second half overture welcomed "Fall" as the Flashes danced to a series of numbers featuring "Autumn Leaves." "Dem Bones," "Football Time," and, "Halftime." The "Winter" section brought "Frosty, the Snowman," with Susan Venus as "Frosty," danced by the Flashes. All the Flash Officers followed with a routine to "Winter in the Park." The band and twirlers performed to "Sleigh Ride," with the finale by the band and Flashes to "Winter Wonderland."

Both the band and Flashes now faced the prospect of an upcoming school year with new directors as Mr. Ingram and Mrs. Bryant bid them farewell. Mr. Ingram was hired as Supervisor of the Instrumental Music Program at Texarkana ISD and Director of the Texas High School bands.

Sarah Smith, GHS Band member noted:
> *Our Floorshows were spectacular! Our band won Sweepstakes two years in a row. Sweepstakes, awarded after concert band contests, meant staying to see who won, even though we knew we would be very late returning to GHS. Both years, we returned after midnight and were met by the Flashes cheering and hugging us…showing appreciation and love.*

Elizabeth Henson (Green) recalled:
> *As American Flag Bearer, I placed black ribbon streamers at the top of the post to pay homage to President John F. Kennedy during the annual Christmas parade. We were all touched deeply by his tragic death.*

Carol Johnston (Grady) shared these memories:
> *I began my desire to be a Flash at a very young age. In the early 50s, we lived on west Lee Street and next door, to my delight, was a member of the early Flashes, a drummer, under Gussie Nell Davis. I can still remember her uniform and loved the "hat!" Memories of my mother and I going to the Floor Show every year, I can almost hear the joke about the Little Moron cutting a hole in the rug! In junior high, our family friend, Mary Mac Park-*

er, became a Flash, and I was in the company of several Flashes. I was in awe! My dream came true in 1962 when I became a Flaming Flash. We were presented as Southern Belles and waltzed with our boyfriends. The cowboy hat was the one most often worn by Flashes. The hat that I loved and only wore one time was the big furry one as Lt. Colonel, which I presented to Miss Jane Ramsey my senior year. I can still do four eight counts of "Tuxedo Junction!" I loved being a Flaming Flash! The tradition continues!

Camille Pickens (Toro) recalled:

When the senior Flash officers came to "tap" us early one Saturday morning in February 1964 to be new officers for the 64-65 season, Rose Crim and I were spending the night together at her home. We couldn't stand the thought of one of us getting "in" and the other one "not" and then making that phone call as to who got "tapped." Fortunately, the officers all came to Rose's home and Elizabeth Henson (Green) tapped me for the American flag position and all "tapped" Rose twice for the Texas flag since Jan Wood had left the position vacant. It was such a joyous moment as we would be officers together!

Outgoing American Flag Bearer Elizabeth Henson (Green), passes the hat to Camille Pickens (Toro) Spring 1964

Gay Kinnamon

Following months of tragic headlines and upheaval, news of war spilled across the newspapers, over the airwaves, and on television, with North Vietnam, the aggressor. Some of the media highlighted the good news of the abolishment of the poll tax with the ratification of the 24th Amendment, and the Nobel Peace Prize awarded to Dr. Martin Luther King, Jr., civil rights leader.

Popular songs that lifted the spirits were "Chim Chim Cheree," "Fiddler on the Roof," and "Hello, Dolly!" The Beatles were making news, movies, and music everywhere they went, especially with "I Want to Hold Your Hand." The Watusi, Frug, Monkey, Funky Chicken, and similar varieties of the Twist pulled the youth into discos to watch "go-go" girls dance in mini skirts and patent leather boots. At the movies, "Bond...James Bond," broke many hearts.

Bob Cartwright accepted the position as new band director at GHS in fall of 1964 and talked with Bob Ingram, his friend from college band days, about the current band program and responsibilities. Mr. Ingram informed him of the work involved with producing a floorshow annually. Mr. Cartwright was up to the challenge and began band practice in earnest, but was in for some surprises before the end of the school year.

Gay Kinnamon was hired in fall of 1964 as Flash Director and was not aware of the many demands of that position. Her training was in physical education, but had no experience working with precision dance/drill teams. She was a strict disciplinarian in the classroom and extended those rules to Flash activities.

The Flash Officers had already worked out halftime routines and just needed coordination with Mr. Cartwright, who was happy to help. These officers knew their responsibilities and were up to the challenge after their drill team camp experience in Karnack (East Texas). Camille Pickens (Toro) stated:

> *We had special matching outfits made so we could all look fabulously coordinated. We looked fantastic, but the mosquitoes almost carried us away. It was hot as blazes... "bake your brains out" kind of temperatures. We sweated profusely... yes, sweated. We were beyond "glowing" as Southern ladies! We used bottles of Absorbine Junior for our tired, aching muscles.*

Flaming Flashes for 1964-65 were:

Head Majorette (Colonel)	Nancy Smart
Senior Majorettes (Lt. Colonels)	Betty Bransom
	Jane Ramsey
United States Flag (Major)	Camille Pickens
Texas Flag (Major)	Rose Crim
School Flag	Mary Mac Taggart

Corps Officers

First Lieutenant	Linda Walker
First Sergeant	Jeannie Henson
Corporal	Susan Hackney

Managers were Kathy Young, Rhonda Green, Jane Graves, and Patsy McClure.

1964-65 Flashes

Wanda Adkins	Sandra Darnell	Paula Knowles	Kay Sport
Sue Ann Alexander	Dionne Deaton	Patricia Miller	Cheri Steen
Margaret Apperson	Glynda Downs	Kathy McClanahan	Sherron Stevens
Cinda Barker	Mary Ella Durrett	Stephanie McGarry	Betty Tucker
Carol Barnes	Rosa Foster	Sherrie Narramore	Carol Turner
Beverly Bower	Candy Frazier	Ruth Nix	Marcia Vallancy
Pam Branton	Sharon Hackney	Gertrude Plunkett	Patsy Vaughn
Janet Bray	Susan Hackney	Linda Raymon	Linda Waddle
Debbie Braziel	Peggy Harper	Marla Reid	Linda Walker
Reba Cathey	Sharon Head	Marilyn Reneau	Ann Winsett
Vicki Chapman	Jeannie Henson	Patricia Rhodes	Wrynn Woodard
Candy Clifton	Karla Hitchcock	Jennie Robinson	
Barbara Coker	Pat Holloway	Anna Rosetti	
Paula Crockett	Carol Jaco	Judy Routh	

Drum Major Gary Guttery led the GHS Band with Illana Cathey as Band Sweetheart. Bobby Holmes was Band Captain and Lieutenants were Johnny Morris, Mike Nichols, and Charles Weis. Farrell Freeman continued as Band Manager. Twirlers were Karla Blount, Diane Alexander, Karen McMillon, Alicia Burton, Jenny Pullen, and Patricia Burton.

The rigorous training the officers had experienced prepared them for the whole year. Gay Kinnamon was not prepared as a drill team director and led by enforcing rules or creating new ones to assert her authority.

Sharon Hackney (Leonard) wrote:

> *Mrs. Kinnamon would not allow any Flash to appear in public in our hair rollers (and cute roller caps), and one friend remembered that she would make us line up well before the half time on the sidelines when it was really cold, because she did not want us "shivering" on the field when we performed.*

Before long, parents of the Flashes began commenting about the strict rules and inconsistent enforcement of those rules. The parents called for a meeting with Principal Flewharty and Mrs. Kinnamon near the end of football season. Following that meeting, Mrs. Kinnamon resigned as Flash Director before the end of the semester. Once again, the Flashes were on their own to keep their organization going.

GHS administrators moved quickly to search for a replacement for Ms. Kinnamon. As they soon learned, it's not easy to find a drill team/physical education teacher quickly. They needed someone desperately.

Patricia Danaher

Ms. Danaher, recently discharged from military service, accepted the position as director. She felt her military experience would be an asset and keeping them disciplined would not be a problem. The precision dance routines might have been problematic, however, a choreographer, Janet Stimson, who served the year prior, was hired to take care of these issues.

During the fall 1964, Mr. Cartwright and Gay Kinnamon had accepted an invitation for the Band and Flashes to march in the Cotton Bowl Parade on New Year's Day and perform in the halftime show. Ms. Danaher was in shock, but Mr. Cartwright took charge to make everything go smoothly. He recalled:

> *One of the many highlights of my time at GHS came early during my tenure when the Band and Flashes were invited to march in the Cotton Bowl Parade and take part in the halftime show on New Year's Day 1965. It was a very cold day, but everyone enjoyed the experience. During those years, the band supplied the music to accompany the Flash routines for all the football games and the floorshow. Sometimes it was a challenge to find band arrangements to some of the pop music of the day, but we usually managed.*

Ms. Danaher, according to Flash members, was "out of her element." Meetings with the outgoing principal, Mr. Flewharty did not resolve the issues needing to be addressed. He had taught for eight years at GHS before being named as Principal in 1943. The search had already begun for his replacement.

Following a parents' meeting, Janet Stimson, whose Air Force family was assigned to Ling Temco Vaught Company in Greenville, now L-3, was named to direct and choreograph the Band and Flash Floorshow for spring 1965. She had choreographed the 1964 Floorshow and was familiar with the program. She and Mr. Cartwright soon had command of the situation. Plans were made, music was selected, routines were arranged, and costumes were designed or ordered from a dance catalog by Marjorie Ethridge.

The theme for the March 18, 19, 20, 1965 show was "Come Fly With Us." As Jan Stimson worked with the Flashes and Mr. Cartwight, Ms. Danaher, aided by the Flash Officers, worked through the process of selecting new officers and new members for 1965-66.

Bill Rust, emcee, welcomed the crowd as the band played the overture, "Come Fly With Us" prior to the Junior Flashes' dance routine to "This Could Be the Start of Something Big." The program, divided into sections, began with "Country Holiday." The Flashes danced to "Little Bit O'Cockney" (England), followed by "The Campbells Are Coming" by the twirlers (Scotland). Ireland featured the Flash Officers dancing to "Lucky Lassies," and the Flashes dancing the "Liechtensteiner Polka" for the country of Germany.

Section Two, "Continental Capers," featured the countries of France, Spain, and Italy, as the Flashes danced to "Chevalier," "Flamenco Guitar," and "Tarantella." Presentation of new members of both groups followed.

"East of the Sun" opened the second half of the show featuring the countries of Turkey (Flashes), Japan (Senior Flashes), China (Flashes), and Siam (Flashes). A section called "Side Trip" featured the Flash Officers and Drum Major Gary Guttery performing to "Calypso Caribbean."

The last section, "Homeward Bound," included Hawaii, Alaska, and Stateside with "War Chant" by the Flashes, "Skater's Waltz" by Betty Bransom and Farrell Freeman, "Button Up Your Overcoat" by the twirlers. Cheerleaders Deanna Darby, Jill Prather, Vicki Smith, Sherry Pennington, Pat Dawson, and Myra Miller, plus Flash Managers Patsy McClure, Kathy Young, Rhonda Green, and Jane Graves performing to "Bossa Nova, Beatles, and Bop."

The Flashes danced to "This Is My Country" for the finale and the entire cast closed the show with "All God's Chillun." All breathed a sigh of relief as another successful show ended a rather hectic year for the Flashes.

Nancy Smart (Johnson) had many wonderful memories to share:
> *At a time before Title IX ushered in girls' athletics, Flashes was one of the few options for girls to become active, and, yes, even competitive. Tryouts in the gym with a number pinned to your red gym suit were nerve-wracking, but performing at football games, pep rallies, and floorshows was absolutely exciting. The thrill of becoming Head Majorette seemed like the capstone to my high school years. I still have the red boots and hat! I particularly remember a beautiful fall day when we traveled to Dallas to perform at the State Fair of Teas. The beautiful blue sky and the crisp fall air seemed electric when we marched into the fair grounds and performed in front of the Hall of State. Even fifty years later, I always hum a few bars of "Peter Gunn" whenever I walk across the Hall of State plaza.*

Camille Pickens (Toro) commented on several special moments.
> *When I was little, we lived about twelve blocks from the football field. I would be playing in the backyard and listening to the band rehearse and wanted to be there with them! Friday nights were electric! The whole town came alive! After I first saw the Flashes perform at a football game, I knew I wanted to be one just like my Momma (Mae Merrick Pickens). She had to play a drum when she was a Flash in 1938-39. Thank goodness they dropped that requirement by the time I got to high school. All we had to do was kick above our heads with our toes perfectly pointed and then do the splits!*

I was so PROUD to be asked to carry the American flag! Before every game, drummers would strike up a loud drum roll as I marched slowly and reverently onto the football field to the fifty-yard line with the other two flag bearers six paces behind me. As I made my final firm step and came to a halt, I felt honored and humbled to be able to hold that flag! It represented so much that all the brave men and women before us had fought for. It seemed as if time had stopped for a brief instant. You could hear a pin drop. Every eye was on that flag and every heart was crossed with a cap, a helmet, or a right hand...then we began to sing the National Anthem as the band played.

Another special moment for me in March 1965 was the Tyler Rose Parade. I was so excited about going to Tyler to march with the Flashes because Momma (Mae Merrick Pickens) had marched with the Flashes at the Tyler Rose Parade in 1939! I was standing there with my flag, ready for them to tell us where to line up, when a man came up and asked me if I would come to the front of the parade and lead the entire parade! I could not even answer him...I was in shock. I think I mumbled something about his asking permission of our Flash Director, Patricia Danaher. She agreed and off I went to lead the ENTIRE PARADE! All I could think about the whole way was Momma. Tears just flowed down my cheeks as I walked the parade route and people stood up to salute or put their hands over their hearts.

After the parade, I received two magazines. I was shocked and amazed! Someone had taken my picture in an earlier parade and there it was...already printed on the magazine cover for the Tyler Rose Parade! A few months later, I received a copy of Texas Highways with my picture on the cover of that magazine...leading the Tyler Rose Parade!

Kay Sport (Denman) shared these memories.

I was a member of the Flaming Flashes from 1963-1965. My sister, Sue, was also a member while I was in my junior year and she was a senior. We always had a lot of fun riding the school buses to the out of town football games and other events. I remember that we were divided into groups and we would also practice our dances on Saturday mornings at our squad leader's home. Our weekly Friday night performances usually were strictly dance routines, and we very seldom had any kind of props to use except at the Homecoming game. We always included a contagion, or domino...as we called it back then. The people in the stands seemed to really like those. During pep rallies, we sat in the stands as a group and did hand jive routines. Those were always fun.

I remember that the Flashes went to march in the Tyler Rose Parade each of those years, and we also went to perform on stage at the Texas State Fair both years. Being a member of the Flashes was so much fun and hard work too, especially in the spring when we were preparing for the Band and Flash Floor Show! We performed for three nights. We had to have all our costumes handmade for the shows. My mother did not know how to sew, so we had to find a seamstress and have ours made.

During the two years that I was a Flash, we had three different directors. That wasn't such a good thing, but we carried on with the leadership of our officers. We also had to pay for our Flaming Flashes jackets our senior year. I still have mine, even though it doesn't fit anymore! I would not trade my time being in the Flashes for anything!

1965-66 saw continued outbreaks of violence in the South and in Los Angeles as the fight for civil rights continued. Anti-Vietnam protesters also marched across the country as casualties mounted. President Lyndon Baines Johnson was overwhelmed with national and world issues. The "British Invasion" was in full swing as hordes of adoring teenage fans screamed loudly during performances of "The Beatles," "The Animals," "The Monkees," and various groups who gave "Elvis" a run for the money. Strains of "A Hard Day's Night," "Eleanor Rigby," and "Ballad of the Green Berets" were heard across the land and in the homes and cars of most Americans. "Flower Power" was also spreading across the country as the "Hippie" movement lured many teenagers away from their homes and families.

During all the tumult, the space program and the Flashes kept moving forward. Soviet Cosmonaut Leonov left his spacecraft for the first walk in space, followed by America's first two-person mission as Gemini 3 took astronauts Virgil "Gus" Grissom and John Young into space for about five hours. Astronaut Edward White followed in Gemini 4 and completed a twenty-one minute spacewalk. The space race continued in 1966 with the Soviets and the United States both completing successful soft landings on the moon. Not distracted by this competition, the Flashes prepared for another year under the direction of Patricia Danaher. Leaders included:

Head Majorette (Colonel)	Candy Clifton
Senior Majorettes (Lt. Colonels)	Peggy Harper
	Ann Winsett
United States Flag (Major)	Debbie Braziel
Texas Flag (Major)	Dionne Deaton
School Flag (Major)	Patricia Miller
First Lieutenant	Carol Barnes
First Sergeant	Cheri Steen
Corporal	Sherrie Narramore
Managers	Jane Graves, Marla Reid, Jean Garber, Winnifred Rogers

Members of the Flashes

Judy Allen	Sandra Darnell	Margaret Henson	Linda Raymon
Margaret Apperson	Kathy Dawson	Karla Hitchcock	Marilyn Reneau
Cinda Barker	Glynda Downs	Paula Knowles	Jenny Robinson
Marsha Bell	Mary Ella Durrett	Londa Ledbetter	Judy Routh
Beverly Bower	Candy Frazier	Patricia Meador	Sue Rowe
Pam Branton	Kathy Fulks	Ginger Moser	Carol Turner
Janet Bray	Wanda Garner	Kathie McClanahan	Jill Vaughn
Janis Caldwell	Susan Gover	Stephanie McGarry	Linda Waddle
Linda Chapman	Carolyn Gray	Ruth Nix	Karen Wall
Vicki Chapman	Sharon Hackney	Debbie Orr	Wynn Warren
Paula Crockett	Sharon Head	Jennifer Price	Wrynn Woodard

Leading the GHS Band was Drum Major Mike Nichols with Dottye Pickrell as Band Sweetheart. Henry Hunt was Band Captain with Alan Doshier (Senior Lieutenant), Phil Mullinix (Junior Lieutenant), and Jimmy Hulsey (Sophomore Lieutenant). Head Twirler Karon Battle led twirlers Cindy Alcorn, Colleen Ernest, Debbie Jones, Marcia Rieber, and Randi Rust.

Mr. James Covert, new principal at GHS, was amazed to see all the work involved with the Band and Flashes. He relied on the advice of his vice principal and secretary to keep him informed as to the traditions and expectations for both groups. He understood most of the band procedures, but was quite lost when it came to dealing with the Flashes and their parents.

With a successful football season and parade appearances behind them, the Band and Flashes began preparations for another floorshow. Few realize the amount of time and effort required to present the annual extravaganza, but Bob Cartwright soon discovered the extent of involvement required.

The Annual Band and Flash Floorshow was one of the community highlights of the spring. It was very popular and people I met on the street started asking about the theme we had chosen at the beginning of the year, and our planning started almost as soon as school started. At that time, it was held in the high school gym around the first of March. This was a perfect venue. The gym had permanent bleachers with a short wall and railing separating the seating. This made it perfect for decorating and separating the seats from the floor. For floorshow week, the gym was turned over to the Band and Flashes and it was off limits to the student body. The Band and Flash students did the decorations and lighting. The Flash Director supervised the decorations, and I, along with a crew of band guys, installed the lighting and lighting dimmer board that was rented from a theatrical lighting company in Dallas. Students in the Band and Flashes did all the artwork. Some of the artists that come to mind were Gary Head (now one of the leading artists for Hallmark) and Johnny Clements, from the band, and Marcia Livesay from the Flashes. They did outstanding work, and the

> *backdrops were very professional. They highlighted the theme of the show. The Flash Director took care of the choreography for the Flashes, and Sandra, my wife, choreographed the twirler routines for the floorshow, as well as all the routines they performed during football season... all without pay, I might add (bless her heart).*
>
> *Bill Rust was the Master of Ceremonies for all the shows during my years as band director. Bill was a master of script writing, timing to connect the acts together... which helped to keep things moving to fill for all the costume changes, and allow the students to move to their positions on the floor in the dark. The week was busy getting the gym decorated, installing the lighting, and having as much done as possible for the Wednesday night dress rehearsal and camera night. The performances were on Thursday, Friday, and Saturday nights, and the gym was pretty much full every night. It has been estimated that as many as 3000 people were in attendance for the combined three performances. There were many people from outside Greenville that attended the shows. They were an outstanding public relations event, not only for the Band and Flashes, but for the school district and community as well.*

On March 18 and 19, 1966, the Band and Flash "Revue" made its debut with Bill Rust at the helm as emcee. Gloria English served as choreographer and Ron Newsome was Lighting Director. The band opened the show followed by the Senior Flashes dancing to "In a Chinese Temple Garden" featuring Judy Routh. The Stage Band played "Polka Dots and Moonbeams," featuring trombone soloist, Mike Nichols. The Flash Officers followed with "The Creeper" leading the Flashes in the next routine to "Goofus." The band played "Misty" just prior to the presentation of new members of both groups.

The band opened the second half with "Señor, Señor" followed by the Flashes dancing to "Fascination." As the band finished playing "Fascination," the Flash Officers readied themselves for their routine to "Mexican Hat Dance." Next, the Flashes executed a precision marching drill to "Washington Post," followed by the twirlers' routine to "Sometimes I'm Happy." The band flowed into "Mancini" as the Flashes readied for the "Can Can"... a truly grand finale.

Gussie Nell Davis, originator of The Flaming Flashes, continued to be an influence for the group. No matter where the Flashes traveled, Gussie Nell's name was usually included, either in news articles or by word of mouth. In 1965, Gussie Nell Davis received the Certificate of Citation bestowed by the State of Texas House of Representatives. Her tenure at Greenville High School was noted at those ceremonies, and her fame as originator of the first precision dance and drill team in the nation, The Flaming Flashes, was lauded.

Robert Ward, Class of 1966 recalled his mother's tenure as a Flash.
> *My mother, Ruth Kathryn Sadler, was a Charter Member of The Flaming Flashes under their originator, Gussie Nell Davis. She often talked about that first year. The excitement of being a part of the new group, especially*

since the football team was so great, was truly remembered by her. With all the hard work, hot uniforms, make-up requirements, and traveling in hot weather; she said it was well worth it. Mom continued to communicate with Gussie Nell until Gussie Nell's death. She was such an influential person in "her girls" eyes. As one who also graduated from Greenville High School, there are many memories of the time I watched the performances of The Flaming Flashes... long may they march!

With the closing of another floorshow and the ending of another school year, Ms. Danaher decided to step down as director of the Flashes. Once again, the administration began their search for a new Flash Director.

Mary Jane Vance, who had served as their director in 1960-61 (her BC "before children" years), was now the proud mother of two amazing children, and had returned to teaching (her AD "after diapers" years). [*Author's Note:* Superintendent Wesley Martin contacted me about the possibility of returning as Flash Director for 1966-67. After serious consideration and engaging a dedicated nanny, Eula Lowrey, for Chip and Missy, I agreed to return to GHS.]

Ginger Moser, Marsha Bell, Janis Caldwell (1966-67)

Mary Jane Vance

Seeds for civil right sown on Bloody Sunday in 1965 grew into political support for the landmark Voting Rights Act cultivated by President Lyndon B. Johnson. While strife and protests in the nation over civil rights and the Vietnam War made the headlines, few noticed the success of Dr. Michael E. De Bakey in Houston making medical history with his successful artificial heart operation and Astronaut Edwin E. "Buzz" Aldrin's successful 129-minute spacewalk out of Gemini 12 in 1966. 1967 saw Dr. Christian N. Barnard perform the world's first human heart transplant and NASA suspend all manned space flights, after three astronauts died in a fire on the launch pad.

Martin Luther King, Jr. led an anti-Vietnam war march in New York and riots broke out in Cleveland, Newark, and Detroit.

The process of integrating the Greenville Schools had begun. Supt. Wesley Martin and GISD Trustees wisely decided to provide all students a "choice" as to which schools to attend. The schools were considered "separate but equal." Twelve students from Carver High School, including Earl Thomas and Gene Mack, chose to complete their senior year at GHS. All public schools remained open. The faculty and administration at GHS was not integrated. The ninth grade was also moved to the GHS campus...that made for a very crowded situation.

So many female students were "out of pocket," so I asked permission to start a GHS Pep Squad to foster a training ground for future Flashes and provide physical activities plus involvement in school spirit. Uniforms were homemade...red knee-length skirts, a red blazer worn over a white blouse, and special white gloves with red palms for "hand routines" in the stands.

Folk music, rock and roll, and the "hippie move-

Mary Jane Vance

ment" continued to spill over the country and around the world. Television programs moved from "Father Knows Best" to programs that included more violence. The Age of Innocence was passing before our eyes.

Strong traditions continued to be the focus of The Flaming Flashes as I inherited a strongly motivated group of Flash Officers and Flashes in 1966-67.

Head Majorette (Colonel)	Sue Rowe
Senior Majorettes (Lt. Colonels)	Kathy Fulks
	Jennifer Price
American Flag Bearer (Major)	Marsha Bell
Texas Flag Bearer (Major)	Ginger Moser
School Flag Bearer (Major)	Janis Caldwell
Lieutenant	Wanda Garner
Sergeant	Margaret Henson
Corporal	Judy Allen
Managers	Jean Garber, Vicki Philpot
	Sharon Reynolds, Karen Steele

Members

Kitty Attison	Patti Denman	Beth Ann Olds	Denise Reneau
Linda Boswell	Sherry Eckman	Debbie Orr	Elizabeth Renfro
Dianne Bryant	Jacque Edwards	Sue Monroe	Nancy Sansom
Kathy Castleberry	Carolyn Gray	Melanie Marshal	Benita Smiley
Charlotte Causey	Irma Harper	Judy Mason	Carol Stapleton
Connie Click	Elaine Harrington	Pat Long	Jill Vaughn
Georgia Crawford	Linda Hester	Londa Ledbetter	Karen Wall
Debby Cox	Janie Hoff	Sandra Humphreys	
Shannon Davies	Marsha Nelson	Brenda Reeves	

The Flashes had their first experience with Drill Team Camp at Southern Methodist University (SMU) conducted by Gussie Nell Davis and Director Irving Dreibrodt. New routines and working under Gussie Nell Davis excited them all. A new high kick entrance and exit presentation, which included the cartwheel ending in the splits, to "Hey, Look Me Over," was perfected and introduced at the opening football game. The crowd came to their feet for a huge standing ovation. Sue Rowe, Colonel, had never perfected a cartwheel as a child, but with the help of her mother, Jewel Rowe, English teacher at GHS, the many hours of practice in her front yard paid off.

I was delighted to have my friend and former classmate at ETSU during the mid '50s, Bob Cartwright, as a coworker. We both had a great appreciation for good music, a love of dance, and a wonderful sense of humor.

The GHS Band was led by David Howard, Drum Major, and Karla Blount, Band Sweetheart/Head Twirler. Thomas Hogland was Band Captain, aided by Senior Lieutenant Danny Fletcher, Junior Lieutenant Fagg Sanford and Sophomore Lieutenant Joe Weis. Gary Bradford was Manager, and Alan Ackles served as Announcer for both groups. Head Twirler

Karla Bount led twirlers Karon Battle, Carol Bledsoe, Colleen Ernest, Debbie Jones, and Judy Pullen. Randi Rust and Tammie Braswell served as alternates.

A busy fall schedule with the Flashes, GHS Pep Squad, GHS Cheerleaders, teaching physical education and health classes, plus caring for our children, ages two and four, kept me busy, and my health began to suffer.

Selection of new officers and Flashes for the coming year, plus the planning, designing of costumes, rehearsals, etc., for the annual floorshow scheduled for March 17-18, 1967, were pressing issues. A trip to kidney specialist, Dr. George Hurt, revealed a fungus feeding on my right kidney... creating a blockage resulting in high fever and digestive distress. Surgery was necessary... but was postponed... the show must go on.

"Continental Swing" was the selected theme. Music was selected. Current and new Flash Officers Sue Rowe, Shannon Davies, Nancy Sansom, Beth Ann Olds, Jacque Edwards, Kathy Castleberry, Irma Harper, Kathy Fulks, and Marsh Bell were named Assistant Choreographers

Bill Rust, our loyal emcee, welcomed the crowd on opening night as the band played "America the Beautiful." The Flashes followed with a rousing routine to "Yellow Rose of Texas," and the band continued with "Ode for Trumpet" featuring Mike Mason as soloist. The Flash Officers continued with a dance to "Lonely Bull" followed by the Junior Flashes lifting spirits with their routine to "Way Down Yonder in New Orleans." The twirlers western routine to "Don't Fence Me In" was followed by the present and new Flash Officers' rendition of "Buttons and Bows." A Senior Specialty number to "Chicago," by Senior Flashes Carolyn Gray, Londa Ledbetter, Debbie Orr, Jill Vaughn, and Karen Wall, was a hit. Following "The Kingfish" by the Stage Band, the Flashes did a precision march/dance routine to "Giant." Presentation of new members of both groups followed.

Sounds of "Strategic Air Command" filled the room followed by the Flashes specialty routine to "What A Country." The twirlers flew across the floor to "Wings of Victory," and the Flash Officers did an interpretive dance to "Exodus—This Land is Mine." David Howard narrated the story of "Threnody" followed by a lovely solo, "You'll Never Walk Alone," by Linda Boswell. The band played "American Civil War Fantasy" followed by the finale to "Stars and Stripes Forever," resulting in a standing ovation.

Before leaving in May for surgery at Baylor, a copy of *The Lion,* the GHS annual, was handed to me during a special presentation. I was very surprised to learn the GHS 1967 Annual was dedicated to me. Doctors gave me a fifty-fifty chance of survival, and I opted for the "better fifty." The Flash Officers were constant visitors, much to my delight. My gratitude and appreciation for them "bringing me through" 1966-67 will never be forgotten.

Several changes took place at GHS during the summer of 1967. Principal James Covert left for another position and Mr. William R. Dendy was hired as principal. Mr. Bill Walters, teacher and coach, was named Assistant Principal. Mr. L. P. Waters, former principal at Carver High School, became Assistant Principal at GHS. Carver High School was being closed, but the elementary campuses remained in operation for the next stage of integration of the schools. The GHS faculty was also integrated to accommodate the growing number of students. The Carver High Band was blended with the GHS Band. Hard rock

> **Southern Methodist University**
>
> **Certificate of Achievement**
>
> This Certifies that
>
> _Mary Jane Vance_
>
> Satisfactorily Completed the
> Pep Squad and Drill Team Course
> at
> Southern Methodist University
>
> _Summer Session_
>
> _Gussie Nell Davis_   _Irving Dreibrodt_
> INSTRUCTOR   DIRECTOR

and "soul' music hits made the charts regularly. Aretha Franklin was everywhere… and we loved it. R – E – S – P – E – C – T was a perfect song for the Flashes and Pep Squad for "hand signal" routines.

The month of June was needed for a recuperation period. Planning, scheduling, selection of music was completed by early July. The Flashes were excited about attending Drill Team Camp at SMU again, with Gussie Nell Davis, and trying to win the Southwest Drill Team Competition. Daily bus rides to Dallas, wearing their new red practice uniforms on a hot bus, did not deter these determined Flashes. The Flash Officers had worked with their squads during July and were ready for SMU in August. I have never seen anyone work so hard to win the competition… and they did. The "Award-Winning Flaming Flashes'" coveted trophy rests in its case at GHS to this day as a reminder of their efforts. Each time they step on the field or perform in public, their "title" is announced with pride. In recognition of their efforts, I designed a banner proclaiming this honor and selected two Flashes to serve as Banner Carriers to display on the field, at parades, or other public events.

Before the school year began, Gussie Nell Davis invited me to Kilgore Junior College for a weekend work session. She had a "soft spot" for The Flaming Flashes and wanted to share some ideas with me. I don't believe we slept at all that weekend. She was a ball of fire and kept going on with her many stories and ideas. I was truly inspired by this bundle of talent and energy.

Football season began with a "bang" under the guidance of Head Coach Larry Hogue, in his second year at GHS. He used a fierce defense and a balanced offense to become the terror of District 6-AAA. (His wife, Betty, took over Janet Stimson's dance studio to the delight of many.) The crowd went wild when the Lions beat the Lake Highlands Wildcats (Richardson) 21-19. A winning football season spurred the Band and Flashes on to excellent performances, both on the field and at public events.

Leading the award-winning Flaming Flashes for 1967-68 were:

Head Majorette (Colonel)	Shannon Davies
Senior Majorettes (Lt. Colonels)	Sherry Eckman
	Irma Harper
American Flag (Major)	Nancy Sansom
Texas Flag (Major)	Beth Ann Olds
School Flag (Major)	Melanie Marshall
Lieutenant	Marsha Nelson
Sergeant	Jacque Edwards
Corporal	Kathy Castleberry

Manager was Debbie Wrenn. Gordy Davies served as Announcer, and Denise Holloway was an Honorary Flash. Members were:

Patti Bench	Jan Dawson	Shannon Marshall	Patti Sansom
Jan Berry	Betsye George	Janet McCartney	Ann Stewart
Mary Bryant	Toni Gossett	Sandra McCutchen	Janet Stovall
Kay Burr	Reba Graham	Cindy McKay	Benita Smiley
Janis Carpenter	Elaine Humphries	Judy Mason	Carol Stapleton
Connie Clock	Sandra Humphreys	Sue Monroe	Jan Treadway
Georgia Crawford	Karla Key	Kay Odeneal	Loretta Turner
Debbie Darnell	Karol Koger	Denise Reneau	Marilyn Williams
Phyllis Darnell	Debbie Lacy	Debbie Robertson	Terry Yarborough

Ronnie Carpenter, Drum Major, led the GHS Band and Karon Battle continued as Band Sweetheart. Jimmy Hulsey and Fagg Sanford served as band co-captains. Lieutenants were Mike Mason, Brent Worthen and Claude Higginbotham. Head Twirler Karon Battle led twirlers Coleen Ernest, Debbie Jones, Coletta Bolick, Marcia Reiber, Randi Rust, and Cindy Alcorn.

The race for space continued as the Apollo 7 spacecraft, launched from Cape Kennedy, carried three astronauts for an eleven-day orbit around Earth ending in a successful splashdown in the Atlantic Ocean.

The race for presenting another successful floorshow was also in motion. "Fantasia" was the theme for the March 22-23, 1968 floorshow...after all...it was Mickey Mouse's fortieth birthday! Assistant Choreographers Shannon Davies and Cindy McKay were ready. Special Assistants Kathleen Barlow and Becky Beggs, Cheerleaders, had performed their magic, the GHS Art Department with Mrs. Sharon Rhodes in charge, were set with the decorations. Following weeks of preparation, music and costume selection, plus rehearsals, Bill Rust, emcee, opened another magical delight for the public.

The band opened with "Walt Disney Overture" followed by the Flashes dancing to "Once Upon A Dream." Mike Mason, Alyce Schrimsher, and Connie Owens highlighted the band's playing of "Bugler's Holiday." The Junior Flashes delighted the crowd with "I've Got No Strings," and the enchantment continued with the Flash Officers routine to "Following the Leader," with Shannon Davies as Peter Pan. Shannon remained on the floor for a solo dance to "A Dream Is A Wish Your Heart Makes," sung by soloist Denise Holloway. The Senior Flashes charmed the crowd with their version of "Toyland." Alyce Schrimsher (trumpet), and Fagg Sanford (tenor saxophone), were featured as the band played "Summertime." The twirlers amazed the audience with their version of the Seven Dwarfs to "Heigh Ho." A Flash Specialty routine featured Shannon Davies, Cindy McKay, Jan Treadway, Debbie Lacy, Karla Key, Patti Bench, and Patti Sansom dancing to "Satin Doll." The band played "I've Got Plenty of Nothin'" just prior to the precision march/dance routine by the Flashes to "March of the Toys." Presentation of new members for both groups followed.

The second half included the Flashes dancing to "Jolly Holiday" followed by the twirlers and their lovely rendition to "Waltz of the Flowers." The Flash Officers picked up the tempo with "Anchors Aweigh," and the band continued with "Man of La Mancha." A colorful routine by the Flashes was done to "Let's Go Fly A Kite," followed by the Stage Band's version of "Walkin' on the Wolfgang." Present and new Flash Officers delighted the crowd with "It's A Small World" just prior to the finale by the entire cast.

Bob Cartwright recalled recently:

> *There were many clever routines from both groups, and, after over forty years it is hard to remember them. One that comes to mind was a twirler routine that used Snow White and The Seven Dwarfs as the theme and the costumes were of the seven wearing papier-mâché heads made and painted by the Art Department.*
>
> *The floorshows were a lot of work, but I have many fond memories of working with all the different directors and all the many students that participated. The students gained much valuable experience in working together for the common goal of creating and giving the best possible performance, and I know they will never forget the feeling of a job well done.*

Pat Long (Burns) included some "Flashbacks":

> 5. *Bus Trips: How great it was for all my fellow Flashes and me to sing "My Girl," "Help Me, Rhonda," "Stop, in the Name of Love," "Town Without Pity," or "Hang on Sloopy," at the top of our lungs. The metal walls of that bus only added to the beautiful notes that we were putting out as we road-tripped to another performance. And who could forget finding a way to modestly change into and out of our uniforms with those wheels rolling?*
> 4. *Camps: From summer camps in our own back yard to summer camps at SMU, we learned AND created some great choreography. There was always an individual critique at the end of the day. I still remember the day my squad leader said, "You left hook cutely!" It sounded like somebody was stretching pretty far to find a compliment for me that day!*
> 3. *The Christmas Parade: Let me just throw out a few words so that a mental image can be formed: December weather, nighttime, long parade route, small Flash uniform...enough said.*
> 2. *Football Games: What a thrill it was to stand on the sidelines in bright*

stadium lights getting ready to do our Flash entrance to the center of the football field. We had smiles glued on our faces, eyes wide and bright, and the notes of our opening, "Hey, Look Me Over," tickling our ears. While we marched, we knew that those sharp head snaps, killer 'contagions' and amazing high kicks were sure to bring a lot of applause from both sides of the field. Friday night was the terror of anticipation and the joy of performance all rolled into one!

1. *Life-long Friendships: My Number One Flashback has to be the friendships that were formed during those Flash days that have remained to this day. We really did and still do, love each other. What a treasure to have the friendship of those girls and of you, our wonderful leader. YOU made all these memories possible.*

Obligations to my family were pressing me to move in another direction. Our son, Chip, was about to enter the first grade, so I needed to return to an elementary classroom to assure our schedules were aligned. My family needed me, and, as we all know, family comes first, but I will always remember my family of Flashes.

Linda Brantley

Our nation was overwhelmed with strife. President Johnson had announced he would not seek another term. The recent assassinations of Dr. Martin Luther King, Jr., and Robert F. Kennedy, who had just won the Democratic primary in Los Angeles in his bid for president, rocked the world.

Riots and protest continued as a weary world tried to find solutions. The only seemingly bright spot in the news was the wedding of Mrs. Jacqueline Kennedy to Greek shipping magnate Aristotle Onassis in 1968. The inauguration of Richard Nixon as 37th President of the United States in 1969 opened the year to new beginnings, starting with the withdrawal of troops from Vietnam. The "Age of Aquarius" extended the "hippie movement" into another year.

Mrs. Linda Brantley, a self-assured young woman, took charge of the Flashes, who had already proved they were winners. Leading were:

Colonel	Cindy McKay
Lt. Colonel	Marilyn Williams
American Flag (Major)	Debbie Lacy
Texas Flag (Major)	Mary Bryant
School Flag	Shannon Marshall
Lieutenant	Debbie Darnell
Sergeant	Kay Odeneal
Corporal	Patti Bench
Managers	Alice Anderson
	Kathy Mizell
Announcer	Dennis Moon.

Lt. Col. Jan Treadway did not complete the year as an officer. The position was not filled that year.

Flash Members

Lana Barker	Teresa Gooch	Kathy Odom	Anne Stewart
Kay Burr	Reba Graham	Mary Beth Parrott	Karen Treadway
Becky Byers	Becky Kilmer	Laura Pitts	Loretta Turner
Paula Campbell	Laurie Lester	Terrie Reid	Cindy Wacasey
Janis Carpenter	Ginger Morgan	Debbie Robertson	Debbie Whitehead
Mary Eichner	Kathie Moser	Gail Ruble	Debbie Wrenn
Betsye George	Laura Murray	June Sanford	

Drum Major L. R. Miller led the band with Randi Rust, Band Sweetheart and Head Twirler. Band Captain was Lee Terrell. Lieutenants were Larry McInnis, Claude Higginbotham, Brian Jacks, and Paul Story.

The Band and Flashes' full football season was capped by their television appearance at the Pecan Bowl in Arlington and their pre-game appearance at the Dallas Cowboy-New York Giant football game in the Cotton Bowl in Dallas. They also performed in the Tyler Rose Parade and the State Fair of Texas, plus their usual assignment of leading the Greenville Christmas Parade.

March 14-15, 1968 were the dates for the Annual Band and Flash Floorshow with "Happiness Is…" as the theme. Chosen as Assistant Choreographers were Cindy McKay and Marilyn Williams. Special Assistants were Alice Anderson and Kathy Mizell. Johnny Clements took charge of the decorations. Bill Rust, emcee, took command as the band played "Night Flight to Madrid Overture." A rousing performance by the Flashes to "Can Can" let the crowd know they were in for a treat. "Moon River" was followed by a specialty routine by the Senior Flashes that flowed into "What Now My Love" performed by the twirlers. The Flashes swam into "By The Sea" with their routine culminated by the Stage Band playing "Seventh Son of A Seventh." The Flash Officers did their magic to "That Old Black Magic" followed by "Contrapuntal Baby" by the Stage Band. The Junior Flashes danced to "I Enjoy Being A Girl" prior to the annual presentation of new members.

"Heat Lightning" by the band opened the second half while the Flashes prepared for their next number to "Sleigh Ride." The twirlers danced to "Music to Watch Girls By" before the Flash Officers performed to "The Look of Love." A band selection, "I Left My Heart in San Francisco," brought the Flashes back to dance to "I Like Mountain Music." Present and new Flash Officers danced to "Circus Attractions" prior to the finale by the entire cast.

Gussie Nell Davis made the news again by being named "Texas Woman of the Year" by the Texas State Civitans. Once again, The Flaming Flashes were hailed since Gussie Nell was the originator of the nation's first high school precision dance/drill team.

Another year rolled by rather quickly as Mrs. Brantley continued as Director. Flash Officers had already completed their training at camp along with the Flashes. Flashes for 1969-70 included:

Head Majorette (Colonel)	Cindy Wacasey*
Senior Majorettes (Lt. Colonel)	Paula Campbell
United States Flag (Major)	Mary Eichner
Texas Flag (Major)	Mary Beth Parrott
School Flag (Major)	Laurie Lester
Lieutenant	Lana Barker
Sergeant	Gail Ruble
Corporal	June Sanford
Banner Carriers	Becky Kilmer, Kathy Odum
Managers	Vanessa Lassiter, Nancy Siergiej, Marlene Shippy
Announcer	Larry Linenschmidt

Members of the Flash Corps

Mary Adams	Teresa Gooch	Ellen Kanazawa	Mary Price
Becky Boswell	Rebecca Graham	Marcia Livesay	Terrie Reid
Jacqueline Cooper	Sherry Hassell	Maria Mahrer	Carla Smith
Dianna Craig	Gail Heard	Laura Murray	Evelynn Walden
Paula Crowell	Patricia Hill	Marlene McClellan	Dean Weldon
Beverly Dennis	Jeannie Hilton	Frances MacPeak	Debbie Whitehead
Carla Ende	Judy Horton	Laura Pitts	
Lisa Erwin	Brenda Isham	Rebecca Pierce	
Judy Gayner	Candy James	Ginny Priest	

*Ginger Morgan, named as Head Majorette (Colonel) for 1969-70, did not return to Flashes. Cindy Wacasey, who was Senior Majorette (Lt. Colonel), was moved into the position of Colonel. The Lt. Colonel's position was not filled.

Drum Major Claude Higginbotham led the GHS Band and Marcia Reiber, Twirler, was Band Sweetheart. Band Captain Jimmy Langley took charge of Lieutenants Mike Rhodes, Rusty Averitt, and James Coffman. Twirlers were Jean Spradling, Linda Brown, Marcia Reiber, Sharon Cathey, Kathy Blount, Coletta Bollick, Cathy Deaton, and Brenda Alexander.

On October 29, 1969, the Supreme Court ruled an end to segregation. Try-outs for the Flashes included members of all races for the first time.

March 23-24, 1970, was set for the Annual Floorshow with the theme "Blues in the Night." Bill Rust, emcee, had the house lights dimmed as the band opened with "Shades of Blue," followed by a routine by the Flashes to "Birth of the Blues." The band picked up the tempo with "Red's White and Blue March" followed by the twirlers' routine to "Aquarius." The Flash Officers and their escorts continued with "I Could Have Danced All Night." The Junior Flashes followed with a snappy routine to "Ballin' the Jack." The Stage Band featured soloists during "Blues One More Time," followed by the twirlers' routine to "Oh! You Beautiful Doll." The Flashes delighted the crowd with their next routine to "Tuxedo Junction," followed by the Stage Band playing another specialty number to "Far Down Below." The Senior Flashes danced to "Good Morning Starshine" prior to the presentation of members.

"Festivo" by the band brought the crowd back to their seats as the Flash Officers prepared to dance to "Hawaii Five-O." The twirlers danced to "Basin Street Blues," and were followed by a special routine by the Flashes to "So Nice." A specialty selection by the band, "People," featured soloists Bobby Andrews (vocal) and Claude Higginbotham (trumpet). Present and new Flash Officers danced next to "Me and My Shadow." The band played "Blue Tail Fly" prior to the finale, "Bye, Bye, Blues," by the entire cast.

The end of another show signaled the end of another school year as the Flashes worked with Mrs. Brantley to prepare for 1970-71.

NASA made progress in the race for space in 1970-71, although disasters raised questions in the minds of many. US Apollo 14 and 15 became the third and fourth groups to explore the moon's surface. Student protests against the Vietnam War resulted in the killing of four by the National Guard. The world bear market in the US for eight years touched bottom when the Dow-Jones dropped to 631. On a lighter note, Burt Bacharach scored high in the realm of music with two Academy Awards for the score of *Butch Cassidy and the Sundance Kid* and the song "Raindrops Keep Falling on My Head." "Fiddler on the Roof" became the longest running musical on Broadway history, surpassing the 2,844 performances of "Hello Dolly."

The Flaming Flashes proved to be more than just entertainers as special projects for local charity and veterans groups involved them in various activities during the year. Anytime the community needed a uniformed group to assist with civic or charitable activities, they called upon the Flashes, who, if their schedule allowed, would proudly offer their services.

The Flaming Flashes were featured again in the *Dallas Times Herald* with Miss Gussie Nell Davis, who began working with the group in 1928 prior to setting their charter in 1934 as the first high school precision dance and drill team in the world. Flash Officers and members for 1970-71 were:

Colonel	Maria Mahrer
Lt. Colonels	Candy James, Mary Price
United States Flag (Major)	Jeannie Hilton
Texas Flag (Major)	Carla Smith
School Flag (Major)	Rebecca Graham
Lieutenant	Lisa Erwin
Sergeant	Brenda Isham
Corporal	Marcia Livesay
Banner Carriers	Mary Adams, Evelyn Walden
Managers	Wrenda Foster, Kay Smith

Members of the Flash Corps

Mary Adams	Susan Hayes	Cindy Marshall	Jamie Tarpley
Carol Bandt	Gail Heard	Phyllis Matthews	Wanda Taylor
Becky Boswell	Patricia Hill	Cheryl McCoy	Jeanita Tidwell
Nancy Burchett	Janet Hooper	Frances McPeak	Evelyn Walden
Dee Carter	Janet Hooper	Judy Nicholson	Dean Weldon
Lisa Cranko	Judy Horton	Lal Ocakoglu	Rita Winsett
Carla Ende	Karen Kaden	Rebecca Pierce	Jan Yarborough
Rosalie Fitzpatrick	Beth Langston	Ginny Priest	
Tricia Hammett	Vanessa Lassiter	Carol Reynolds	
Gail Hartford	Gail Lightfoot	Jackie Stiles	

The GHS Band was led by Drum Major Larry Woodall with Cathy Deaton as Band Sweetheart. Band Captain Rusty Averitt was assisted by Lieutenants Steve Watkins, James Coffman, and Ronald Steen. Twirlers were Knel Parsons, Kathy Blount, Jean Ann Spradling, Sharon Cathey, Linda Brown, Cathy Deaton, Brenda Meador, and Brenda Alexander.

"A Night at the Movies" was the theme for the March 12-13, 1971 show. Marcia Livesay took charge of the decorations and the Flash Officers choreographed the show. The band opened with "How The West Was Won" followed by the Flashes dancing to "Paint Your Wagon." A "Mancini Medley" was played by the band followed by the Flash Officers' routine to "The Good, The Bad, and The Ugly." The twirlers amused the crowd with "Barnum and Bailey's Favorite" before the Stage Band played "Fly Me To The Moon." The Junior Flashes delighted the audience with a routine to "Thoroughly Modern Millie" followed by a specialty number by the Stage Band. The Flashes continued with their rendition of "Yellow Submarine" prior to the presentation of new members of both groups.

The second half opened with the band's version of "Incantation and

Rosalie Fitzpatrick

Dance" followed by the Flashes taking the floor with "Viva Max." An interesting routine to "Kemo Sabe" by the twirlers led to the next routine by the Senior Flashes to "March of the Siamese Children." The Flash Officers upped the tempo with "If You Could See Me Now" followed by the band's rendition of "Thanks For The Memory." The current and new Flash Officers took charge of the floor with "Stars and Stripes Forever" prior to the finale featuring the entire cast in "There's No Business Like Show Business."

Another successful show was completed, but there was still much to do in closing one school year and moving forward to another. With the Flashes now integrated to include all races, the Flash Officers carefully trained the new officers to take over their duties for the coming year. The new officers, in turn, began working with their squads at their homes each weekend in preparation for another football season. Practice was intended to make them perfect...their ultimate goal.

The band's ambitious campaign to finance a trip to Florida's Festival of Five Flags in Pensacola was accomplished with hard work by the members and help from the community. They also won their tenth consecutive First Division rating in UIL marching competition. Bob Cartwright recalled:

During the playing of "Stars and Stripes Forever," the flute players performed the piccolo solo in unison using three piccolos, which really enhanced the number.

1971-72 presented many challenges for the nation with ratification of the 26th Amendment to the US Constitution giving 18-year olds the right to vote. The US economy was still strained and unemployment continued to rise. In 1972, District of Columbia police arrested five men in the Watergate complex ushering the start of the "Watergate Affair." On a happier note, the Dallas Cowboys defeated the Miami Dolphins, 24-3, to win the Super Bowl!

Football "rules the roost" in Texas. The win by the Cowboys spurred the GHS Lions to win more games. The football season ahead meant work, not just for the Lions, but for the Band and Flashes also. Mrs. Brantley and Mr. Cartwright carefully studied the football schedule and their calendars to provide an outstanding season of halftime shows. 1971-72 Flashes were:

Colonel	Carol Reynolds
Lt. Colonels	Karen Kaden, Judy Nicholson
US Flag (Major)	Carol Bandt
Texas Flag (Major)	Cindy Marshall
School Flag (Major)	Jan Yarborough
Lieutenant	Susan Hayes*
Banner Carriers	Jamie Tarpley, Rita Winsett
Managers	Donna Neal, Donna Walden, Pam Harmon

*Positions of Sergeant and Corporal were eliminated.

Members

Julie Bridges	Gail Hartford	Nancy Murray	Sherry Vinson
Nancy Burchett	Dianah Hill	Deborah Nelson	Patsy Wagley
Dee Carter	Janet Hooper	Lynne Rowe	Sylvia Wilkerson
Mary Cowling	Pud Lauderdale	Ann Rutherford	Rita Winsett
Rosalie Fitzpatrick	Beth Langston	Debbie Simpson	Ginni Worthen
Gwen Fleming	Jan Lovell	Kay Smith	Kim Yarbrough
Ginger Garrett	Pam Morris	Jamie Tarpley	
Patty Harrington	Cathy Morrison	Jeanita Tidwell	

Drum Major Tobby Watkins led the GHS Band and Gayle Aston was Band Sweetheart. Band Captain was Max Herron and Lieutenants were Ronnie Adcock, Richard Tharp, Douglas Bench and Mike Bridges. Twirlers included Brenda Alexander, Bonita Baker, Kathy Blount, Linda Brown, Sharon Cathey, Tina Graves, Debbie Kilgore, Brenda Meador, Knel Parsons, and Kathy Pope.

The theme "Adventures in Astrology" opened on March 17 and 18, 1972, with Bill Rust at the helm as emcee. Selections from "Hair" were played as the opening followed by a Flash routine to "Those Were the Days." The band continued with "Second Suite in F" as the Junior Flashes prepared to claim the floor dancing to "Salute to Cancerian Composers." The twirlers perked up the beat dancing to *"El Cumbanchero,"* and a specialty number by the Stage Band followed. Flash Officers revved the pace with "Light My Fire," and the Stage Band echoed with "Baby, Please Don't Go." The twirlers spun around to "Going Out of My Head" prior to another Stage Band pleaser. The Senior Flashes followed with the dance to "Games People Play" prior to the presentation of new members.

"Introduction and Fantasia" opened the second half and the current and new Flash Officers continued with "Bicycle Built for Joy." The band kicked up the sound with "Tournament of Trumpets" before the Flashes danced to "Take Me Out to the Ballgame." Ronald Steen, pianist, played selections from *Love Story,* and the Flashes continued with a routine to "Vehicle" followed by "Salute to the Armed Forces" by the twirlers. Flash Officers continued dancing to "Moon Children Medley" prior to the finale by the entire cast to "Aquarius."

Mrs. Brantley decided to leave GHS at the end of the year and congratulated the Flashes on their exceptional versatility in statewide performances. These Flashes attended the drill team camp at SMU in July, where they won second place for their famous high kick routine. National Drill Team Day gave them the opportunity to perform during the pre-game activities of the SMU-Arkansas game. They also performed at the State Fair, the Tyler Rose Parade, and the Christmas Parade. Their willingness to share their time and talents for civic and charitable events was lauded by community leaders.

Carol McDonald

Republican President Richard M. Nixon was reelected President in 1972 with a near-record landslide vote. Democrats won majorities in both the Senate and House of Representative. The stage was set for a political stalemate. By Spring 1973, President Nixon was embroiled in the Watergate investigation resulting the resignation of his top aides, Haldeman and Ehrlichman. The media chose to spotlight Watergate issues while Apollo 16 astronauts; John Watts and Charles Duke spent 71 hours on the moon's surface, later the Apollo 17's feat broke their record by more than three hours.

GISD administrators met to find a new high school principal, vice-principal, and a new Flash Director. They felt fortunate that Bill Walters, serving as Vice Principal at GHS, would provide for a smooth transition. Coach Kenneth Gibson became Vice Principal. Mrs. Carol McDonald was hired in May. The GISD Board of Education also hired Linda Holmes as Associate Director for the GHS Band. Early in June, the Flash Officers attended drill team camp at the University of Oklahoma and earned a first place and two second-place awards in competitions. They began working with their squads in preparation for football season upon their return.

The 1972-73 Flaming Flashes membership roster follows:

Colonel	Patty Harrington
Lt. Colonels	Ginger Garrett
	Nancy Murray
US Flag (Major)	Lynn Rowe
Texas Flag (Major)	Pam Morris
School Flag (Major)	Gwen Fleming*
Lieutenant	Dianah Hill
Banner Carriers	Judy Bridges, Mary Cowling
Managers	Debbie Ferrell, Pam Harmon,
	Donna Holmes

*First African-American Flash Officer

Members of the Flash Corps

Lisa Alexander	Maureen Friedman	Deborah Nelson	Shannon Shirey
Terri Bost	Debbie Goodrich	Linda Oxford	Cheri Vinson
Linda Booher	Holly Hale	Doris Perry	Jennifer Withers
Julie Bridges	Darcie Krider	Laura Pierce	Gini Worthen
Mary Cowling	Beverly McFarlin	Jane Reynolds	Luann Wacasey
Keli Collins	Barbara Motley	Melody Roach	Sylvia Wilkerson
Debbie Converse	Cathey Morrison	Dometric Stephens	Patsy Wagley
Susan Darnell	Karen Moser	Janis Steele	Kim Yarbrough
Peggy Everhart	Margaret Myers	Kay Smith	
Cecelia Foote	Brenda Norwood	Sheila Shirey	

GHS Band Drum Major Ronald Steen led the band through its paces with Cindy Stephens, Band Sweetheart, at his side during parades. Band Captain Hank Clark worked with Lieutenants Richard Tharp, Ricky Terrell, and Randy Steen. Twirlers were Carol Averitt, Bonita Baker, Carol Dearing, Sandy Goode, Gwen Fleming, and Dianah Hill.

"From Stage to Screen" opened on March 9 and 10, 1973, with Bill Rust as emcee. Cole Porter selections drifted around the gym before the Flashes took the floor to "Little Bit of Luck." The Symphonic Band played "English Dances" with the Junior Flashes following to the lively strains of "Fiddler on the Roof." The twirlers rocked the crowd with "It's Not Unusual" followed by the Stage Band's rendition of "It Was a Very Good Year" with Perry Jones, guitar soloist. The Flash Officers took control with "Mod Squad" followed by the Stage Band with "Festival Rock Blues." The twirlers "Put on a Happy Face" to the crowd's delight and Senior Flashes danced to "Super Star" prior to the annual presentation of new members.

Combined bands played "Slaughter on Tenth Avenue" to draw the crowd back to their seats for the second half. Present and new officers followed dancing to "How the West Was Won." The Concert Band continued with "Overture for Winds" followed by a Flash routine to "I Ain't Down Yet." Bob Cartwright, Band Director recalled the next portion.

> *Ronald Steen performed Mendelssohn's "Piano Concerto" accompanied by the band by playing his personal grand piano that was rolled onto the gym floor during the blackout. The crowd was overwhelmed.*

The "Casino Royale" routine by Flashes provided color and excitement before the twirlers marched in to "Seventy-Six Trombones." Flash Officers provided an interpretive dance to "The Men" followed by the Symphonic Band's rendition of "Salute to Bacharach and David." The finale by the entire cast brought forth a standing ovation.

Watergate, the Vietnam War, the Middle East, and the economy dominated the headlines and television news reports in 1973-74. The Dow Jones stock exchange index fell to its lowest level since 1970. Economic growth slowed to almost zero in most industrialized nations. Fighting in the Middle East between Arabs and Israelis escalated. Spiro Agnew, Vice President, pleaded "no contest" and resigned his office. Gerald Ford was named as his replacement. President Nixon continued to deflect Watergate issues.

Greenville citizens looked to the football season to find relief from the daily news. Mrs. McDonald and Mr. Cartwright moved forward.

Nine awards were won by the Flashes at Gilliam Drill Team Camp at Cisco Junior College during the summer months, and Flash Officers also won awards at two separate drill team camps prior to September.

Flashes ready to kick off the 1973-74 year were:

        Colonel...Jane Reynolds
        (Lt. Colonel Melody Roach did not return.)
        US Flag (Major) ....Linda Oxford
        Texas Flag (Major) ....Shannon Shirey
        School Flag (Major).........................Sheila Shirey
        Banner Carriers...............................Barbara Motley
                                          Jennifer Withers
        Managers..Judy Fletcher, Janet Green,
                                          Cindy Hamilton, Jamie Wallace

Flash Corps Members

Lisa Alexander	Maureen Friedman	Barbara Motley	Janis Steele
Terri Bost	Debbie Goodrich	Margaret Myers	Debbie Wacasey
Linda Booher	Karen Hale	Cathy Poppe	Valerie Wade
Rhoda Brown	Deborah Hamilton	Ann Randolph	Debbie Warren
Debbie Converse	Lucy Johnson	Susan Ridings	Debbie Warren
Susan Darnell	Liz Lasley	Renda Shields	Teresa Whitney
Doyle Dietz	Darcie Krider	Cindy Smith	Melva Williams
Peggy Everhart	Debbie Martin	Debi Smith	Jennifer Withers
Cecelia Foote	Theda Moore	Kay Smith	

Marty Andrews, Drum Major, led the GHS Band and Ricky Terrell was Band Captain. Lieutenants were Gerald Gilstrap, Webber Woodall, and Scott Weaver. Twirlers were Carol Averitt, Lori Baker, Nancy Chapman, Carol Dearing, Sandy Goode, Debbie Harris, Debbie Patterson, Debbie Stewart and Sherry Watson. The position of Band Sweetheart was not filled. The GHS Band won three superior ratings during fall marching contests.

"Holidays on Parade" opened on March 8 and 9, 1974, with Bill Rust as emcee. Flash Officers did the choreography and assisted Gary Head with the decorations. Combined bands played "Mac Arthur Park" as an overture before the Flashes entertained with their routine to "Christmas." The Symphonic Band continued with the first movement of "Incidental Suite" prior to the Flashes dance to "Thanksgiving." The twirlers performed to "Valentine's Day" and the Stage Band followed with "One Fine Morning." Flash Officers dashed across the dark gym floor to spook the crowd with a routine to "Halloween." The Stage Band continued with "McPherson's Freak" before the twirlers took the floor with their Labor Day routine. The "Fourth of July" routine by the Flashes ended the first half followed by the presentation of new members.

"Marching Up Broadway" opened up the second half followed by the "May Day" dance by present and new Flash Officers. "Tocata for Band" by the Concert Band led to the Senior Flashes routine to "St. Patrick's Day." A tuba quartet to "Puff, the Magic Dragon" was followed by the Flashes dancing to an Easter number. The twirlers' "April Fools Day" dance charmed the crowd and was followed by the Junior Flashes' routine to "Chinese New Year." A Glenn Miller Medley by the combined bands led to the finale, "I Love A Parade," by the entire cast.

The hot topic for summer 1974 was the resignation of President Richard Nixon when the release of the Watergate tapes revealed damaging details of his involvement. Gerald R. Ford was named as the 38th President of the United States in early August. Nelson Rockefeller, former governor of New York was nominated as Vice President. The "co-conspirators" in the Watergate scandal were convicted and sentenced. Across "the pond" in 1975, Margaret Thatcher became the leader of the British Conservative Party. On an upbeat note, *A Chorus Line* was named the best musical by New York Drama Critics.

Summer camps kept the Flashes occupied with training, competition, and days of squad practices at individual homes. All routines must be perfected by mid-August and uniforms must be ready for all events.

A busy football season demanded the attention of the Band and Flashes as they prepared for performances. The Flaming Flashes for 1974-75 were:

Colonel	Valerie Wade
US Flag (Major)	Debbie Wacasey
Texas Flag (Major)	Doyle Dietz
School Flag (Major)	Cindy Smith
Banner Carriers	Lucy Johnson
	Deborah Hamilton
Managers	Cathy Gandy, Janet Green, Terry Samples, Cindy Whittington
Announcer	Kento Gibson

Members of the Flash Corps

Claudia Bloom	Barbara Gassaway	Jennifer Meeks	Leah Thompson
Nancy Clements	Diane Harris	Melissa Morgan	Judy Wardlaw
Rita Dabbs	Teresa Harrison	Sherry Moseley	Debbie Warren
Robin Dabbs	Donna Harvey	Shannon McGinlay	Cindy Woodall
Dana Darby	Cynthia Hayter	Lynda McDonald	Tammy Whitlock
Julia Dietz	Mary Horn	Liz Nicholson	Teresa Whitney
Kathy Eldridge	Heidi Hake	Tracie Patterson	Melva Williams
Sherry Ely	Martha Jacobs	Pam Pickens	Rhnea Wright
Debbie Everhart	Liz Lasley	Kim Poteet	Sherry Wright
Betty Gandy	Susan Little	Ann Randolph	
Carol Gantt	Lisa Martin	Terri Spradling	

Drum Major Bobby Graff led the GHS Band and Carol Dearing was Band Sweetheart. Band Captain Brian Ward was aided by Lieutenants Scott Weaver and Karl Shackelford.

Twirlers were Carol Averitt, Lori Baker, Nancy Chapman, Carol Dearing, Sandy Goode, Debbie Harris, Debbie Patterson, Debbie Stewart, and Sherry Watson.

"Those Were the Days," theme for the 1974-75 show, opened on March 14-15, 1975, with Bill Rust as emcee. Flash Officers directed the choreography. The combined bands delivered a rousing overture to "New Ragtime Follies" followed by the Flashes rolling to "Rock Around the Clock." The Symphonic Band slowed the tempo with "Incantation and Dance" before the Flash Officers' comedic act to "Be A Clown." Steve Reynolds, guitar soloist, was featured with the Stage Band playing "Blues for B.B" just before the Flashes ramped up the beat with "Boogie Woogie Bugle Boy." The Stage Band continued with "The Suncatchers" featuring Steve Reynolds (guitar) and Brian Ward (tenor sax). "The Charleston" livened the beat as twirlers performed just prior to the presentation of new members…ending the first half.

"Great Hits of the 60s" opened the second half and the Flash Officers followed with their "Boogie Like" routine. A "Dedicatory Overture" by the Concert Band led to "Flash Back" danced by the twirlers. Present and new Flash Officers danced to "Me and My Shadow" and the Senior Flashes followed with "Doin' What Comes Naturally." The twirlers performed to "The Entertainer" before the entire cast joined forces for the finale.

Changes were on the way for the Flashes as Mrs. McDonald decided to leave GHS. The past three years had brought many experiences into her life that she would take to her next position. The Flashes anxiously awaited news of their next director as they moved into squad practice sessions for the coming year.

Miss Gussie Nell Davis, originator of The Flaming Flashes, made headlines again as the Houston Contemporary Museum of Art honored her for creating a "living art form." Her former Flashes in the Greenville area were delighted to read this news, as she always gave credit to her beginnings at GHS.

Pam Clayton

The movie *Jaws* gave the public a "distraction" from all the issues of Watergate, the Middle East, Vietnam, the economy, and rising oil prices. Americans wanted to be entertained and wanted an "escape" from the daily news. They were ready for football.

Mrs. Pam Clayton accepted the position as Flash Director and reported for duty. Flash Officers had already organized members into squads and were working on marching, dancing, and high-kicks to be ready for football season. Leaders and members were:

Colonel	Judy Wardlaw
US Flag (Major)	Shannon McGinlay
Texas Flag (Major)	Liz Nicholson
School Flag (Major)	Rhnea Wright
Banner Carriers	Tracie Patterson, Leah Thompson
Managers	Terri Boarman, Carla Thomas

Members of the Corps

Marjorie Adams	Sherry Ely	Suzette Holland	Kim Poteet
Cindy Baughn	Betty Gandy	Mary Horn	Delores Schuler
Claudia Bloom	Darla Goad	Susan Little	Wende Skinner
Sharon Brown	Penny Harmon	Donna Johns	Karen Smith
Nancy Clements	Diane Harris	Lisa Martin	Terri Spradling
Kim Cozine	Teresa Harrison	Charlotte Mason	Tami Vinson
Rita Dabbs	Donna Harvey	Lynda McDonald	Debbie Wallace
Robin Dabbs	Nancy Hayter	Jennifer Meeks	Cindy Woodall
Dana Darby	Marie Hill	Melissa Morgan	Janet Woodard
Janet Diggs	Stacy Hoerth	Pam Pickens	

Drum Major Craig Smith did an outstanding job of leading the GHS Band for 1975-76. Band Captain Scott Weaver and Lieutenants Jeff Walters, Karl Shackelford, and Mike Huggs assisted. Lori Baker was Band Sweetheart and Twirlers were Lori Baker, Bonita Bandy, Marcella Bryant, Nancy Chapman, Susan Cvitanovich, Teri Greaves, Kelly Higginbotham, Donna Jackson, and Debbie Stewart. Ron Hoes served as Associate Director.

"Let Freedom Ring," the theme for March 12-13, 1976, honored the celebration of our nation's bicentennial. Flash Officers did the choreography for members and Donna Harvey, Art Department, assisted Flashes with the decorations.

Bill Rust, emcee, set the tone for the combined bands to play "America the Beautiful" followed by the Flashes performing to "1776 Overture." Red, white, and blue spotlights flashed everywhere as the Symphonic Band presented "Festive Overture." Flash Officers graced the floor performing to "Saints in Concert" followed by the Stage Band, featuring Steve Reynolds (guitarist), playing "Silver Morning." The twirlers picked up the pace with their dance to "Love Will Keep Us Together" followed by the Stage Band's rendition of "The Way We Were" featuring Craig Smith, trombone soloist. The Stage Band picked up the tempo with "Fly Me to the Moon" followed by "Thank You, Band" featuring Steve Reynolds (guitar), Ken Shackelford (trumpet), Mike Brown (flugelhorn), and John Wilson (drums). The twirlers changed the mood with "Davy Crockett" followed by the Junior Flashes dancing/marching to "This Land is Your Land" just prior to presentation of new members.

Tracie Patterson (Bjorkgren) found this in her memory bank.

> *Being a member of the Flashes created a lot of fond memories. If my friend, Jane Reynolds, had not encouraged me to try out, I would have missed the best two-year of my high school life. The greatest honor was bestowed upon me by Carol McDonald when she selected me as one of the Banner Carriers my senior year. I loved to dance, and this was the perfect outlet for me and I cherish being a pert of such a great organization. My only regret was not trying out for Flash Officer. I went on to try out for the Kilgore College Rangerettes, since Gussie Nell Davis had started the Flaming Flashes, but I was too tall. Gussie Nell was very particular about her "line" and I am 6' tall...the next girl was 5'8" tall and I would have stuck out like a sore thumb.*

Bob Cartwright had been directing the GHS Band since 1964 and decided to resign and purchase McKay Music Co. He had worked with six different Flash Directors and had the information for conducting the annual floorshow memorized. Mrs. Clayton had one year of experience in this area, but was thankful that Mr. Cartwright would be nearby, if she needed his expertise.

Leonard (Lenny) Walker came on board as GHS Band Director in 1976, and Mrs. Pam Hansen was also hired as his Associate Director. The band began practice sessions the first week in August under new leadership.

Jimmy (James Earl, Jr.) Carter was elected 39th President of the United States, narrowly defeating Gerald Ford, incumbent. One of his first acts, following his inauguration in 1977, was to grant pardons to almost all American draft evaders of the Vietnam War era. North and South Vietnam had reunited in 1976 after 22 years of separation. Carter warned citizens to control energy consumption or suffer a national catastrophe. Americans spent more time at the movies seeking relief from depressing news with films like "Star Wars" or "Saturday Night Fever." The world of fantasy and disco had arrived.

Football season was also a delightful distraction and a way of life for many. The GHS

Band and Flashes were always the main focus to draw the crowds, especially when the team was not winning.

The Flaming Flashes for 1976-77 included:

Colonel	Penny Harmon
US Flag (Major)	Darla Goad
Texas Flag (Major)	Nancy Hayter
School Flag (Major)	Wende Skinner
Banner Carriers	Marie Hill, Stacy Herath
Managers	Kelly Ball, Tammy Lytle

Members

Marjorie Adams	Kim Cozine	Carolyn Manton	Kelly Smith
Betty Barcoe	Aletha Davis	Charlotte Mason	Debbie Stephens
Cindy Baughn	Kathy Dennis	Janet Murley	Leighanne Tillery
Kimberly Boshear	Kerry Dodds	Paige Patterson	Tami Vinson
Sharon Brown	Manette Fitzpatrick	Kim Pittman	Dana Wallace
Cheryl Brown	Debbie Gantos	Venita Price	Janet Woodard
Nelda Campbell	Suzette Holland	Lori Rumage	

Drum Major Tony Chandler, assisted by Band Captain Karl Shackelford, led the GHS Band. Lieutenants were Scott Nixon, Mike Huggs, and Robert Graff, while Kelly Higginbotham served as Band Sweetheart. Twirlers were Bonita Bandy, Gloria Bolling, Marcella Bryant, Susan Cvitanovich, Teri Greaves, Kelly Higginbotham, Brenda Ussery, and Angie Wein.

The Flashes provided the choreography and decorations for "Little Bit of Country...Little Bit Rock 'n' Roll" which opened March 11-12, 1977, with Jerry Bench as announcer. The opening numbers "I Write the Songs" and "Mandy" led to the first dance by the Flashes to "Bad Blood." Following "Fanfare and Allegro" by the band, the Flash Officers took the floor with "Let 'Em In." "Tater Patch" by the Stage Band led to the twirlers' routine to "A Fifth of Beethoven." The Stage Band continued with a specialty number to the love theme from *Lady Sings the Blues* followed by a piano solo by Mike Huggs, "I Can't Stop Lovin' You," as the Senior Flashes did an interpretive dance. "Corazon" by the Stage Band led to "The Ballad of Jed Clampett" performed by the twirlers. The Flash Officers and Banner Carriers danced to "Jive Talkin'" followed by the annual presentation of new members of both groups.

The band opened the second half with "MacArthur Park" followed by the Flashes dancing to "Wabash Cannon Ball." The playing of "Rhinestone Cowboy" led to the Junior Flashes' routine to "Your Mama Don't Dance." The twirlers continued dancing to "I Could Have Danced All Night" and were followed by the present and new Flash Officers dancing to "When You're Hot You're Hot" prior to the finale by the entire cast.

Travel on the Concorde supersonic transport between New York, Paris, and London was offered in 1977-78. The "Jet Set" could fly faster around the world. "Cowboy Fever" ran rampant as the Dallas Cowboys beat the Denver Broncos, 27-10, to win the Super Bowl. Football continued to be "King" in Texas. The "fever" was contagious as the Band and Flashes prepared for football halftimes.

Flashes and their officers included:

```
Colonel ........................... Manette Fitzpatrick*
US Flag (Major) ................. LeighAnne Tillery
Texas Flag (Major) ............. Debbie Stephens
School Flag (Major) ............ Janet Murley
Banner Carriers ................. Kathe Dennis, Kelly Smith
*First African-American Colonel
Manager .......................... Judy Jacobs
```

Members of the Corps

Kim Boshear	Aletha Davis	Denise Newhouse	Amy Shirey
Karen Brooks	Diane DeVeny	Jennifer Nicholson	Lisa Smith
Cheryl Brown	Janis Fletcher	Page Patterson	Dana Wallace
Nelda Campbell	Paige Garrette	Patty Patterson	Lisa Wallace
Alice Cantrell	Tammy Grider	Penny Pickle	Julie Ward
Penny Clarkson	Jennifer Harrison	Venita Price	Mary White
Julie Coker	Linda Hawes	Lori Rumage	Fran Wright
Michele Comer	Michele Hill	Julie Schwene	
Kelly Crabtree	Dawn Mitchell	Kelly Sheffield	
Kristy Curtis	Dana Mize	Shelly Shepherd	

Tony Chandler led the GHS Band as Drum Major, assisted by Band Captain, Kevin Banks. Lieutenants were Kay Boshart, Sandra Linerode, and Jeff Hancock. Band Sweetheart was Benita Peavey and twirlers were Dana Willis, Kristy Wagoner, Jan Baker, Angie Wein, Teri Greaves, Anita Clinton, Donna Cartwright, Carla Maldonado, Bonita Bandy, and Ellen Hendricks.

"Showtime," the theme for March 17-18, 1978, was choreographed by Flash Officers. Judy Jacobs supervised and made most of the decorations. Jerry Bench served as emcee.

"Star Wars Medley" played by the band led to the "Rockford Files" danced by the Flashes. The second routine featured the Flash Officers dancing to "Hot Line" followed by the theme from "Barney Miller." The twirlers danced next as the Stage Band played the theme from "Charlie's Angels." The Senior Flashes danced to the strains of

Flash Colonel Manette Fitzpatrick

"Free Again" followed by the Stage Band's rendition of the theme from "The Man" featuring Phillip Perser on the drums. The twirlers continued with a routine to "23 Skidoo" followed by the Flash Officers and Banner Carriers dancing to "Welcome Back." Presentation of new members was completed prior to intermission.

A medley of Broadway show-stoppers opened the second half, and the tempo increased as the Flashes performed to "Cabaret." Another band number led to the Junior Flashes and their dance to "Don't Rain on my Parade." Angie Wein, piano soloist, played selections from *Love Story* leading to the new Flashes' performance to "Coke Adds Life." The band continued with a medley from *The Sound of Music* leading to present and new Flashes with their interpretive dance to "Sesame Street." The twirlers performed to "Gold" between two band selections before the finale, performed by the entire cast, closed another exciting floorshow.

Lori Rumage (Keith) shared her memories.

> *The floorshow my sophomore year, when we were inducted into the Flashes, was special for a girl from the North to learn how to do a real "Southern" curtsey and wear a full ball gown! My son has that picture in his living room. I loved the high kicks we did and how graceful they were. Summer camps were wonderful, but the best memory was of the night our "big sisters" kidnapped us in the middle of the night to let us know we had made the Flashes! I struggled with my weight. Each Wednesday, Mrs. Clayton made me step on that ugly scale and weight. One pound over the weight limit and I would not perform that week. So, like any dysfunctional eater, I abstained from eating on Sunday through Tuesday, then gorged the rest of the week until the weekend. I only missed one performance! Being a Flash was the highlight of high school.*

Gussie Nell Davis made headlines again in 1978 when she was recognized as Distinguished Alumnae of Texas Woman's University. The newspapers always included the fact that Miss Davis had begun her career in Greenville, Texas, as the originator of The Flaming Flashes…the first high school precision dance/drill team.

The movie *Grease*, starring John Travolta, created a stir across the nation. Disco lounges thrived and the people were "movin' and grooving" at every opportunity. The music was everywhere and clothing trends were impacted. President Jimmy Carter, Israel's Premier Begin and Egyptian President Sadat agreed on a peace treaty at Camp David. Egypt was expelled from the Arab League. Carter later met with USSR President Brezhnev and signed the SALT-2 arms limitation treaty in Vienna. Carter felt it was a "victory," but Congress felt differently.

No matter what was happening in the world, the Band and Flashes still prepared for football season. 1978-79 was no different, however, one major change was made. There would no longer be designated flag bearers. All officers, with the exception of the Colonel, would hold the rank of Major, and the number was increased by one. Leaders, selected the year prior, reported for duty.

Colonel	Jennifer Nicholson
Majors	Dana Mize, Shelly Shepherd
	Lisa Smith, Fran Wright
Banner Carriers	Kelly Crabtree, Penny Pickle.
Managers	Gala Turner, Debbie Stidham

Flash Corps

Kathy Baker	Shauna Clark	Linda Hawes	Patty Patterson
Carrie Bostick	Michelle Comer	Michelle Hill	Lisa Pennington
Sarah Bowman	Kristy Curtis	Jennifer Johnson	Tammy Poteet
Maura Bracken	Dianne DeVeny	Debbie Kuykendall	Lesa Prince
Karen Brooks	Teri East	Dawn Mitchell	Kelly Sheffield
Lachelle Butler	Andrea Ellsworth	Holly Narramore	Teri Vinson
Stacey Carter	Karen Fletcher	Denise Newhouse	Katy Wallace
Cheryl Clark	Chele Goode	Melanie Nussbaum	Lisa Wallace

Two Drum Majors, Jeff Hancock and Jim Collins, were selected to lead the GHS Band. Band Captain Sandra Linerode worked with Lieutenants Kathleen Floyd, Dana Willis, and James Folks. Band Sweetheart was Sandra Linerode. Twirlers were Jan Baker, Donna Cartwright, Anita Clinton, Lisa Ewell, Ellen Hendricks, Carla Maldonado, Becky Morrow, Kristie Wagoner, Cheryl Wheeler, and Dana Willis. Kita Richardson was Twirler Advisor, and Bonita Baker served as Choreographer. A Flag Corps, added to the GHS Band, consisted of Angela Benzi, Susie Bobbitt, Melissa Brooks, Barbara Horan, Sharon Linerode, Christine Martin, Janice Neatherlin, and Terri Pearson. Gordon Cloutier became Associate Director of the band.

Tammy Prather and Andrea Thomas completed the artwork for the decorations, so "Anything Goes" opened on March 30-31, 1979, with local radio personality, Rich Reneau, as Narrator. The opening number, "Tie A Yellow Ribbon" by the band, led to a special routine by the Flashes to "It's So Easy." The Flag Corps followed with a colorful flag routine to "Sabre Dance" and the Flash Officers continued with their routine to "Fifty Ways to Leave Your Lover." Completion of "Live!" by the band brought in the twirlers for a dance to "Pink Panther," featuring Peter Morgan on trumpet. The Stage Band exploded with the theme from *Star Trek* followed by "Sweet, Sweet Smile" with the Senior Flashes performing. "The One and Only" by the Stage Band, featured Tammy Prather on the flugelhorn, followed by the twirlers' routine to "Shadow Dancing." "Sgt. Pepper's Lonely Hearts Club Band" by the Stage Band led to a routine by the Flash Officers and Banner Carriers to "Runaround Sue," closing the first half and beginning the presentation of new members for both groups.

The band opened the second half with a Mancini "Spectacular," and brought forth the Flashes for a specialty routine to "All In the Family." Another Flag Corps routine to "Championship" led to a routine by the Junior Flashes to "Still the One." The band continued with "In The Mood" before the new Flashes took the floor to "Hey There, Good Times." Present and new Flash Officers followed a band number with their routine to "I'm Popeye the Sailor Man" adding levity to the program. The twirlers danced to "Copacabana" after the band played "The Golden Age of Rock and Roll." Playing of "South Rampart Street Parade" brought forth the finale by the entire cast and the end of another great show.

Shelly Shepherd (Longacre) shared these memories.
> *I am a second generation Flash. My mother, Betty Love (Shepherd) served in 1954-56, and I have a special memory of my cousin, Holly Narramore (Dodds) being in the squad with me. (So much fun for our family!) My very best memory is the day that we, as officers, won The Spirit Stick at Officer Camp at North Texas State University! A matching memory was of the football season ending with our being Co-District Champs!*

Lisa Smith (Aly) shared these memories.
> *I loved the Band and Flash Floorshows! All of the wonderful music, beautiful costumes, spotlights, the emcee in a "tux," and the excitement we all felt those two night each spring. Football games! Wearing those genuine cowboy boots and marching across the grassy (and sometimes muddy) football fields... doing our pompom routines in the stands... cheering out team on... marching in the Greenville Christmas parade... pep rallies... hand or pompom routines in the bleachers. We all wanted our football team to win so our school superintendent, Wesley Martin, would throw several shiny red apples into the bleachers during the pep rally! Fun times!*

Once again, Miss Gussie Nell Davis made headlines... this time with her retirement as director of the Kilgore Rangerettes after 29 very active years. Several former Flashes, Ruby Moran (Gladewater), Greenville residents Rosabelle (Williams) Warren and Mary Virginia Duck (who attended college with Gussie Nell), recalled their years as a Flash under Gussie Nell's leadership and how much knowing Miss Davis had impacted their lives. Miss Davis may have left the Rangerettes, but her influence on Greenville and the Flashes will never be forgotten.

Leonard (Lenny) Walker chose to leave GHS at the end of the 1978-79 school year, so a new band director must be hired. The search was on, and it was not long before GHS had a new band director... a delightful person... Mr. Bill Goodson!

The "space race" continued with the discovery of a ring around Jupiter by Voyager I spacecraft. Two Soviet cosmonauts in Salyut 6 returned after a record-breaking 175 days in space. President Carter restricted grain sales to the USSR to protest the Soviet invasion of Afghanistan. Carter also broke off diplomatic relations with Iran as members of the U.S. Embassy were held hostage. The popular song "This Is It" seemed to punctuate a national response to national issues.

The retirement of Wesley N. Martin as superintendent in 1980 led to the hiring of Dr. Arnold Oates. Changes were in the air.

The GHS Band, Flashes, and football season wait for no one. As time marched on, so did they. The Flashes began their year in June when they all traveled to the University of Houston for summer camp and earned two "Superior" high kick awards, one award of "Excellence" in jazz, and the title of "Best Precision Drill Team." Flash Officers attended Kilgore Junior College officers' camp and won "First Division High Kick." Lesa Prince (Colonel) and Laschelle Butler were named as outstanding officers.

With several awards to their credit these Flash Officers were ready to lead The Flaming Flashes directed by Mrs. Clayton.

Colonel	Lesa Prince
Majors	Lachelle Butler, Debbie Kuykendall, Melanie Nussbaum, Katie Wallace
Banner Carriers	Carrie Bostick, Karen Fletcher
Managers	Phyllis Eastup, Kristie Kesler, Phyllis McMurtree

Members of the Flash Corps

Maura Bracken	Diann Clark	Karen Johnson	Susan Roberts
Susan Brodton	Ernie Cowgill	Kim Key	Cindy Saenz
Susan Burgin	Denise Edgerton	Brenda Lytle	Denise Stapleton
Stacey Carter	Christi Ellis	Mary McCaw	Lisa Summers
Tamye Chandler	Terri Harral	Tina Miles	Robin Wilemon
Ami Chetlin	Christa Horn	Tammye Poteet	
Cheryl Clark	Jane Jacks	Marcy Ritter'	

Drum Majors Karen McPherson and Jim Collins were assisted by Dana Willis with help from Lieutenants Jeff Hancock, Christie Hammett, and Denard Gilstrap. Donna Cartwright, Head Twirler, led twirlers Kristy Wagner, Tori Collins, Lisa Ewell, Jan Baker, Anita Clinton, Becky Morrow, Dana Willis, Sharon Cartwright, and Carla Maldonado. Flag Corps Captain, Donna Jeter, was aided by Lieutenant Sherry Morgan. Tammy Prather was Band Sweetheart. Laurencio Arroyo served as Associate Director of the GHS Band.

"Heaven Knows What," the theme of the March 28-29, 1980 show, was full of lively music. Some of the numbers included "One," "Boogie Wonderland," "Twelfth Street Rag," "Blame it on the Boogie," "Birth of the Blues," and "Rockjazz March," to name a few. The program followed the traditional pattern of performances prior to the presentation of new members of both groups before the intermission. The grand finale always brought the crowd to their feet for a standing ovation.

Lachelle Butler (Johnson) recalled these experiences.

Football games, pep rallies, floorshows, early morning practices, uniforms, boots, and hats—each memory makes me smile. I must admit that a tear comes to my eyes every time I hear the Flashes sing, "We are the Flashes." I have been fortunate to be able to continue feeling like a part of the Flashes since my sister, Lori Butler, has been their director for the last 25 years. Once a Flash…always a Flash.

Melanie Nussbaum (Weisenfeld) had these thoughts.

It seems like yesterday we were singing our Flash song. I attended the floorshows as a young girl. Mother always told me that I wanted to take dance lessons so I could become a Flash. It was what I always wanted and was lucky enough to have that dream come true. I am forever grateful for the friendships, the confidence, and the fun times that being a GHS Flash gave to me.

Susan Brodton (Essary) added these remarks:
I have such fond memories of camp, practices, parades, competitions, performances, floorshows, etc. I enjoyed pushing myself harder to be the best at what we did. We worked hard and were proud of our accomplishments. I made lifelong friends and am still thankful that I participated in this talented group.

"Dallas" fever swept across the world in 1980-81 as people wanted to know "Who shot J.R.?" Almost ninety million viewers were left wondering. In the political arena, Ronald Reagan, nominated by the Republicans as their choice for president, chose George H. W. Bush as his running mate.

June 1980 saw the Flash Officers at Kilgore Junior College for officer training with the Rangerettes. Karen Johnson and Susan Roberts were named "Outstanding Officers." Later, the entire corps traveled to the University of Houston for summer camp and received two "Superior" high kick ribbons and one award of excellence in jazz. Colonel Susan Roberts received the "Best Officer" award. Leaders and members for 1980-81 included:

Colonel	Susan Roberts
Majors	Karen Johnson, Tina Miles, Marcy Ritter
Banner Carriers	Senior Flashes (as needed for parades)
Manager	Phyllis Dunmon, Michelle Miller, Libby Speyrer.

Members of the Corps

Angie Ayers	Denise Edgerton	Mary McCaw	Cindy Saenz
Joy Bolin	Kim Evans	Melinda Moore	Kristi Sherrill
Bobbie Brooks	Tammy Green	Vetrice Mulkey	Rhonda Singleton
Lori Butler	Holly Brown	Jamie Patterson	Lisa Summers
Tamye Chandler	Terri Harral	Patty Prather	Renee Watson
Ami Chetlin	Christa Horn	Vickie Price	Sheri White
Diann Clark	Brenda Lytle	Frankie Priest	Julie Young
Ernie Cowgill	Christi Manmett	Gaye Priest	

About one hundred band members began practice in August under the superior direction of Bill Goodson and Laurencio Arroyo for 1980-81. At summer camps, the Flag Corps and Twirlers learned new techniques and routines. Drum Majors Chris Miles and Bill Toles, assisted by Senior Captains Tori Collins and Mark Hare, had more help from Connie Ramsay and Denard Gilstrap, Junior Lieutenants, and Sophomore Lieutenants, Barb Cutting, Rachel Madkins, and Brian Swiggart. Lisa Ewell (Head Twirler), Glenda Gilbert (Flag Corps Captain), and Tori Collins (Band Sweetheart) completed the roster of leaders.

The annual floorshow, March 13-14, 1981, entitled "Howdy, Texas" opened with the rousing selection, "Big 'D'," by the band followed by the Flashes performing "Hot Stuff." The traditional order of acts and presentations followed with the "Cotton Eyed Joe," "Southern Nights," "Dallas," "Wabash Cannonball," and the theme from *Giant* as some of the selections leading to the grand finale.

In national news, Sandra Day O'Connor became the first female judge of the US Supreme Court. Few could tear themselves away from the television screen as the world watched the royal wedding of Prince Charles and Lady Diana Spencer. They continued to watch as the first U.S. space shuttle, "Columbia," completed its maiden flight successfully. In other news, scientists identified Acquired Immune Deficiency Syndrome (AIDS).

Dr. Arnold Oates left for another district and Mr. Bill Kennedy took over as GISD Superintendent. Changes were made to the curriculum, administration, with others to follow. A new high school, under construction on Lion's Lair (Terrell Road & Sayle) would be ready by Fall 1983. The high school building would be a middle school, and the junior high would serve as an intermediate campus.

Mrs. Clayton and Mr. Goodson moved forward with their plans for the 1981-82 football season. The world could be falling apart, but the football season would continue...after all, this was Texas!

Ready for the 1981-82 year were:

Colonel	Kristi Sherrill
Majors	Lori Butler, Melinda Moore
	Gaye Priest, Julie Young
Banner Carriers	Holly Brown, Sherri White
Managers	Phyllis Dunmon, Melisa Rials
Flash Guards	Wayne Feezor, David Hunsucker
(New Positions)	Jerry Weathers, Tyler Veak, Kevin Bost

Members of the Flash Corps

Wendy Abbott	Amy Dennis	Karen Morris	Becky Sagebiel
Lorie Bolch	Manya East	Veatrice Mulkey	Carol Thomas
Joy Bolin	Kim Evans	Donna Palmeri	Amy Tillery
Bobbie Brooks	Lisa Housewright	Sheri Pickens	Kelly Wendfeldt
Holly Brown	Rachel Hyatt	Patty Prather	Sherry White
Olivia Brown	Lesa Jenkins	Robin Purgerson	
Mary Carter	Julie Mathews	Ylicia Richards	
Laura Clark	Jill Morris	Carla Royal	

The officers began early in the year by going to officer camp at SMU "Superstar Officer Drill Team" camp where they won thirteen "Superior" and twelve "Excellent" awards. The Corps attended Golden Gulf Drill Team Camp in Houston where three "Superior" awards were earned.

Drum Majors Denard Gilstrap and Chris Miles put the GHS Band through their paces aided by Glenda Gilbert, Sharon Cartwright, Kim James, Jenny Henrickson, Kristi Reynolds, Jay Minmier, Donny Hodgson, Miles noble and Jeff Phillips. Sharon Cartwright was Band Sweetheart. Outstanding member was Jesse Smith who made All-State Band for two consecutive years.

The "Magic of Music" held on March 12-13, 1982, was the result of months of hard work by the Band and Flashes and created a magical, musical event that has grown more spectacular with the passage of time. The show followed the traditional format and included some of these musical selections: "Carol Burnett Fantasy," "Hot Lunch Jam," Over the Rainbow," On Broadway," "Feels So Good," "Stars and Stripes Forever," plus a specialty tap routine by the Flashes where the beat of the taps created most of the music for the dance with accompaniment by the Stage Band on percussion.

Kristi Sherrill (Hoyl) shared these thoughts:
> *Waking up early for practices...laughing and cutting up with all the girls in the Flashes...working on the routines to perfection...bright red lipstick...the nervous thrill just before you perform under the bright lights at football games...the boots...the hat...the wonderful hat!*
>
> *We were all so nervous trying out for the famous Flaming Flashes. We lined up in the hallway of the old high school practicing the routine for no one wanted to make a mistake. We made friends for life.*
>
> *Floorshow was hard work, but we got to showcase all our hard work and talent. The band was such a terrific partner. I learned a great deal about leadership that still serves me well today. It was extraordinary.*

Lori Butler had these memories.
> *I'll never forget: being on the line with Mary McCaw, Kristy Sherrill, Christa Horn, and Jamie Patterson; laughing until we cried when Mary's wig flew off at the Lake Highlands' football game; tearing my panty hose at the Sulphur Springs game and Leah Rita Sherrill Tillotson rescued me (She took hers off and gave them to me because I had already given my extra pair away and my mom was not wearing any!); being presented as a new Flaming Flash during my sister's senior year (Major Lachelle Butler); and, making Flash Officer.*

Mary (Missy) Vance Spears expressed her thoughts via email.
> *When my mother asked me to submit my thoughts and memories of the Flaming Flashes for her newest book, my first reaction was that I could not, since I was a cheerleader and never on the drill team. Her persuasive skills convinced me. Most persuasive were her comments reminding me that I was surrounded by Flashes (I was their Mascot in 1968-69.) all my life. As a young girl, I was fascinated by their performances. The showstopper was always their synchronized high kicks that always received a standing ovation. The dedication and respect that these young ladies had for their "sisters," the school and community was inspirational, not just for me, but for so many others in our community. When thinking of the Flashes who touched my life in some way, two words come to mind to describe them..."excellence and dedication."*

Television, movies, and the news media influenced opinions. By the end of 1982, over 28 million homes in the US had cable and the term "couch potato" surfaced. Drive-in movie theaters, popular in the '50s and '60s, made way for movie theaters with larger screens to show films like *Chariots of Fire,* Academy Award winner. Music, marching, and dancing were at the heart of the Band and Flashes. Strong traditions kept the programs moving in the constant pursuit of excellence. Pam Clayton and Bill Goodson continued challenging students. The Band and Flashes were prepared.

Colonel ....Jill Morris
Majors..Lorie Bolch, Laura Clark,
                                                 Amy Dennis, Julie Mathews
Manager..Michelle Clark

Members of the Corps

Wendy Abbott	Manya East	Lesa Jenkins	Carla Royall
Susan Ball	Stacey Frazier	Dee Ann Jones	Staci Shanks
Brandy Boswell	Dawn Fritschen	Karen Morris	Amy Tillery
Sharon Burgin	Kim Fritschen	Rebecca Nicholson	Amy Wallen
Amy Casstevens	Jana Garner	Lori Norfleet	Sheri Ware
Susan Chapman	Stacy Gilstrap	Kristi Norris	Melanie Warren
Annette Cleveland	Janet Girdner	Daphne Norsworthy	Jana Williams
Becky Cole	Marla Goodwin	Susan Payne	Dawn Woodson
Bridget Comer	Carla Grose	Sheri Pickens	Valerie Wright
Stephanie Cummings	Rachael Hyatt	Elaine Porter	Lisa Reames
Debbie Detter	Barbie Jackson	Emily Ramsey	Ylicia Richards
Sherry Diggs	Patrice Jackson	Kelly Ritter	
Darlena Drake	Janet Jacobs	Kara Robinson	

Drum Majors Jenny Henrikson and Sarah Faulkner led the GHS Band and were assisted by Senior Captains Beth Henrikson and Brian Swiggart. Junior Lieutenants were Kim James and Brian McCool, with Christy Ward and Mike Norris serving as Sophomore Sergeants. Melanie Cartwright, Head Twirler, led twirlers Beth Henrikson, Shelley Churchill, Cindy Morphew, and Sara Faulkner. Leading the Flag Corps were Debbie Avers and Sherry Barnes. Jenny Henrikson was Band Sweetheart.

Miss Gussie Nell Davis was honored once again at GHS during homecoming festivities for October 1982. First organized as Flaming Flashes by Miss Davis in 1932, but not chartered until 1934, Gussie Nell was truly impressed with her "creation" and their continued successes and accomplishments. She was "flabbergasted" that the people of Greenville remembered her.

Ronnie Green recalled:

> *Following the pep rally in the GHS gym, I drove my dad's Model A roadster, and Gussie Nell rode in the homecoming parade from the school to the downtown pep rally at the Hunt County Courthouse in the rumble seat. I stopped in front of the courthouse to let her out, and before I could help her out of the rumble seat, Gussie Nell had already stepped out of the rumble seat onto*

Daphne Norsworthy (Hyatt) and Stacy Gillstrap (Piña), 1982.

a round chrome piece on the fender (made for that purpose) and jumped down from there! (Miss Davis was a "spry" septuagenarian at the time.

In 1983, the series *M*A*S*H* ended after 251 episodes, and the world watched as NASA launched its Space Shuttle "Challenger" with Sally Ride, the first American woman in space, and Guion Bluford, first Black astronaut. Michael Jackson ruled the music world with "Beat It" and "Thriller." Disco dancing was still going strong with "Flashdance" at the top of the charts.

"Lights, Camera, Action" opened on April 29-30, 1983, with outstanding artwork completed by Janet Jacobs, Sarah Faulkner, and Katie Ferguson. "Holiday for Winds," the overture, led to a musical extravaganza throughout the traditional program. A wide selection of songs included "Boogie Woogie Boy," "Fame," "Physical," "Satin Doll," "*La Bamba*," "Ballin' the Jack," and "Thunder and Blazes," to name a few. All-State Band members Chris Chipman and Jesse Smith impressed the crowd with their talents on the alto sax and trombone, respectively. Another floorshow was "put to bed," and the Band and Flashes were ready to celebrate another successful year.

Lisa Reames (Morquecho) shared these memories.
> *I will never forget the fun times with my friends at drill team camp...the floorshows...football halftime performances...the pep rallies. The Flashes celebrated their 50th that year and we hosted a reception for Miss Gussie Nell Davis! Most of all, I cherish the lifelong friendships I made. Thanks for the memories!*

The USSR was dubbed the "evil empire" by President Reagan who moved forward to put the Strategic Defense Initiative ("Star Wars") in place. Reagan signed legislation to make Dr. Martin Luther King, Jr.'s birthday a national holiday from January 1986 onward. In May 1984, Reagan and other heads of state visited the site of the D-Day invasion to commemorate its 40th anniversary. In technology, the compact disc was launched...changing the way data, music, and movies are recorded. Michael Jackson won eight Grammy's to break the record. "Thriller" sold over 37 million copies.

The award-winning Flashes continued winning awards wherever they performed. At

Al Gilliam's Drill Team Camp (HSU), Abilene, and SMU Super Star Drill Team Camp, they won numerous "Superior" ribbons for jazz, high kick, prop, novelty, and "Outstanding" awards for high kick, jazz and precision drill/dance.

The Award-Winning Flaming Flashes for 1983-84 included:

    Colonel .... Valerie Wright
    Majors .... Patrice Jackson, Rebecca Nicholson
                        Emily Ramsey, Kelly Ritter, Staci Shanks
    Manager .... Michelle Clar

Members of the Corps

Kristi Baker	Su Fang	Leah McCullough	Jill Smith
Susan Ball	Stacy Frazier	Cindy Morphew	Tracey Thompson
Anne Banner	Kim Fritschen	Kristi Norris	Dristi Wallace
Sharon Burgin	Janet Girdner	Karen Oldham	Amy Wallen
Stephanie Cameron	Marla Goodwin	Elaine Porter	Melonie Warren
Susan Chapman	Johnette Graff	Kristi Reeves	Dianne Watts
Becky Cole	Michele Guinn	Kara Robinson	Jana Williams
Lorie Davis	Jennifer Jackson	Kim Sandlin	Dianne Worrell
Anet Cleveland	Tanya Kerbow	Mary Sawyers	Kenna Wright
Sherry Diggs	LuAnne Manning	Janet Sizemore	
Darlena Drake	Stephanie Martin	Jeannie Smith	

  Drum Majors Sarah Faulkner and Brian McCool were aided by the following officers: Senior Captains–Katie Ferguson, Jeff Phillips, Dennis Garth, and Leanne Gray; Junior Lieutenants–Mandy Shackelford, Steve Gregg, Layne Russell, and Katie Hardaway; Sophomore Sergeants–Michelle Ryder, Bedri Wilderom, Christy Ward, and Mike Norris; and, Freshman Sergeants–Michelle Fischtziur, Jeff Thompson, Erin Reese, and Jimmy Littlefield. Head Twirler, Kim James, and Flag Corps Captain Tammy Holley completed the list. Kim James was also Band Sweetheart.

  "Strike Up the Band" and "Dance" was the theme for April 27-28, 1984. Artwork was completed by the GHS Art Department, Sarah Faulkner, and Katie Ferguson. Following the traditional program format, the band opened with "Americans We," followed by the Flashes dancing to "Strike Up the Band. "Beat It!" by the twirlers, "Puttin' on The Ritz," "Rock Around the Clock," "McCaviity, the Mystery Cat," "Getaway," "Flashdance," "Beer Barrel Polka," and "Mr. Touchdown USA" were included. The show concluded with a twinge of sadness as Mrs. Clayton announced her resignation as director. More changes were in store for GHS for the coming year.

  The Flashes knew the drill to prepare for the coming year and organized the Corps into squads so officers could begin training the new members for football season. Organization was the key, which opened the lock of long-standing traditions of The Flaming Flashes.

Betty Ballard

Technology was on the rise in 1984-85. Apple launched its microcomputer (with mouse) making computer use in the home a wave of the future. Communication avenues exploded. Disney World, Florida, celebrated Donald Duck's fiftieth birthday. The economy continued to suffer, and by the end of 1984, over seventy banks in the USA failed...the highest rate since 1937. In 1985, President Reagan began his second term in office and the space shuttle "Atlantis" made its maiden flight.

Greenville High School had a new principal. James Weatherall, a seasoned educator known for his fairness and sense of humor, was the first Black Principal at GHS. He was a fan of "all things that are good for students." The Band and Flashes were at the top of his list.

Besides a new principal, the Flashes had a new director. Betty Ballard had several ideas for making changes. The Flashes traveled to HSU, Abilene, where they won several "Superior" and "Excellent" ratings. The Flash Officers earned the "Best Officer Group" award and Colonel Diane Watts won the "Best Officer" award. Officers also attended camp at SMU. Squad practice, which had been ongoing during the summer months, began to intensify in August. Daily morning practices at the high school were repeated during squad practice at the home of each officer. They had to be perfect.

The Flaming Flashes for 1984-85 and their Officers were:

Colonel	Dianne Watts
Lt. Colonel (reinstated position)	Angie Hemby
Majors	Stephanie Cameron, Johnette Graff, Michelle Guinn, Tonya Kerbor
1st Lieutenant	Micki Ice
Banner Carriers	Kim Moser, Janet Sizemore

Anne Banner, selected as Major in Spring 1984 left. No Managers or Flash Guards were listed.

Members of the Corps

Theresa Anderson	Lori Davis	Dawn McKinney	Karen Schorr
Lori Avery	Shawn Fang	Alison Noble	Jeannie Smith
Jeri Bonham	Shelbye Gilstrap	Karen Oldham	Jill Smith
Stephanie Bostick	Angie Hope	Emily Patterson	Tracy Thompson
April Bowes	Jennifer Jackson	Cindy Ray	Evonne Toiiver
Sue Brown	Shelonda Johnson	Christi Reeves	Kelly Toms
Julie Cartwright	Nicki Kusewitt	Sara Robinson	Kristi Wallace
Kathryn Clifton	Lu Ann Manning	Kim Sandlin	
Lea Ann Copeland	Cindy Morphew	Mary Sawyers	

Drum Majors for the GHS Band were Kevin James, Katie Hardaway, and Christy Ward. Senior Captains included Byron Black, Steve Gregg, Leslie Farmer, and Mandy Shakelford. Serving as Junior Lieutenants were Mike Norris, Laura Davis, and Traci Hillis. Sophomore Sergeants were Larry Green, Eric MacDonald, Michelle Fischtzier, and Tammy Mehew. Freshmen Sergeants were Nathan Roberts, Travis Washington, Sharon Ball, and Shelly Carwile. Head Twirler was Karen Hopewell. Flag Corps Captains were Michelle Ryder and Jennifer Cox. Katie Hardaway was Band Sweetheart.

"Rock, Roll, and Remember," scheduled for April 29-30, 1985, had everyone "shakin', movin', and groovin'" as the beat rocked the gym. George Fudgen, local educator and Black artist, and Kevin James handled the artwork for the show. Jim Hodo, Narrator, got the crowd's attention for the Flashes' routine to "Bandstand Boogie." The twirlers followed with "Sweet Georgia Brown," followed by "Ninety Nine Red Balloons" by the Junior Flashes. The second half, following presentation of new members, rocked the gym with "Jailhouse Rock," "Breakdance," "Rock Around the Clock," and others, before closing with "Basin Street Blues."

Shelbye Gilstrap (back) and Theresa Anderson

Before one could say, "Elvis has left the building," Betty Ballard decided to resign as director, and, within weeks, Bill Goodson, Band Director, also decided to leave. Whatever was "going around" must have been contagious because Superintendent Bill Kennedy also hit the road. Band and Flash parents were all shaking their heads wondering who would be leaving next.

Mary Patterson & Sarah J. Wright

The Flashes and Officers had already made plans to attend summer camp at SMU, and most had already paid their camp fees. Confusion reigned. A new director, Shannon Karr, was selected, but could not report for duty until she finished contract responsibilities at Caddo Mills ISD, where she was director of their drill team and must take them to summer camp. Two of the Flash parents, Mary Patterson and Sarah Jane Wright (employed by GISD), decided to take charge of the situation.

Mary Patterson recalled:

> We had a meeting with the girls beforehand to make arrangements, get parental permission, and provide a list of what they should take to camp. I think Mrs. Karr helped with that. At the time, I was the librarian at Bowie Elementary School, and was involved with the Flashes because our daughter, Emily, was selected as Major for the coming year. Julie Cartwright was the Colonel, but her mother, Carolyn, was teaching at the university that summer and could not go. Jamie Wright was a new Flash. Sarah Jane and I were friends and both employed by Greenville ISD. We decided to ask Mike Cardwell, Acting Superintendent (since Mr. Kennedy left), if he would allow us to take the Flashes to camp at SMU. He was very receptive and agreed, saying that they deserved to go, and they would, if he had to take them himself. That was a statement I could never forget. He appointed us as temporary directors (volunteers) and arranged for a school bus to transport them to Dallas, and Mr. James Evans, Elementary Principal and Director of Transportation, drove the bus daily to cut costs. We were

never given written contracts and were not paid for our services, because we were already under contract with GISD. In those days, we did not think about having a separate contract. Today, if we took a group of students to camp for two weeks, we would need to have blood drawn and be thoroughly checked by an approval committee. I was glad I drove my car to SMU on some of the days, as I was constantly leaving to pick up hose and other items that some of the Flashes needed, but forgot. I felt sad for them when we arrived. Most of the other drill teams had directors who were young or had been Kilgore Rangerettes. Somehow, we conquered the tasks with hard work and prayer. Our Flashes looked good, performed well, and won many awards. We were so proud of them. I learned, the hard way, that being a Flash Director is a horrific responsibility. Praise to all of you who have accepted the call!

At SMU Superstar Line Camp, the Flashes earned "outstanding" awards. They could not have participated without the valuable assistance of Flash parents, Mary Patterson and Sarah Jane Wright, who served as volunteer directors for the summer. Their time, efforts, patience, and assistance was greatly appreciated and will never be forgotten.

[*Author's Note:* Other memories shared by Mary Patterson were not only highly amusing, but quite detailed. They were not included in this writing, but may be shared in public reviews at a later date.]

Shannon Karr

President Ronald Reagan, with a landslide victory over Senator Walter Mondale (Minnesota) by winning every state (except Mondale's) and Washington, D.C., received more accolades during inaugural festivities in 1985. Films such as *Amadeus, Ghostbusters, The Killing Fields,* and *Romancing the Stone,* targeted a wide variety of theatergoers. The wreck of the "Titanic" in North Atlantic waters was filmed by underwater cameras...another "first." Disasters struck in 1986 when a reactor at Chernobyl blew up causing the world's worst nuclear accident and the space shuttle "Challenger" exploded seconds after launch, killing 11 astronauts.

More changes were noted at GISD with the arrival of a new leader, Superintendent John Wilson, new Band Director, James Coffman, and new Flash Director, Shannon Karr. Mrs. Karr, with twenty years of experience, directed the Caddo Mills Foxettes for 17 years and served as staff member of the ETSU Summer Drill Team Camp for twelve years. She held a Bachelor of Science degree from Texas Woman's University and a Master's of Education from ETSU (now Texas A&M-Commerce). Parents were tired or a "revolving door" directorship for the Flashes, and her qualifications were quite impressive. There was work to be done with no time to waste...the football season was fast approaching.

The Flaming Flashes for 1985-86 included:

Colonel	Julie Cartwright
Lt. Colonel	Angie Hemby
Major	Emily Patterson
Captain	Allison Noble
1st Lieutenant	Micki Ice
2nd Lieutenant	Evonne Toliver
Jr. Corporals	Abbie Black, Tricia Mize
Managers	Karolyn Ford, Scarlett Hamilton

Members of the Flash Corps

April Adams	Leslie Brown	Shelonda Johnson	Jana Rudd
Theresa Anderson	Rowena Burnett	Sebrena Lewis	Shelly Stailey
Jo Berke	Tina Cole	Tammy McCarty	Sherilyn Stefancik
Amy Bolch	Jacque Ellis	Carrie Nolan	Shawn Washington*
Shawn Blythe	Kristi Harper	Lori Ray	Jamie Wright
Kelly Bolton	Kim Hicks	Joan Reed	

*Banner Carrier

Mr. James Coffman, new Band Director for 1985-86, put the GHS Band through their paces. Mr. Arroyo continued as his Associate. Drum Majors were Christy Ward, Julana Crom, and Michelle Fischtziur. Flag Captains Michelle Ryder and Jennifer Cox led the Flag Corps. Band Officers were Joe Melendez, President; Librarian, Cathy English; Transportation, Frankie Melendez; and, Property, Joslin Arrington. Traci Hillis was twirler, and Christy Ward was Band Sweetheart.

"A Salute to Texas—Our Heritage," to honor the Texas Sesquicentennial, opened on March 14-15, 1986, with "Laredo" as the overture followed by the Flashes' precision drill/dance routine to "The Yellow Rose of Texas." Other routines presented by the Flashes included "The Trolley Song," "Five Foot Two," "The Heat is On," "Dallas," "San Antonio Rose," "Carioca," and, "Ragtime Cowboy Joe." The finale, "Deep in the Heart of Texas," made for a rousing "standing ovation" finale. The program followed the usual format with presentation of new members held before intermission.

Change was in the air once more. James Coffman, Band Director, decided to leave GHS. Band parents met with the administration to express their concerns that the band needed a director to help in the recruiting and rebuilding process. Their concerns were answered with the hiring of Mr. Larry Miears for Fall 1986. Mr. Miears adopted the slogan, "The Pride Is Back," to initialize enthusiasm and the rebirth of the band as "The Lion Pride Band of GHS." Mr. Laurencio Arroyo, in his eighth year with GISD, continued as Associate Director and was a stable force in rebuilding the GHS Band.

During the summer of 1986, the Flashes attended camp at East Texas State University where they received a "Superior Squad" trophy for the "Most Entertaining Military" precision marching drill. Sherilyn Stefancik won "Miss East Texas Drill Team" title and four others, Rowena Burnett, Abbie Black, Jamie Wright, and Tricia Mize were semi-finalists. The Officers attended camp at San Marcos where Jamie Wright was named "Miss Half-time USA." The group received "Champion Dancer" ribbons, "Best All-Round Group," "Best Technique and Style" awards, and First Place for a high-kick routine. At Halftime Production Invitational Competition in Arlington, they won a First Division rating.

Early in the 1986-87 school year, Mrs. Mary Virginia Duck, retired teacher and member of the Hunt County Historical Commission Board, continued work on documenting the validation of The Flaming Flashes as the first precision dance/drill team in Texas (and the world). Mrs. Duck, a former physical education teacher in Greenville, and other former Flashes on the Commission, felt that documentation was critical before making the assertion that The Flaming Flashes were the "first" in Texas and the world. Commission members agreed. A query letter to the Superintendent of Schools in Orange, Texas, was sent for clarification.

P. O. Box 313
Greenville, Texas. 75401
Oct. 3, 1986

SUPT. OF SCHOOLS
ORANGE, TEXAS 77630.

Dear Sir;

The Hunt County Historical Commission Board is making a study concerning the organization of the Girls Drill Team in our High School by Miss Gussie Nell Davis in 1934.

To receive a marker for this work we need to know about the drill team started in the Orange High School with Mr. Stark contributions toward it.

I was living in Port Arthur, Texas in 1936 and I was under the impression your school had this drill team about that time.

We were writing the history about being the first in Texas to have a Girl's drill team, but we must clear this with your school to be accurate in this matter.

Please have someone that can research this matter and give us this information as soon as you can, as we are in the process of writing our history at this time.

We do not wish to claim the position of being first, if there is a question about the organization.

I finished College with Mrs. Stark and this is why I knew about their interest and work with the team. I understood he was a retired army man and he supported the group in many ways.

Enclosed is a stamped envelope to send me this information. We will appreciate anything or any information you can send to us.

Sincerely,
Mary Va. Williams Duck
Mrs. Mary Va. Duck (H.B.)

A prompt response to Mrs. Duck's query verified that The Flaming Flashes appeared to hold the title of being the "first."

> **WEST ORANGE-COVE CONSOLIDATED INDEPENDENT SCHOOL DISTRICT**
> P. O. Box 1107
> ORANGE, TEXAS 77630
>
> October 8, 1986
>
> Mrs. Mary Va. Duck
> Post Office Box 313
> Greenville, Texas 75401
>
> Dear Mrs. Duck:
>
> Thank you for your interesting letter. I contacted Nelda Stark, and she reports that the planning for the Bengal Guards took place in 1935 and that their first performance was in 1936.
>
> It would appear, then, that the drill team in Greenville was first. We congratulate you on your present efforts to gain this desired recognition and wish you the best of luck.
>
> Sincerely,
>
> *Ken Armstrong*
>
> Ken Armstrong, Executive Director
> Secondary Education
>
> KA/nlg

The Flaming Flashes for 1986-87 included:

  Colonel...Jamie Wright
  Majors..Carrie Nolan, Sherilyn Stefancik,
        Tricia Mize, Jana Rudd
  Manager..Karolyn Ford.

Corps Members

April Adams	Tina Cole	Sebrena Lewis	Amy Tarpley
Brenda Ball	Shannon Davis	Kim Nolan	Sherrie Wallace
Abbie Black	Heather Duvall	Shelia Pohl	Delonna Wilburn
Shawn Blythe	Sharla Edwards	Liz Ransom	Heather Wilcoxson
Leslie Brown	Jacque Ellis	Yolanda Rector	Jennifer Williams
Teri Brown	Julie Ellis	Melanie Rhodes	Tina Young
Rowena Burnett	Sharen Hopewell	Karen Royall	
Kristie Chapman	Stephanie Hunt	Melissa Sherrill	
Cheri Coats	Brandee Jenkins	Alicia Spaulding	

Drum Majors included Head Drum Major Michelle Fischtzhur, Justin Arrington, and Shelley Carwile. Flag Captain was Robin Wilson. Instead of officers, Mr. Miears selected a Band Council with Michelle Fischtziur, Fred Aimes, Kim Hale, Sandra Skillerns, Krissa Ross, John Chipman, Shelley Carwile, David Chetlin, and Frankie Melendez as members. Band Sweetheart was Michelle Fischtziur.

"In Rhythm with American Classics," opened March 12-13, 1987, with "76 Trombones" as the overture. The Flashes performed next to "Fun, Fun, Fun" as the traditional program format produced music and routines to "Fascinating Rhythm," "Physical," "New York, New York," and "A Night in Tunisia" prior to the Presentation.

The second half opened with the Officers dancing to "Boogie Woogie Bugle Boy" and the band continued with music from "American Bandstand." The Flashes danced to "Flash Dance," "Hound Dog," "Wabash Cannonball," and "Mickey Mouse Parade" before the finale by entire cast to "America, the Beautiful" and "Stars and Stripes Forever." No one remained seated by the end of the show…red, white, and blue colors dominated the big finish.

Jamie Wright (Burns) recalled:
> *I was a young Flash mascot when I was six years old, at the request of my beloved grandfather, Wesley N. Martin, Superintendent of GISD. He had the same red uniform made especially for me! From then on, I had my heart set on becoming the Colonel of The Flaming Flashes, and, in 1986-87, I was given the privilege of wearing the RED hat…and a sequined one at that! Being a Flash was an amazing experience from the initiation…being taken in the middle of the night…to summer camps…to the Director I adored…Mrs. Shannon Karr. May the Flaming Flashes forever reign in all their glory!*

Larry Green, Jr. shared the following:
> *I never knew what it was like to not play music in high school. I made*

lifelong friends. Jazz Band, in particular, was memorable. We recorded songs for an album called "Silver Jasmine" led by our dedicated director, Laurencio Arroyo. We performed well against Dallas area bands at the UTA and TCU Jazz Festivals. The floorshow is a great tradition at GHS...a unique way for the Flaming Flashes, Concert Band, and Jazz Band to blend their talents.

Whitney Houston and Madonna dominated the popular music world in 1986 and continued to be queens of popular music. "Bad," by Michael Jackson, was also topping charts. *Platoon* won the Academy Award for best picture. In 1987, Vice-President George H. W. Bush announced his candidacy for President of the United States. Television time was filled with campaign ads and debates.

No one debated the performances of The Flaming Flashes. Their precision drills and dancing brought out the crowds to football games, parades, charitable events...anywhere they appeared. Mr. Larry Johnston, new GHS Principal, congratulated Mrs. Karr on their achievements. 1987-88 Flaming Flashes were:

Colonel..Karen Royall
Majors..Brenda Ball, Amy Tarpley,
　　　　　　　　　　　　　　　　　Brandee Jenkins, Deionna Wilburn
Manager..Kelly Ball. Members included:

Renita Allen	Cheri Coats	Stephanie Hunt	Leslie Pugh
Ginny Banner	Jacque Cobbs	Cathy Konderia	Yolanda Rector
Stephanie Blair	Shannon Davis	Patty McFarland	Melanie Rhodes
Amy Brooks	Sharla Edwards	Tricia Nichols	Bobette Stogner
Amberly Brown	Michelle Farmer	Paige Payton	Sherri Wallace
Dorsey Brown	Judy Hoffman	Jill Pitts	Heather Wilcoxson
Teri Brown	Sharen Hopewell	Jennifer Poole	Jennifer Williams

"On Broadway" opened on May 6-7, 1988, with "Everything's Coming Up Roses" followed by the Flashes' high-kicking routine to "There's No Business Like Show Business." "Fascinating Rhythm" led to the Flash Officers' routine to "Live." Following the songs "On Broadway" and "Summertime," featuring Jason Scott on bass trombone, the Flashes performed to "One." The Jazz Band, with Pam Avers (Trumpet), Sammy Toliver (Tenor Sax), and the entire saxophone section played "42nd Street" followed by presentation of new members of both groups.

"Ease On Down The Road" opened the second half with the Flashes performing. The Flag Corps' routine to "Fame" was followed by "Yankee Doodle," (Flashes); "America," (Flag Corps); "Mame," (New and Current Flash Officers); and, "Singing in the Rain," by the new Flashes. "Mem'ries" by the band led to "That's Entertainment" and the finale by the entire cast.

GHS was sad to see Assistant Band Director Laurencio Arroyo leave at the end of the year. He was an effective leader of students and was an outstanding director of the Jazz Band.

Democrats chose Michael Dukakis and Lloyd Bentsen, and Republicans tapped

Vice-President George H. W. Bush and Dan Quayle for the November 1988 Presidential Election. In 1989, the world mourned the loss of Irving Berlin, popular American songwriter; Mel Blanc, "carton voice" of Bugs Bunny and Daffy Duck; and, Lucille Ball, American film and television star. Everyone loved "Lucy." Technology returned their works for our enjoyment.

Tricia Nichols, Judy Hoffman, Beverly Sealy, Jackie Westwood, Kristen Head, and Laura Livesay returned to the Eurobowl in London, and were recognized as being part of the world's oldest high school precision dance and drill team. The Flashes were also excited to be part of a campaign stop by Michael Dukakis in Greenville, as presidential candidates usually went to large cities like Dallas, and seldom came to Northeast Texas.

The Flaming Flashes for 1988-89 included:

Colonel	Melanie Rhodes
Majors	Judy Hoffman, Heather Wilcoxson, Tricia Nichols, Ginny Banner
Managers	Charlotte Corcoran, Kesha Gassaway

Members of the Flash Corps

Christina Adams	Wendy Gilley	Holly King	Jennifer Milton
Renita Allen	Kristen Head	Kimm Knowles	Jill Pitts
Amy Brooks	Misty Hite	Cathy Konderla	Carol Robinson
Darla Case	Shawntay Holmes	Misty Linton	Beverly Sealy
Jacque Cobbs	April Hudgeons	Cristi Little	Mindy Smith
Carrie Davis	Jennifer Jaco	Laura Livesay	Cherish Stanley
Elise Earnhart	Shannon Johnson	Kim Massey	Samantha Vaughn
Julie Fuller	Jennifer Jones	Bridget McClure	

Band Director Larry Miears welcomed Mike Ferguson aboard as Assistant Band Director for the GHS Lion Pride Band. Drum Majors Charlene Shields (Head), Bambi Fields, and Stevanne Ellis led the band to All State Orchestra and All State Jazz Band competitions. Band Sweetheart was Stevanne Ellis, and the Band Beaux was Hector Lara. Class Representatives were: Kalynn Ross and Lori Abell (Freshmen); Debbie Collin and Keith Freeman (Sophomores); Amy Abell and Matt Hunt (Juniors); and, Krissa Ross and Mike Stephenson (Seniors).

In March 1989, the 71st Texas Legislature honored The Flaming Flashes for their "longevity and continued tradition." Texas Representative William (Bill) Thomas, who authored this resolution and proclamation, recognized The Flaming Flashes as the "original precision drill team in Texas." The Flaming Flashes, Director Shannon Karr, and a number of Greenville dignitaries and parents, traveled to Austin for the official reading of House Bill No. 50 by Representative Thomas.

"Golden Memories" opened March 10-11, 1989, with "Pledge of Allegiance" by the Concert Band, and the Flashes "upped" the tempo with their routine to "Puttin' On The Ritz." The Jazz Band kept the tempo going with "Carnival" followed by the Flashes' routine to "Big Spender." The Flag Corps got everyone "In The Mood," for feature twirler, Kristi Powers,

House of Representatives

H.R. No. 50

R E S O L U T I O N

WHEREAS, The citizens of Texas can take great pride in the accomplishments of the Greenville High School Flaming Flashes drill team; and

WHEREAS, This award-winning student ensemble has been exciting audiences for the past 57 years and is recognized internationally as the world's oldest precision-dance drill team; and

WHEREAS, On March 10-11, 1989, the Flaming Flashes will again display their tremendous talent and showmanship as they perform in the Greenville High School Band and Flash Floor Show; and

WHEREAS, The theme of this year's show is "Golden Memories: 50 Plus Years of Band and Flash"; as in the past, traditional long dresses will be worn for the formal occasion and the new members of the team will be presented; and

WHEREAS, The Flaming Flashes drill team was founded in 1932 by Gussie Nell Davis, who was later to establish the state's famous Kilgore Junior College Rangerettes; and

WHEREAS, It was through her early work at Greenville High School from 1932 to 1939 that she developed the distinctive precision-dance style that continues to influence many high school and college drill teams today; and

WHEREAS, Under Ms. Davis's direction, the Flaming Flashes introduced their trademark "Peruna Strut" while charming audiences at the 1934 Cotton Bowl and later at the Texas Centennial celebration in Dallas; and

WHEREAS, Many current members are carrying on the family tradition started when their mothers and grandmothers proudly represented Greenville High School on the drill squad; and

WHEREAS, The Flaming Flashes have won numerous honors competing in Texas and have toured extensively, performing before enthusiastic American and European audiences; and

WHEREAS, The discipline, self-confidence, and leadership gained through participation in this worthy activity have enabled many young women to pursue successful careers and make valuable contributions to their communities; now, therefore, be it

Resolution from the Texas Legislature proclaiming the Flaming Flashes as the state's original precision drill team.

RESOLVED, That the House of Representatives of the 71st Legislature of the State of Texas hereby honor the distinguished achievements of the Greenville High School Flaming Flashes, and extend to the current team members best wishes for success in the future; and, be it further

RESOLVED, That an official copy of this resolution be prepared for the Greenville High School Flaming Flashes as an expression of the high regard of the Texas House of Representatives.

Thomas
Gib Lewis
Speaker of the House

I certify that H.R. No. 50 was adopted by the House on February 2, 1989, by a non-record vote.

Betty Murray
Chief Clerk of the House

and "Watermelon Man." The Flashes got "Bad" shaking to the next numbers followed by the Jazz Band with "Samba de Haps," and continued with "That's All" just before intermission was announced by Narrator, Andy Bench.

Presentation of new members of both groups followed intermission, which was followed by the Flashes' dance to "Can Can." The Flag Corps kept the beat going with "Rockin' Robin" followed by "Parade of the Wooden Soldiers" by the Flashes. New and current Officers danced next to "Me and My Shadow" followed by the new Flashes' routine to "By The Sea." A Mancini Spectacular led to the finale, "Sempre Fidelis," performed by the entire cast.

In 1989-90, General Colin Powell became the first Black American named as Chairman of the Joint Chiefs of Staff. NASA launched the "Galileo" space probe to Jupiter, and the USSR sent its 2,000th Cosmos satellite into outer space. Weary television viewers escaped to the movies to see *Batman, Driving Miss Daisy,* and *When Harry Met Sally,* among others.

In Spring, 1989, the Greenville community and high school students were shocked by the sudden death of one of their favorite GHS administrators. Mr. Kenneth (Ken) Gibson died suddenly, leaving a void in the hearts of many. Students dedicated the 1989-90 annual as a memorial to Mr. Gibson.

More changes occurred at GISD when Dr. John Wilson, Superintendent, decided to leave in May 1989, and Gilbert (Gib) Weaver became Superintendent of Schools for 1989-90. Mr. Larry Miears and his assistant, Mike Ferguson, remained at the helm of the GHS Band and Mrs. Shannon Karr continued as Flash Director.

The Flaming Flashes for 1989-90 included:

Colonel	Christina Adams
Lt. Colonel	Jill Pitts
Majors	Mindy Smith, Jacque Cobbs
	Jennifer Jones
Manager	Edna Singleton

Members of the Flash Corps

Darla Case	Wendy Gilley	Holly King	Amanda Robinson
Charlotte Corcoran	Angie Hales	Kimm Knowles	Carol Robinson
Carrie Davis	Kristen Head	Cristi Little	Shelly Skinner
Kendria Davis	Rae Hicks	Laura Livesay	Deanie Smith
Heather Day	Ashley Hill	Bridget McClure	Jean Smith
Elise Earnhart	Shawntay Holmes	Angie McDaniel	Meredith Snyder
Shanna Ellis	April Hudgeons	Lori Medford	Meredith Snyder
Jennifer Fuller	Betsy Hurst	Linda Morquecho	
Julie Fuller	Jennifer Jaco	Sabra Roberts	

Leading the GHS Lion Pride Band were Drum Majors Wylie Creech, Philip Holmes-Head, and Jason Spivey. Twirler was Kristi Powers.

Miss Gussie Nell Davis made headlines with news of the Fiftieth Birthday celebration of the founding of the world famous Kilgore Rangerettes. Gussie Nell left Greenville in 1939 for Kilgore to teach what she practiced and perfected in Greenville. Additional honors were bestowed on the founder of The Flaming Flashes when she was inducted into The Texas Women's Hall of Fame in Austin on March 27, 1990. Other inductees were: Jane Wetzel, Terry Hershey, Governor William P. Clements, Jr., Dr. Ruth Guy, Dr. Judith Craven, Lucia Madrid, First Lady Barbara Bush, First Lady of Texas Rita Clements, and Margaret Forbes.

"Let's Go to the Movies" opened on May 11-12, 1990, with entire cast performing the opening number. "Rocky's Theme," played by the Jazz Band, led to the Flag Corps' routine, to "Pink Panther."

The Flash Officers danced to a space medley from *Star Trek* and *Star Wars* followed by the Jazz Band's rendition of "Misty." The Flashes revved up the tempo with "Bat Dance" and "Johnny's Mambo." The Jazz Band's version of "Cable Vision" led to the presentation of members of both groups.

"Fiddler on the Roof" by the Concert Band was followed by "Hang 'em High." The Flag Corps' routine to "Power of Love" and the Concert Band's medley of "Rainbow Connection" and "Over the Rainbow" led to the new and current Officers' routine to "Danger Zone." The new Flashes' dance to "Greased Lightnin'" led to "Raiders of the Lost Ark" by the Concert Band and the finale, "Hooray for Hollywood," performed by the entire cast.

Mindy Smith (Hamilton) shared these memories:
> *Being a Flaming Flash was something I was so proud of...an honor and a privilege. We worked so hard, but it yielded such joy and gave us friendships that will never be forgotten. I wouldn't trade them for the world! I have such fond memories of the annual Floorshow. I distinctly remember having Gussie Nell Davis attend the 1988-89 performance and was so nervous, hoping she would approve of our production. I recall what a little spitfire she was! Floorshows were so much fun to do. I loved teaming up with the band...the costumes, lighting, music and choreography were awesome! I get a little skip in my heartbeat thinking about marching out on the field and performing "Hey, Look Me Over." There's nothing like it! Shannon Karr was strict and expected us to always do our best, but she loved us like we were her own daughters. I am so thankful that she had such high expirations of us and showed us that we should always do everything with excellence to make us worthy of the rich heritage of The Flaming Flashes.*

Lori L. Butler

In 1990-91, the outbreak of the Gulf War caused an international spike in the stock market. Health issues, with the spread of AIDS, also captured headlines. Hollywood stars and popular singers pooled their talents to raise funds for the World Health Organization (WHO). In other news, actor/director Kevin Costner's film, *Dances with Wolves,* won seven Oscars and "Best Film," "Best Screenplay," and "Best Director," at The Golden Globe Awards. The film, *JFK,* (about President Kennedy's assassination) reopened controversy regarding Lee Harvey Oswald's role.

In local news, Lori L. Butler, was hired to be the twentieth director of The Flaming Flashes. Previously with the Royse City ISD for one year as teacher and cheerleader sponsor, Miss Butler was the second Flash Director to have been a former member of the Flaming Flashes and a Flash Officer. She brought with her, not only her experience as a Flash, but a love for the organization. A member of the Greenville community since she was in Kindergarten, Miss Butler knew and appreciated the legacy of the Flashes and their traditions. She was delighted to be selected and could hardly wait to begin working with the Band and Flashes. GISD administrators were pleased with her credentials and felt they had made the right choice.

Mascot Lori Butler, Abbott, Texas

The 1990-91 Flashes and Officers were:

Colonel	Jennifer Jones
Majors	Heather Day, Ashley Hill, Julie Fuller
Manager	Missy Law

Members of the Corps

Jennifer Acuña	Angie Hales	Laura Livesay	Lisa Pugh
Hayley Banks	Kelleigh Head	Stacy Lorance	Angie Reynolds
Dedra Cathey	Kristen Head	Courtney Mayner	Amanda Robinson
Carrie Davis	Meagan Hemby	Bridget McClure	Carol Robinson
Kendria Davis	Kristi Hood	Angie McDaniel	Shary Shelton
La Shun Denmark	Betsy Hurst	Lori Medford	Tonna Shuler
Allison Doughty	Joanna Jaco	Linda Morquecho	Jean Smith
Elise Earhart	Holly King	Carmen Peña	Misti Stephenson
Sara Elder	Brandi Landrum	Julie Pitts	Mindi Warren

Members of the Band Council included: Keith Freeman, President; Drum Majors Christin Frank and Amanda George; Jennifer Neatherlin, Flag Corps Captain; Jan Miller, Flag Co-Captain; David Warren, Senior; Chanell Stephenson, Junior; Kelly Courns, Sophomore; and, Niki Hennager, Freshman. Band Sweetheart was Christin Frank and Band Beau was David Warren.

"A Stroll Down Disney Lane," opened on March 13-14, 1991, with "The Star Spangled Banner" as the overture, followed by the Flashes in a delightful routine to "Zip-A-Dee-Doo-Dah." Flash Officers continued dancing to "Muppet Theme" with Daniel Smith on the piano. Flag Corps members twirled banners to "It's A Small World," followed by Sophomore and Junior Flashes' routine to "Chim-Chim-Cher-ee." The Jazz Band played "Harlem Nocturne" followed by "Thumper's Song" danced by the current and new Flash Officers prior to the traditional presentation of new members.

The second half opened with the Flashes' dance to "Little Mermaid," followed by "Under the Sea" routine by the Flag Corps.

Senior Flashes continued with "Black Hole." The band played "Pete's Dragon" prior

Jennifer Jones (Moody)

to the new Flashes' routine to "Disney Showcase." The full cast concluded with "Disney March" as the finale. Narrator for the show was Robert Jolly.

In 1992, the maiden voyage of the space shuttle "Endeavor" made headlines and half the world watched on television. The US space shuttle, on its 48th flight, set a record with ten days and 21 hours in space. The race continued. The Democratic Party selected Bill Clinton, former Governor of Arkansas to run against incumbent, George H. W. Bush. *Silence of the Lambs* won five Oscars. News in GISD included the hiring of James Fuller as GHS Principal, since Larry Johnston's departure.

With a year's experience as Flash Director under her belt, Lori Butler, faced the school year with confidence and enthusiasm. She handpicked these officers and members of the corps and was ready for the 1991-92 year. Officers and members included:

```
Colonels......................Heather Day and Ashley Hill
Majors.........................Kendria Davis, Angie Hales, Betsy Hurst,
                               Lori Medford, Amanda Robinson, Jean Smith
Manager......................Latisha Dean.
```

Members of the Flash Corps

Jennifer Acuña	Joanna Jaco	Jill Mangram	Corrie Ray
Christi Britton	Dondi Gibson	Amber Marsh	Doc Ray
Chrissy Brown	Patty Johnson	Courtney Mayner	Molly Schwartz
Cicely Burns	Tasha Johnson	Angie McDaniel	Addie Shepherd
Debra Cathey	Brandi Landrum	Stefani Mitchell	Sonya Skillerns
Chyuonna Daniels	Stacy Lewis	Carmen Peña	Yvonne Ulm
Nina Dixon	Amanda Loehr	Julie Pitts	Alison Weis
Allison Doughty	Amber Lovell	Lisa Pugh	Patricia Williams

Drum Majors for the GHS Band were Greg Hensley and Zara Courns. Band Director Larry Miears worked with Band Assistants Mr. West and Mr. King. His goal for the year was to acquire new band uniforms for the membership for the 1993 season.

Miss Gussie Nell Davis, in an article published in *The Flare,* the Kilgore College News (Thursday, 24 October 1991, p. 8) gave a detailed account of how she originated The Flaming Flashes in Greenville, Texas, before leaving for Kilgore in 1939, after being called by Dr. B. E. Masters to begin a similar group at the college as a way to attract female students. She will always be remembered as the compelling force that gave Greenville High School the first precision dance/drill team in the world.

"Hot Shoe—Gum Shoe Review" opened May 10-11, 1992, with Mr. John Sutton, a former member of the GISD Board of Education and vocalist with various bands, singing "The Star Spangled Banner." The Flashes followed with their dance routine to "One" from *A Chorus Line.* The Flash Officers upped the tempo by dancing to "Fame" followed by two numbers by the Jazz Band. A "Disney Showcase" featuring current and new Flash Officers was enjoyed by the crowd prior to the traditional presentation format of new members of both organizations.

Following intermission, the Flashes danced to "Ease on Down the Road" and the Flag

148 *Flashes Forever*

Corps performed to "Peter Gunn." "Axel F" was a routine done by the Senior Flashes and the Junior Flashes followed with their dance to "Copacabana." After playing "Dances with Wolves," the new Flashes pulled out their umbrellas as props for "Singing in the Rain." The finale to "Stars and Stripes Forever" involved the entire cast.

In the November presidential election, Democrats William (Bill) Clinton, and Albert (Al) Gore were elected President and Vice President of the United States, respectively. Changes were underway once more as preparations for the January 1993 inauguration were made in Washington, D.C., for Bill and his First Lady, Hillary, to claim the White House. The Hollywood "elite" looked forward to participating in the festivities. In other news, American scientists, Jerry Hall and Robert Stillman cloned (for the first time) two human embryos with identical genetic blueprints. The world was shocked.

Flaming Flashes for 1992-93 included:

Colonel .... Jennifer Acuña
Majors .... Dedra Cathey, Allison Doughty
　　　　　　　　　　　　　　　　　Amanda Loehr, Courtney Mayner
　　　　　　　　　　　　　　　　　Lisa Pugh, Alison Weis
Manager .... LaCondra Goyens

Corps Members

Susana Aquirre	Anita Farris	Stacy Lewis	Carrie Salamon
Angie Bagwell	Jamie Frazier	Carmen Peña	Molly Schwartz
Kim Brooks	Dondi Gibson	Tracy Pettingale	Veronica Stephens
Chrissy Brown	Joanna Jaco	Julie Pitts	Mindi Warren
Tobi Carr	Emily Johnson	Alicia Pryce	Amber Watkins
Cyndi Coker	Patty Johnson	Corrie Ray	Tara Wright
Tameka Davis	Jeanny Kane	Katrina Rogers	

Mr. Larry Miears continued as Band Director with the addition of new Assistant Director, Steve Weger. Drum Majors for 1992-93 were Zara Courns, Emily George, and Brian Miears. Band Council Members included: M. Williams, L. Courns, B. Speer, C. Beaver, L. Smith, A. Gillham, E. George, J. Eargle, B. Miears, and A. Williams.

"Yesterday Once More" opened on May 21-22, 1993, with "The Star Spangled Banner," followed by "Rag" from "First Suite" by the Flashes. The Flag Corps continued with Mambo Jambo" followed by "Stardust" danced by the Junior Flashes. The Jazz Band played "Groovin' Hard" which led to "Popeye, the Sailor Man" by the current and new Flash Officers. The traditional program format led to presentation of new members prior to intermission.

A rip-roaring "Can Can" by the Flashes opened the second half and the Flag Corps completed a "Tribute to Glenn Miller." Senior Flashes danced to the "Charleston" before the band's rendition of "Raiders of the Lost Ark." Flash Officers rocked the house with "Jailhouse Rock" and the new Flashes followed with a routine to "Zip-A-Dee-Do-Dah." The finale made the crowd go wild as the Flashes led with "Peruna" followed by the rest of the cast.

1993-94 the most spectacular trial in criminal history against O. J. Simpson, pro football star, who was accused of killing his wife was televised for the entire world to watch.

South African activist Nelson Mandela was elected President in its first democratic election. The world celebrated the support of human rights.

These 1993-94 Flashes were ready for football season:

        Colonel .... Jamie Frazier
        Majors .... Angie Bagwell, Cyndi Coker
                                                  Emily Johnson, Tracy, Pettingell
                                                  Katrina Rogers,, Veronica Stephens.
        Managers .... LaCondra Goyens, Deanna Moore.

Members

VeronicaAnderson	Kathy Diviney	Tiffany Huey	Shelly Skelton
Roxy Baker	Sherry Dollison	Patrice Johnson	A'Lesha Smith
Kim Brooks	Anita Farris	Landra Joseph	Pam Smith
Charmaine Byres	Antria Goyens	Jeanny Kane	Willette Stiggers
April Campbell	Jennifer Green	Lisa Montgomery	Farika Watson
Tobi Carr	Rhonda Griggs	Shanda Perkins	Chandra Wright
Cassie Cook	Tammy Hammond	Dierdra Pryce	Tara Wright
Tameka Davis	Danielle Hartley	Shannon Reyes	
Holly Deas	Dacia Hicks	Stacie Ricther	

"Salute To America" opened on May 13-14, 1994, with "The Star Spangled Banner" followed by a precision dance/drill/high kick routine to "Stars and Stripes Forever." The Color Guard (Flag Corps) got the crowd "In The Mood," and the Senior Flashes wowed them with "Anchors Aweigh." "'Round Midnight" by the Jazz Band led to the current and new Flash Officers' dance to "Engine #9." Two numbers by the Jazz Band led to the presentation of new members prior to intermission.

"American Salute" opened the second half as the Flashes' military routine had everyone clapping. The Color Guard continued with music from *Star Trek* followed by the Junior Flashes' display of precision marching skills to "Air Force Theme." A moving rendition of "God of our Fathers" by the band led to an upbeat routine by the Flash Officers to "Boogie Woogie Bugle Boy," followed by the new Flashes' raising the roof with "Yankee Doodle Boy." "America the Beautiful" flowed into an "Armed Forces Medley" with the entire cast and special guests (honored veterans) for the finale.

In world news, the "space race" continued with Valery Polyakov, Russian cosmonaut, setting a world record... 438 days in space. Seven American

Tyisha Fletcher (Nelson)

astronauts, on the space shuttle Endeavor, stayed in flight for seventeen days. Citizens were horrified when a federal building in Oklahoma City was bombed...killing almost 200 persons. The Ebola virus in Africa spread across the Equator. The populace looked to the world of entertainment for some relief.

Many Texans welcomed the football season as an "escape mechanism" from world and local issues that surrounded them.

Miss Butler and Mr. Miears were ready to provide that relief via halftime performances by the GHS Band and Flaming Flashes.

Members of the award-winning Flaming Flashes were:

Colonel	Danielle Hartley
Majors	Veronica Anderson, Tammy Hammond, Tammy Hammond, Stacie Rischer, Shelly Skelton, Chanda Wright
Manager	Courtney Carter

Members of the Flash Corps

Elizabeth Acuña	Tyisha Fletcher	Kristy Lee	Willete Stiggers
Roxy Baker	Ashley Hamilton	Kara Lorance	Marcie Stevenson
Candie Beaver	Monica Hite	Rashanda Mata	Whitney Thomason
Brandi Brown	Tiffany Huey	Stephanie Money	Dana Walker
Kristy Cotton	Jennifer Jones	Deirdre Price	Lacey Waters
Kathy Diviney	Patrice Johnson	Jane Ray	Farika Watson
Sherry Dollison	Tia Johnson	Shannon Reyes	Timilya Wilkerson
Saniqua Drennon	Emily Jordan	Misti Rogers	
Nichole Ehn	Jennifer Kent	A'Lesha Smith	
Jenny Ellis	Deane Lee	Pam Smith	

The Lion Pride Band had a fascinating year with the addition of Jill Dougherty, feature twirler. The Pride's theme of "Hook" had the Color Guard as the "Lost Boys," and the drummers as "Pirates." Head Drum Major Melissa (Missy) Welch (Peter Pan), Junior Drum Major Megan Cude (Wendy), and Senior Drum Major Tommy Poulter (Hook), dubbed their feature twirler (Jill Dougherty) "Tinkerbell," as she led them on a merry chase across the field.

"Around the World in Eighty Minutes" opened on May 12-13, 1995, with "The Star Spangled Banner," followed by the Flashes' routine to "Dallas." Their "travels" followed the traditional floorshow program that included music from Africa, Hawaii, Tunis, France, Mexico, the Caribbean, South America, Ireland, Israel, and New Orleans. "Semper Fideles," by the entire cast, closed the show.

Shelly Skelton (DeLay) shared these memories:

I loved my years with the Flaming Flashes. I gained many friends and lots of confidence. I remember the excitement of making the squad, hard work during practices, the great feeling of accomplishment after our performances, and the pride I had as a Flaming Flash. Some special memories are:

making up my own dance routines for tryouts; the amazing support and encouragement that my family gave me; the dinner with Ms. Butler at the Reunion Tower in Dallas; and, the many, many fun locker room conversations with amazing friends! I enjoyed my high school years, and my time with the Flaming Flashes just made it that much better. Thank you, Ms. Butler and all the Flashes... past, present, and forevermore!

Politics dominated the 1995-96 school year with Democratic candidate Bill Clinton and Republican Bob Dole expressing their views and making public appearances. The media blitz covered everything from Bill Clinton's assertion that he had tried marijuana, but did not inhale, to expressing concerns regarding Dole's age and health issues. The November 1996 election saw Bill Clinton as the winner by a slim margin of fifty percent of the votes cast. Across the "pond," Princess Diana agreed to divorce Prince Charles after three years of separation. Camelot was crumbling. News from Hollywood revealed that Mel Gibson's *Braveheart* won the Academy Award for "Best Picture." Susan Sarandon was named "Best Actress" for her leading role in *Dead Man Walking,* and Nicolas Cage won "Best Actor" for his leading role in *Leaving Las Vegas.*

1995-96 was an eventful year for the Flashes. Members were:

Colonel	Jana Ray
Majors	Elizabeth Acuña, Carole Beaver, Kristy Cotton, Emily Jordan, Stephanie Money, Dana Walker
Managers	Courtney Carter (Head), Emily Thompson, Calicia Heath, Rachell Johnson

Members of the Flash Corps

Brooks Avery	'Saniqua Drennon	Jennifer Kirkham	Amber Richardson
Heather Ayers	Tyisha Fletcher	Dawana Lee	Crystal Romero
Alissa Benton	Lolita Futrell	Deana Lee	Natalie Salamon
Megan Bouknight	Sara Gilley	Lindsey Linkenauger	Desiree Scott
Jennifer Carwile	Andrea Gilmore	Kara Lorance	Mandy Stewart
Kelly Clark	Haley Griffith	Shauna Lynch	T'misha Traylor
Candice Cooper	Ashley Hamilton	Kim Lyner	Mandy Voss
Chamiera Davis	Amber Harris	Patti Meisenheimer	Lacey Waters
Chamyra Davis	Monica Hite	Lacey Morgan	Lachalonda Williams
Tonisha Denmark	Sakarra Hubbard	Mandy Murphy	Melissa Whitlock
Losheda Dillard	Brandi Jackson	Amberly Portwood	
Cheryl Diviney	Lizzy Kilmer	Christy Price	

The Lion Pride Band had about 120 dedicated members. Head Drum Major Jason Miears was assisted by Mary York and Steven Green, juniors. Feature twirler was Brooke Martin. Steve Payne was named to the All-State Band. Band Council members were Jason Miears, Jeremy Drake, Jeremy Wofford, Ann Cloutier, Melanie Eargle, Mary York, and

Steven Green. Captain Melissa Burke and Lieutenant Rachel Miears led the Color Guard. Choreography was by Mika Norlin.

"Super Heroes" opened on May 10-11, 1996, with "The Star Spangled Banner" followed by the Flashes dancing to "Hound Dog." Other "super hero" music presented in the traditional floorshow format included "Robin Hood," "Pink Panther," Peter Gunn," "Batdance," "McCavity," "Raiders of the Lost Ark," "I Love Lucy," "Let's Go to the Movies," "Apollo 13," and "Magnificent 7." The finale included a medley of marches by John Phillip Sousa and included the entire cast.

During Fall 1996, the Rock and Roll Hall of Fame, designed by I. M. Pei, American architect, opened in Cleveland, Ohio. Music of that era filled the airwaves as the nation moved forward to the extravagant inauguration of Bill Clinton as President of the United States.

Tragedy flooded the news with the accidental deaths of folksinger, John Denver, and Princess Diana. Questions regarding those accidents kept the populace glued to their television screens and scanning written media reports. In the music world, the Rolling Stones released their twenty-first studio album "Bridges to Babylon." Many Americans were dismayed when Woolworth closed all its stores.

Miss Butler added a touch of "sparkle" to the Flashes costumes with the addition of red, white, and blue sequined vests as a uniform change to the fringed "V" overlays. New Principal Scott Potter was impressed by the new "touch" and the legendary tradition of Flashes.

The Flaming Flashes for 1996-97 included:

Colonel	Jennifer Carwile
Majors	Heather Ayers, Tonisha Denmark, Sara Gilley, Andrea Gilmore, Haley Griffith, Amber Harris, Lindsey Linkenauger, Patti Meisenheimer
Managers	Calicia Heath, Rachel Johnson, Sheane Stephenson, Laquita Washington

Members of the Corps

Tiffany Ashford	Roshun Daniels	Sakarra Hubbard	Christy Price
Stacie Atkinson	Chamiera Davis	Andrea Hughes	Amber Richardson
Alissa Benton	Chamyra Davis	Brandi Jackson	Tabitha Russell
Megan Bouknight	Paige Davis	Kizma Kelly	Natalie Salamon
Sarah Briggs	Tricia Dickeson	Kim Lynch	Erica Stevenson
Claudia Caro	Cheryl Diviney	Rachel McNellis	Mandy Stewart
Carolina Castillo	Connie Dobson	Britt Melendez	Tanisha Thrash
Courtney Cathey	Angela Driggers	Brooke Melendez	Shelly Vaughn
Sarah Cathey	Candice Echols	Tameca Mitchell	Carmen Walding
Kelly Clark	Lolita Futrell	Whitney Neese	Melissa Whitlock
Jackie Colbert	Amberly Garcia	Mandy Newsome	Lashonta Williams
Latrecia Cole	Holly Hamilton	Heather Palmore	Takeeva Wright

Director Larry Miears and Assistant Director Stephen Weger welcomed Mr. Rene Lera as the second Assistant Director for the Lion Pride Band. Head Drum Major Mary York was assisted by Drum Majors Stephen Green and Scott Mitchell.

"People's Choice," the 60th production of the Annual Band and Flash Floorshow, opened with the National Anthem on May 10-11, 1997, followed by the Flashes' opening routine to "New York, New York," a crowd favorite. The traditional floorshow program contained favorites from past floorshows to the delight of the crowd. A special by the drum line brought the crowd to its feet. They remained standing for the finale to "Stars and Stripes Forever," the all-time favorite of at least fifteen past floorshows.

During Fall 1997 after twenty years from its release, *Star Wars* was back on theater screens. James Cameron's feature film, *Titanic,* also grabbed the attention of theatergoers. In news closer to home, Dr. Herman Smith was named Superintendent of Schools for Greenville ISD and a full football schedule was planned.

The Flaming Flashes approached the 1997-98 year with renewed dedication and pride in being a part of Flash Tradition. Members included:

Colonel	Holly Hamilton
Majors	Stacie Atkinson, Roshun Daniels, Paige Davis, Mandy Newsome, Shelly Vaughn
Managers	Stephanie Gilstrap, Katrina Miller, Sheane Stephenson, LaQuita Washington

Members of the 1997-98 Flash Corps

Karen Anderson	Candice Echols	Rachell McNellis	Jasmine Stiggers
Ladonna Brown	Amber Evans	Brooke Melendez	Heather Tresemer
Latesha Barrett	Nicole Evans	Melandie Mitchell	Carmen Walding
Latrecia Cole	Y'licia Jackson	Andrea Newsome	Joelle Whitney
Tricia Dickeson	Krystal Johnson	Misty Porter	Elaine Williams
Connie Dobson	Kelli Killough	Amber Reagan	
Bridgette Dukes	Sarah Lewis	Erica Stevenson	

The GHS Band, led by Director Larry Miears, had a busy year since the GHS Lions went into play-off season, which meant more performances by the Lion Pride Band led by Head Drum Major Scott Mitchell, assisted by Drum Majors Kimbell Kornu and Julia Andrews. Their hard work and dedication led more members to Four States Honor Band for competitions.

Local and state headlines announced the death of Gussie Nell Davis, at age 87. Founder and originator of The Flaming Flashes and the Kilgore Rangerettes, Miss Davis will live in our hearts forever. Her energetic spirit, innovative ideas, and love for dancing shall never be forgotten. These qualities continue as part of Flash tradition.

"Director's Choice" opened on May 13-14, 1998, with the National Anthem and followed by the "Mexican Hat Dance" performed by the Flashes. Band Director Larry Miears picked his favorites from past floorshow productions. He was leaving, so this show was his final one at GHS and was dedicated to Theda Wright.

During the 1998-99 school year, President Bill Clinton justified the deployment of

415 cruise missiles against Iraq based on "US national interests." Months later, Clinton was faced with allegations of an affair with White House intern, Monica Lewinsky. Special Prosecutor Kenneth Starr, appointed to investigate, wrote a 450-page report that was also published on the Internet. The U.S. House of Representatives began impeachment proceedings…the second time in U.S. history. Clinton was acquitted of the charges of perjury and obstruction of justice by the US Senate.

Miss Butler and The Flaming Flashes marched forward to prepare for the 1998-99 year. Members were:

Colonel	Melandie Mitchell
Majors	LaTesha Barret, LaDonna Brown, Sarah Lewis, Andrea Newsome, Amber Reagan, Jasmine Stiggers, Joelle Whitney
Managers	Tonya Hunt, Monique Lewis, Melissa Mack, Kim Walker

Members of the Flash Corps

Jennifer Bakkum	Amber Dukes	Eugenia Hollingsworh	Guanita Phelps
Brooke Burns	Amber Evans	Y'Licia Jackson	Misty Porter
Noél Chance	Lisa Evans	Krystal Johnson	Angela Richardson
Jennifer Cook	Jaci Ferrell	Amber Kellogg	Ameeka Steveson
Monté Dean	Ashley Fletcher	Maisie Lowe	Tamara Traylor
Naomi Decker	Stephanie Gilstrap	Jing Luan	Dana Tresemer
Kaci Denman	Martha Grimes	Michelle Mahan	Lindsey Turk
Amanda Drake	Sissy Hawkins	Amberly Miller	

Flaming Flashes, 1999-2000

The GHS Lion Pride Band began the 1998-99 year with two new directors...Head Band Director Tony Kullmer and Assistant Band Director Aubrey Williams. Head Drum Major Julia Andrews assisted by Drum Majors Erin Davis and Celia Weddle, led the band.

"70 Years of Dance and Music" opened on May 7-8, 1999, with the National Anthem followed by the Flashes' routine to "Gloria." The various dance numbers and music reflected the period of time since the Band and Flashes were created as complementary groups as the traditional floorshow program was presented.

The entertainment world made headlines in Spring 1999 when *Shakespeare in Love* earned eleven Oscars with Gwyneth Paltrow winning the Oscar for "Best Actress." Stephen Spielberg received "Best Director" for *Saving Private Ryan*. Stuntman Robbie Knievel jumped an almost 230-foot gorge in the Grand Canyon. Rumors were rampant about "impending doom" in this millennial year with 2000 just around the corner. "Life" magazine ceased publication after 64 years. In November, Hillary Clinton was elected to the US Senate...a "first" for a former First Lady.

Flaming Flashes for 1999-2000 included:

Colonel	Brooke Burns
Majors	Monté Dean, Kaci Denman, Jaci Ferrell, Ashley Fletcher, Maisie Lowe, Michelle Mahan, Lindsea Turk
Managers	Stacie Garcia, Tonya Hunt, Hope Lewis, Monique Lewis, Melissa Mack, Kim Walker

Members of the 1999-2000 Flash Corps

Olivia Angel	Denise Gilstrap	Amanda Mitchell	Tami Stevenson
Megan Berry	LaKesha Hendricks	Lauren Owens	Ameeka Stevenson
Kadrine Blakley	Nichola Hickman	Christy Palmore	Kendra Stogner
Jennifer Brooks	Jessica Hightower	Angelic Parker	Katherine Terrell
Jennifer Dean	Jennifer Hobbs	Guanita Phelps	Dana Tresemer
Naomi Decker	Holli Houser	Shaquinta Pitts	Tamara Traylor
Rebekah Dyson	Amber Kellogg	Emily Rackley	Shannon Turner
Amanda Eubanks	Jing Luan	Kat Rawlings	Tameeka Vation
Tia Fields	Abby Marshall	Angela Richardson	LaTisha Williams
Taylor Gafford	Amberly Miller	Jana Sandlin	Leslie Witkofsky

New Band Director Tony Kullmer and Assistant Director Aubrey Williams depended on Head Drum Major Jerry Powell and Drum Major David Gregg to be their "student advisors" during the year. Miss Butler provided assistance and guidance regarding band and Flash traditions to be valued and continued.

"And the Beat Goes On" opened May 12-13, 2000, with the traditional playing of the National Anthem, followed by an opening number by the Flashes to "Boot Scootin' Boogie."

Texas Stadium, 2000: Maj. Nichola Hickman, Erin Richards, Lori Butler, Col. Emily Rackley, and Jacey Johnson.

A "first" this year was the introduction of the Eighth Grade Band as part of the show, under the direction of Mr. Rene Lera, former assistant at GHS. Another "first" was having the band for the coming year, 2000-2001, to play the number for the Senior Flashes' routine to "Hey, Look Me Over," and the new Flashes, who danced to "Tequila!" Presentation of new members, prior to intermission, included members of the Eighth Grade Band.

Amber Kellogg shared these thoughts.
> *I was honored to join the sisterhood of The Flaming Flashes in the spring of 1998. I remember the first time I saw the Flashes perform. I was nine years old and knew I NEEDED to be a part of this group. I made the best friends as a Flash and learned how to be a proper young lady with the help of Lori Butler. My senior year was "the year of the funky colored pom poms." I think they were orange and green!*

In 2000-2001, the "space race" became a joint venture when the US space shuttle, Endeavor, delivered solar arrays to the International Space Station (ISS). Later, a crew of four U.S. astronauts, launched by a Soyuz rocket, arrived at the ISS and settled in for the first long-term presence of humans in space. George W. Bush was elected President with Richard (Dick) Cheney as Vice-President and Colin Powell as Secretary of State. The "dot-com" age began.

Ready for the 2000-2001 season, the Flashes were:

Colonel .... Emily Rackley
Majors .... Lindsay Hamilton, Nichola Hickman,
 Jennifer Hobbs, Holli Houser,
 Christy Palmore, Kathleen Rawlings,
 Shannon Turner
Managers .... Monique Lewis (Head), Stacie Garcia,
 Ali Martin

Members of the Flash Corps

Sonya Amratial	Chelsea Clack	Audrey Key	Jana Sandlin
Olivia Angel	Brittany Clark	Abby Marshall	Melissa Santana
Vashoney Bailey	Adrienne Cowell	Tiffany Mason	Sheena Smith
Megan Berry	Jennifer Dean	Jessica McNellis	Carley Spradling
Kadrine Blakley	Myia Dukes	Sarah Meeks	Katherine Terrell
Jennifer Brooks	Rebekah Dyson	Chasity Miles	Tameeka Vaton
Dametrice Brown	Taylor Gafford	Caryn Minneweather	Jessica Wallace
Cindy Burks	Nicole Goswick	Katie Moore	Jamie White
Rasha Camacho	Carley Griffith	Jocelyn Morris	Jennifer Williams
Kalina Camblin	LaKesha Hendricks	Samantha Philyaw	Latisha Williams
Charity Cross	Jessica Hightower	Shaquinta Pitts	Shaniqua Williams
Nicole Cruise	Nicole Kennedy	Arquetta Robinson	

(Band information not available.)

Flaming Flashes, 2000

"Feel the Music" opened May 11-12, 2001, with the playing of the National Anthem, followed by the Flashes dancing to "Ready to Run." The tradition floorshow program included some of these songs: "Rock Around Tonight," "Get Down Tonight," "Great Balls of Fire," "One More Time," "Frankie and Johnny," "Hey, Look Me Over," "American Woman," "Johnny Be Good," "Rubber Duckie," "The Blues Brothers" (medley), "Boogie Woogie Bugle Boy," "76 Trombones," "The Lion Sleeps Tonight," and closed with the finale to "On Wisconsin."

The worst terror attack in the history of the United States came on September 11, 2001. What should have been the beginning of a wonderful school year for GHS students turned into a time of chaos. The world watched with horror as two hijacked planes struck each of the twin towers of The World Trade Center in New York City, killing over 3,000 people, and, later, another hijacked plane hit the Pentagon and claimed 289 lives. The horror continued as a fourth hijacked plane smashed into a field near Philadelphia with 45 more lives lost. Terrorist leader Osama bin Laden was considered the "mastermind" behind these attacks. A series of anthrax attacks spread fear in America and shut down Congressional operations. Our world changed drastically. Air travel restrictions and security at airports were defined. The Department of Homeland Security was born. The use of the Internet grew with the launching of *Wikipedia*.

No matter what, the Flashes learned that the school year, learning, and the football season must continue...there are laws to be kept and traditions to uphold. Flashes for 2001-2002 were:

Colonel	Katie Moore
Majors	Carley Griffith, Sarah Meeks, Jocelyn Morris, Samantha Philyaw, Arquetta Robinson, Melissa Santana, Carley Spradling
Managers	Elise Corley, Shamiya Hubbard, Jill Morris, Shelby Sidwell, Amber Wade.

Members of the Corps

Claudia Alverado	Nicole Cruise	Haley Houser	Brittany Peters
Vashoney Bailey	Rachel Curling	April Howard	Emily Reynolds
April Boyd	Amanda Dyson	Sheniqua Jackson	Josie Simon
Shekia Brown	Candice Giddens	Audrey Key	Sheena Smith
Jessica Buckley	Kim Gilkinson	Cari King	Deyanira Vega
Tasha Camacho	Maggie Gray	Kim Kongamnach	Jessica Wallace
Calina Camblin	Natalie Gray	Julie Lake	Lakiya Washington
Gloria Caro	Shana Hardaway	Tiffany Mason	Jennifer Williams
Adrienne Cowell	Chakira Hite	Chasity Miles	Shaniqua Williams
Charity Cross	Sharita Hoskins	Julie Moore	Kathryn Wisdom

The Flashes were delighted to have Mrs. Deborah Anderson Hoskins named as Assistant Flash Director. No stranger to The Flaming Flashes, she served as a Flash parent working behind the scenes to make things happen. A 16-year employee of GISD, Mrs. Hoskins was an asset to help mold them into women of the future.

Col. Haley Houser

Other changes included the replacement of Superintendent Dr. Herman Smith with new Superintendent, Mr. William Smith, a former elementary principal at GISD and counselor at GHS. The community welcomed William Smith, the first Black superintendent for GISD, who was later selected as Greenville's "Worthy Citizen."

Rick Lynch was named as GHS Principal.

The GHS Lion Pride Band and The Flaming Flashes went beyond expectations for 2001-2002. Working together to raise funds after being invited to perform at Disney World, they performed at Epcot and marched in the "Dreams Can Come True Parade" at Magic Kingdom during Spring Break. Work began immediately upon their return to finalize plans and practice for the annual floorshow!

"Dance to the Music" on May 11-12, 2002, opened with the National Anthem followed by "Achy Breaky Heart" by the Flashes. The traditional format for the program included: "Battle Hymn of the Republic," "I Want Candy," "George of the Jungle," "I Feel Good," and "Hey, Look Me Over," by the Senior Flashes prior to the annual presentation of new members.

The second portion of the show continued with "Dance to the Music," "Jail House Rock," "Disney Medley," "Play That Funky Music," "YMCA," by the new Flashes, and "Armed Forces on Parade" as the finale involving the entire cast.

In 2002-2003, home computers, laptop or otherwise, the Internet, cell phones, electronic games, and electronic devices were "fixtures" in American homes. The world of information was growing rapidly. We used "Google" to get the "lowdown" on just about any topic. People who were not "connected" were considered "dinosaurs." "My Space" took up more space on the web. We had live reports and "instant replays" of events around the world. Not all of this was good. In the northeastern states and southern Canada, the biggest power blackout in North America's history (over 50 million people without power for over 48 hours) was blamed on computer error and incompetent technicians. "Garbage in...garbage out."

The 2002-2003 Flaming Flashes had the power to keep the flames going as they moved into a busy school year. Members were:

Colonel	Haley Houser
Majors	Amanda Dyson, Maggie Gray, Carol King Julie Moore, Kim Kongamnach, Julie Moore, Brittany Peters, Emily Reynolds
Managers	Amber Wade (Head), Elise Corley, Rebecca Landers, Kim Martin, Jill Morris

Members of the Flash Corps

Callie Angel	Katie Davidson	Elsa Hernandez	Mary Beth Terrell
Rachel Bellotte	Tamesha Davis	La' Dorisha Johnson	Amber Turner
Shekia Brown	Dominique Denmark	Monica Kirk	Naomi Wade
Justina Brigham	Sarah Elliot	Julie Lake	Falon White
Gloria Caro	Emma Giles	Linzy McManus	Billye Williams
Kacie Chambers	Andrea Gray	Shelly McMullen	Laura Williams
Sonya Childs	Natalie Gray	Stephanie Reisor	Kathryn Wisdom
Lara Chitwood	Jeannie Harrison	Felicia Roach	Misty Wood
Rachel Curling	Taryn Heckadon	Lydia Shook	

Band Director Tony Kullmer welcomed David Baggett as new Assistant Band Director. Senior Drum Majors Phillip Harrison, Kris Porter and Kristen Slaes (Head) were assisted by Sophomore Drum Majors Stephanie Roberts and Darryl Montgomery. Color Guard Captain Bonnie Cook and Lieutenant Lisa Berger led members Jennifer Ruthhart, Heather Watkins, Mariah Brand, Shalane Keller, Angela Coleman, and Kathleen Griffiths.

"What Dreams Are Made Of" opened on May 9-10, 2003, with the National Anthem, played by the band and sung by Mary Beth Terrell (Flash). The Flashes' opening number, "All My Rowdy Friends Are Coming Over Tonight," had the crowd clapping to the beat of the music. The traditional floorshow program, highlighted by an amazing drum solo by Richard Kearns, was enjoyed by the audience, as they looked forward to "Hey Look Me Over" by the Senior Flashes signaling the annual presentation of new members. The second half included patriotic music such as "We Are An American Band," by the Flashes, "You're A Grand Old Flag," by the band, and for the finale, "America the Beautiful."

2003-2004 saw US combat forces and their allies conduct an all-out military campaign against Iraq declaring war on terrorism. George W. Bush and Britain's Prime Minister Tony

Mary Beth Terrell, Jacey Johnson, Laura Williams

Flaming Flashes, 2003

Blair stood firmly behind the invasion. Dictator Saddam Hussein fled and was later captured. Border security was increased as the United States attempted to prevent additional acts of terrorism. The skies in Northeast Texas displayed a trail of smoke as the space shuttle Columbia exploded…killing all astronauts aboard. The trail of debris told the sad story of this disaster. As causes were investigated, the world mourned another loss…that of popular comedian, Bob Hope. We can only say, "Thanks, for the Memories."

Another football season rolled around for the 2003-2004 Flaming Flashes. Members were:

Colonel .... Mary Beth Terrell
Majors .... Lara Chitwood, Andrea Gray, Jeannie Harrison, Elsa Hernandez, Monica Kirk, Linzy McManus, Lydia Shook, Laura Williams
Managers .... Kim Martin (Head), LaKendren Jackson, Artie Jennings, Somalia Timmons

Members of the Flash Corps

Callie Angel	Victoria Henry	Malia Milton	Sara Salamon
Justina Brigham	Lauren Hollon	Kelly Narramore	Tiffany Sampson
Kacie Chambers	Amber Ishmael	Franeta Phelps	Heather Sherman
Kacie Cummings	LaKasha Jackson	Danielle Redman	Amber Turner
Katie Davidson	Courtney Johnson	Dayna Reeves	Falon White
Tiffany Echols	Brianne Locke	Stephanie Reisor	Billye Williams
Sydney Harmon	Kaele Lowe	Felicia Roach	Misty Wood
Stacy Harp	La'Ronnica McCurdy	Taylor Robertson	
Rachael Helvey	Angela Miller	Jenifer Ruthhart	

"A Night On The Town" opened May 7-8, 2004, with the National Anthem sung by Mary Beth Terrell (Flash). The Flashes' opening routine to "Any Man of Mine," was followed by "The Girl from Ipanema." "Sing, Sing, Sing," danced by current and new Flash Officers, led to "Back to the Future" by the band. Junior Flashes danced to "Roxie," led to "Hey, Look Me Over" by the Senior Flashes and presentation of new members before intermission.

The second half included "Cell Block Tango" by the Flashes and followed the traditional floorshow format…leading to the end of another successful presentation and the beginning of "goodbyes."

Lord of the Rings made headlines in 2004 by winning eleven Oscars. Charlize Theron won Best Actress for *Monster,* and Sean Penn took the Oscar for Best Actor in *Mystic River.* The world mourned the loss of Ray Charles, who gave us some beautiful music, including "Georgia On My Mind." George W. Bush was re-elected President while the Mars "Rover" landed and began its journey. Many people began "friending" each other after the launch of Facebook on the Internet. "YouTube" entered our e-mail world and became a form of entertainment to be shared with others.

The Flashes were tech-savvy and "Driven to Dance." They were supported strongly by new GHS Principal, Karen Jo Barrow.

Colonel	Sydney Harmon
Majors	Kacie Cummings, Tiffany Echols, Lauren Hllen, Kaele Lowe, Kelly Narramore, Sara Salamon
Managers	Somalia Timmons (Head), Naisha Conerly, Brittany Harlin Ruby Morrow, Shannon Smith.

Members of the Corps

Laci Andreola	Amber Ishmael	Elizabeth McKay	Tiffany Sampson
Dasha Benford	LaKadren Jackson	Angela Miller	Heather Sherman
Latayvia Benford	LaKasha Jackson	Malia Milton	Jazzmen Stephenson
Lauren Carter	Courtney Johnson	Ashleigh Morrison	Katy Wall
Ashleigh Clark	Da'vette Jones	Kendra Otis	Andrea Warren
Kassi Craig	Ashley Kenner	Ashley Owens	Chelsea Whitney
Nicole Eller	Christa Kimble	Zynethia Patterson	Dranay Williams
Marisa Gomez	Jill Landrum	Franeta Phelps	Danyelle Wilson
Victoria Henry	Brianne Lock	Dayna Reeves	Jazmine Wilson
Ali Hickman	Angelina Loredo	Diana Rios	
Crystal Hite	LaRonnica McCurdy	Taylor Robertson	

May 6-7, 2005, rolled around quickly for "Showtime," which opened using the traditional floorshow format. The National Anthem, played by the band, was sung by Ashley Kenner and Ashley Morrison. The Flashes continued with "Hey, Good Lookin'" and moved through two band numbers, "A Closer Walk to Thee," featuring a solo by Justin Griggs, and "Ain't No Mountain High Enough," danced by current and new Flash Officers. Two Jazz

Back row: Nicole Eller, Ashley Owens, Deborah Hoskins (Assistant Director), Allie Hickman, Elizabeth McKay. Front row: Lauren Carter, Christa Kimble, Dasha Benford

Band numbers, "Big Swing Face" and "Norwegian Wood" led to "Crazy in Love" performed by the Junior Flashes. "Pirates of the Caribbean," by the Color Guard, led to "Hey, Look Me Over" by the Senior Flashes and the formal presentation of new members of both groups.

The second half sparkled as the Flashes danced to "Diamonds Are A Girl's Best Friend." Two Jazz Band selections, "Mack the Knife," and "Basie Buddy 'B'," moved into "Mustang Sally" danced by the Senior Flashes. The Flash Officers' routine to "Last Dance" brought a tear or two to senior members before the new Flashes changed the tempo by dancing to "Great Balls of Fire!" The finale, "Armed Forces on Parade," by the entire cast, brought another successful floorshow and end of high school days for many.

In 2005-2006, "flash drives" replaced floppy disks in the world of personal computers. "Worms" began to invade online sites and computer viruses were rampant causing "crashes" and invasions of our personal data. 2006 had many "tweeting" as Twitter was launched. The world watched as Hurricane Katrina crashed into the Gulf Coast leaving New Orleans and other areas completely flooded. Evacuations were chaotic as residents attempted to flee the rages of the storm and the ensuing looting. Thousands were left homeless and many lost everything they had…including family.

Changes in Greenville ISD saw the retirement of Superintendent William Smith and the hiring of Lloyd Graham as his replacement. With a new GISD leader at the helm, the GHS Band also had an addition. Kyle Brenner was named Assistant Band Director to move the GHS Band through its paces.

Miss Butler and Mrs. Hoskins made improvements and adapted to changes as The

Flaming Flashes moved into 2005-2006. They encouraged them to "reach for the sky" as they moved toward graduation and productive lives as they furthered their education.

Flaming Flashes for 2005-2006 included:

    Colonel ....Ashley Owens*
    Majors ....Dasha Benford, Lauren Carter,
                 Nicole Eller, Ali Hickman,
                  Ashley Kenner, Christa Kimble,
                  Elizabeth McKay

*Col. Ashley Owens was a member or the National Dance Team and Miss Butler hopes that she will be her replacement some day.
    Managers ....Monique Riley, Emily Goswick.

Members

Jenny Callies	Amglesha Gray	Ashleigh Morrison	Nicole Teeters
Kendra Camblin	Leslie Heavin	Zynethia Patterson	Stacey Walker
Hillary Champion	Danielle Jones	Katie Powell	Andrea Warren
Lauren Clark	Da'Vette Jones	Amanda Rodriguez	Faith Watkins
Jeanetta Colbert	Addie Latham	Brandy Rumph	Dranay Williams
Dee Collier	Esmeralda Maqueda	Sarah Sanders	Lindsey Williams
Alyssa Davis	Rachel McCraw	Lakeisha Smith	Jazmine Wilson
Eve Gish	Sara McMurray	Robin Stroud	Karlee Wright

  Crystal Kellog, Head Drum Major, led the GHS Band forward during 2005-2006. The Band Council and feature twirler concept were continued for the year and worked closely with Director Kullmer and new Assistant Director Kyle Brenner.

  "That '70s' Show" opened on May 12-13, 2006, with the National Anthem played by Band Director Tony Kullmer. "Sweet Home Alabama," opening number by the Flashes, led to the band's salute to the "Genius of Ray Charles." The Flash Officers' routine to "Aquarius" was followed by "Legends of Elton John." The Junior Flashes countered with "Play That Funky Music" to change the tempo before moving to "Hey, Look Me Over," by the Senior Flashes. A special "musical delivery" by Venita Hickman and Director Kullmer led to the traditional presentation of new members.

  The Flashes wowed the crowd as they danced to "Free Ride" and continued through "Land of Make Believe," "Moulin Rouge Opener" (Color Guard), before the Senior Flashes' routine to "We Are Family." The current and new Flash Officers performed to "Hot Stuff" before the finale by the entire cast.

  In 2006-2007, astronomers demoted the planet Pluto to the status of "dwarf" planet. Gwen Stefani, Will Smith, Kelly Clarkson, Kenny Chesney, and Carrie Underwood continued to dominate the music charts with their respective hit songs. President George W. Bush awarded The Medal of Honor to B. B. King for his many contributions to the world of music. A world economic downturn slipped into 2007 as Apple unveiled the iPhone and Amazon released Kindle. Google Street View was also launched. "Texting" became an "issue" for

Sara Sanders, Eve Gish, Jenny Callies

many. Classroom rules were adjusted accordingly. Mr. Don Jefferies was named as GHS Principal.

The 2006-2007 Flaming Flashes were again prepared through regular summer practice. Availability of technology did not reduce the number of hours needed to perfect a routine. They worked until their famous "high kicks" were perfect. The Flashes were ready.

        Colonel .... Eve Gish
        Majors .... Jenny Callies, Kendra Camlin,
                                            Sarah Sanders, Lindsey Williams,
                                            Karlee Wright
        Managers .... Emily Goswick, Kalan Brookins,
                                            Tameka Clayton, Jasmine Tidwell

Members of the Corps

Lauren Clark	Nicole Teeters	Chelsea DeGarso	AnaKaren Ortiz
Alyssa Davis	Stacey Walker	Ashley Hearne	Lacee Patterson
Leslie Heavin	Dee Dee Collier	Anna Hillman	Katy Perkins
Addie Latham	Kristin Chambers	Catlin Hopson	Amanda Poyner
Sara McMurray	Tyffani Cozine	Nikki Lenz	Mrgan Sandlin
Amanda Rodriguez	Kaylee Dawson	Ashley Neal	Janixa Wrigh

Returning Band Director, Bill Goodson, who served as Director of Bands for GISD from 1979 to 1985, filled the slot vacated by Mr. Kullmer's sudden departure during Fall 2006. Charles Michael Brock, former Choir Director at Greenville Junior High, also returned to serve as Mrs. Goodson's assistant director, along with David Bagget, a "new hire" for Greenville ISD. Miss Butler was delighted with his return, as he was the band director during her high school years when she was a member and officer for the Flashes. Mr. Goodson knew all about the traditions of the Band and Flashes, so it was easy to pick up the pieces and move forward to prepare the floorshow. Mr. Goodson knew exactly what to do, and began to work closely with Head Drum Major Ali Phillips, Miss Butler, Mr. Brock, and Mr. Bagget to develop an exciting program for the Annual Band and Flash Floorshow, scheduled for May 11-12, 2007.

"Broadway Nights" opened with the National Anthem sung by Lindsey Williams and flowed into "America the Beautiful" played by the band. "Any Man of Mine" by the Flashes set the mood for the traditional program of musical selections and dance routines. Some included: "Reflections from 'Cats'," (Band); "Roxie," (Flash Officers); "They Both Reached for the Gun," (Junior Flashes); and, "Hey, Look Me Over" by the Senior Flashes. Presentation followed.

"All That Jazz" danced by the Flashes had the crowd clapping and tapping their feet to the beat. Selections from past floorshows completed the remainder of the program.

Another recession reared its ugly head in 2007-2008 sending the economy into a downward spiral. The price of crude oil jumped to a record high…$147.00 per barrel. Escalation of the price of gasoline soon followed. The world waited to see the results of the first Black to make a bid for the White House. Senator Barak Obama set his cap for that post. Nancy Pelosi was elected as the first woman to become Speaker of the United States House of Representatives.

More changes took place at GHS during 2007-2008. Superintendent Lloyd Graham left GISD and Don Jefferies served as GHS Principal and new superintendent. Mr. Kyle Treadwell was hired as the new GHS Band Director, replacing Mr. Goodson, who was these on special assignment.

The Flashes sported new sequined double-breasted waistcoats for the 2007-2008 school year. Members included:

        Colonel .... Morgan Sandlin
        Majors .... Chelsea DeGarso, Ashley Hearne,
                                                  Anna Hillman, Catlin Hopson,
                                                  Lacee Patterson, Katie Perkins
        Managers .... Kaylan Brookins, Tamika Clayuton

Members

"T"Keyah Alex	Christie Carter	Lynsey Finley	Sydni Spradling
Alex Anthony	Amber Casselberry	Amanda Grady	Sarah Tyler
Becca Brannon	Kristen Chambers	Katherine Kym	Janisa Wright
Rene Brogan	Ambrea Dean	Raven McGrew	
Rimeka Brown	Taylor Ehrhart	Brittani Nelms	
Ganequia Brown	Andrea Eller	Anakaren Ortiz	

With an appropriate theme, "The Show Must Go On," opened on May 16-17, 2008, with the National Anthem and a routine by the Flashes to "Little Betty." A medley of songs by the band led to the current and new Flash Officers dancing to "We've Gone So Far, But We've Got So Far To Go." The Lion Pride Color Guard performed to "L—O—V—E," followed by the Junior Flashes dancing to "You Can't Stop the Beat." "Hey, Look Me Over" led to presentation and the traditional "dance-with-your-parent" event following.

A jazz combo moved into "Nicest Kids in Town" performed by the Flashes. The traditional program with selections from the past continued to the finale by the entire cast. Mr. Treadwell was quite impressed with how organized Miss Butler, Mrs. Hoskins, the Flashes, and the GHS Band were and was amazed by the traditional presentation ceremony and the conduct of all concerned.

Hurricane Ike struck the Gulf Coast with a vengeance in September of 2008, killing over 100 persons on the Texas coast and causing more that $31 billion in damage. Barack Obama, Democrat, was elected as the first Black President of the United States in November. In 2009, the Tea Party began a series of protests about some of Obama's proposed programs. Superintendent Don Jefferies continued as GHS Principal in his dual role for 2008-2009.

The GHS Band and Flashes continued their work in preparation for the football season, parades, charitable events, and the forthcoming floorshow at the end of the year. Leaders were:

Colonel	Christie Carter
Majors	Alex Anthony, Becca Brannon, Rene Brogan, Andrea Eller, Lynsey Finley, Taylor Ehrhart.
Manager	Jamie Ishmal
Flash Guard	Spencer Hill.

Members of The Flaming Flashes

Rae Arnold	Rachel Goswick	Angelica Olivarez	Kaitlin Stanford
Olivia Ash	Allie Hansel	Morgan Phillips	Melissa Webb
Rachel Copeland	Jackly Hansel	Leah Priebe	Maryam Williams
Brionna Davis	Jessica Hunt	Amy Ramirez	Brillion Woods
Lakebrial Davis	Katie Kroncke	Chelsea Reisor	
Jessalyn Dyson	Morgan Millard	Amanda Rudd	

"Remember When" opened on May 15-16, 2009, with the National Anthem and followed a traditional format. "Ladies Love Country Boys," the opening routine for the Flashes led to a medley of Glenn Miller songs followed by the Flash Officers' routine to "Aquarius." "Phantom of the Opera" by the Concert Band was followed by "Jailhouse Rock" danced by the Junior Flashes. The traditional routine to "Hey, Look Me Over" by the Senior Flashes led to presentation of new members of the Band and Flashes.

Intermission concluded with the Concert Band playing "Three Russian Cameos" followed by the Flashes' routine to "All That Jazz." The program continued with favorites from past floorshows leading to the finale by the entire cast.

In 2009-2010, a United States probe discovered water on the moon. Mind control and

2009-2010 Officers: (sitting) Col. Katie Kroncke, Maj. Allie Hansel, Maj. Jacklyn Hansel; (knees) Maj. Jesslyn Dyson, Maj. Morgan Millard; (standing) Maj. Morgan Phillips, Maj. Katlyn Standford.

3-D scanning were introduced to the consumer market. The sudden death of pop star/singer Michael Jackson rocked the world. His physician was later accused of providing an overdose of medication…ending his long career. In April, Deepwater Horizon's catastrophe killed some employees and spilled oil across much of the Gulf of Mexico. "Obamacare" promised to provide affordable health care for all citizens in the United States.

Heath Jarvis was named to serve as GHS Principal. A former GHS student, he proudly supported the Band and Flashes.

Miss Butler and Mrs. Hoskins made sure all was in place for the 2009-2010 year. Flaming Flashes were:

Colonel	Katie Kroncke
Majors	Hacklyn Hansell, Morgan Millard, Morgan Phillips, Kaitlyn Stanford
Flash Mascot	Jacey Johnson
Flash Guard	Spencer Hill

Members of the Corps

Rae Arnold	Bre Davis	Jamie Ishmal	Amanda Rudd
Olivia Ash	Brionna Davis	Raven Lucas	Nikki Strube
Stephany Aguirre	Martezzes Davis	Angelicia Olivarez	Chelsie Wilkerson
Elizabeth Attison	Reecina Davis	Leah Priebe	Melissa Webb
Adria Brown	Lexie Dick	Britney Poe	Noemi Ugalde
Enereida Cerda	Emily Elmore	Jessica Rios	
Rachel Copeland	Rachel Goswick	Laura Risley	
Sheila Crowder	Jessica Hunt	Gladus Rodriguez	

Drum Major Aaron Evans led the GHS Lion Pride Band and was assisted by Lisa Malone. Kyle Treadwell, Band Director, made some changes in order to recruit more students into the program.

"Dance Fever" opened May 14-15, 2010, with the tradional playing of the National Anthem. "Cowboy Cananova," a routine by the Flashes, continued through the usual format for past floorshows. Most of the musical selections contained the word "dance" as part of their titles. Two highlights included the Senior Flashes dancing to "Turn the Beat Around," and the new Flashes with their routine to "Car Wash."

During 2010-2011, Middle East uprisings dominated the news. The Israelis and Pakistanis continued fighting as the United Nations tried to intervene, with no success. In April, the largest tornado outbreak in United States' history wreaked havoc across the nation. By May, news exploded across the world about the successful raid that killed Osama bin Laden. Navy seals were credited for this covert operation. On a lighter note, English singer, Adele, delighted audiences with her enchanting voice that soothed jangled nerves.

Lori Butler continued to nurture her "girls" and cajole them into always doing their best. Flashes for 2010-2011 included:

Colonel	Chelsie Wilkerson
Majors	Adria Brown, Raven Lucas, Laura Risley
Banner Carriers	Stefany Aguirre, Lexie Dick
Flash Guard	Cheston Henry

Members of The Flaming Flashes Corps

Sheila Crowder	Marissa Farquhar	Martezees Davis	Nikita Gautam
Recinna Davis	Jennifer Steward	Nikki Strube	Gladys Orduna
Noemi Ugalde	Lizabeth Perez	Evangelina Arana	Kaitlyn Qualls
Bethany Arnold	Morgan Teves	Victoria Asbury	Amanda Valenzuela
Stefany Calderon	Ashley Weyrick	Yazmin Cerda	Aaliyah White
Alison Davis	DeAndrea Wilderson	Lisa Farquhar	

Mr. Treadwell, Director of Bands, worked with Drum Major Keegan Blackshear to present an outstanding array of music for the football season and the Annual Band and Flash Floorshow.

"Made in America" opened on May 13-14, 2011 with the National Anthem and followed the traditional floorshow format. The Flashes danced the first number to "Giddy On Up" to the delight of the crowd. Other numbers new to the show were: "Short Cut Home," (Concert Band); "Sharp Dressed Man," (Current and new Flash Officers); "Party in the USA," (Color Guard); "Surfin' USA," (Sophomore and Junior Flashes); leading to the annual presentation of new members.

The second half opened with two selections by the Jazz Band followed by the Flashes' routine to "Deep in the Heart of Texas." The Flash Officers continued with "Hawaii Rollercoaster Ride" followed by David Aly and the Concert Band performing "Someone to Watch Over Me." The program concluded with the usual finale.

The world seemed to move from one "war" to another with no sign of relief, so the end of war in Iraq was welcome news in 2011, however, fighting and terrorists continued to create casualties for American troops stationed in that country. The nation was ready for some welcome news, and the World Tour by The Beach Boys for their fiftieth anniversary provided some relief.

The football season was also welcomed in Greenville, Texas, as a great way to escape the "daily doom" broadcasted on television. The Band and Flashes were ready to provide outstanding shows. The Flaming Flashes for 2011-2012 included:

Colonel .... Evangelina Arana
Majors .... Victoria Asbury, Amanda Valenzuela, Ashley Weyrick,
Banner Carrier .... DeAndrea Wilkerson
Flash Guard .... Cheston Henry
Flash Manager .... Peri Redd

Members of the Flash Corps

Jocelyn Arana	Allison Heath	Yazmine Cerda	Alaiyah Nelson
Stefany Caledron	Krystal Lopez	Allison Davis	Kaitlin Qualls
Morgan Crabtree	Lizabeth Perez	Lisa Farquhar	Selena Ugalde
Hailey Finley	Delaney Stewart	Elle Grantan	Aaliyah White
Nikita Gautam	Bethany Arnold	Abigail Hooper	

"Celebration" on May 4-5, 2012, followed the traditional floorshow format. Opening with the National Anthem, new numbers to the program included "Fake I.D.," danced by the Flashes, "Dancing in the Streets," by current and new officers, and "I'm Free," by Sophomore and Senior Flashes. Presentation of new memebers included the "Senior Members Dance" with their parents.

Music in the second half included: "Footloose," "Gravity Wave," "Let's Hear it for the Boys," "Undertow," "Holding Out for a Hero," and, "Celebration." The entire cast wished the crowd, "Good Night!" Later, Kyle Treadwell, Band Director, bid the GHS Band "Goodbye" as he left for Rowlett High School.

In October 2012, "Superstorm Sandy" spread destruction across Northeastern United States creating major damage plus loss of lives. In November, President Obama ran for a second term and was elected by popular vote. April 2013, another tragic day for America, shocked the world as bombs exploded during the Boston Marathon killing several and wounding dozens.

Aubrey Williams, Assistant, was hired as GHS Band's new director. Head Drum Major David Aly, assisted by Daniel Rios, Assistant Drum Major, provided support for the following: Drumline Captain, Ricky Steward; Woodwind Captain, John Shasteen; Brass Captain, Ben Fawcett; Color Guard Captain, Victoria Hoskins; and, Band President, Clay Evans, completed the 2012-2013 Band Leadership Team. Loading Crew Chief was Mason Smith.

The Flaming Flashes for 2012-2013 included:

Colonel	Kailin Qualls
Majors	Bethany Arnold, Allison Davis, Lisa Faraquhar, Nikita Gautam, Lindsey Shepherd, DeAndrea Wilkerson
Managers	Peri Redd, Floretta Davis
Junior Flash	Jaci Dawson
Flash Guards	William Strickland, Chase Vance, Timothy Tooker, David Paulin

Members of the Flash Corps

Jocelyn Arana	Shayla Dennis	Allison Heath	Taylor Lowery
Yazmine Cerda	Ashley Hoskins	Aaliyah White	Nallely Palmores
Lizabeth Perez	Hailey Finley	Kacie Vance	Leslie Portillo
Morgan Crabtree	Maddy Prado	Delaney Stewart	Yesenia Rodriguez
Alaiyah Nelson	Emely Ramirez	Hailey Kizer	Lysette Vega
Abigail Hooper	Crystal Rios	Ruby Chuck	Infiniti Williams
Elle Grantham	Destinee Stevenson	Maria Deleon	
Marissa Brown	Brittany Atherton	DaKeyla Edwards	
Shelby Clements	Krystal Lopez	Ekera Hughes	

"Simply Floorshow" opened with the National Anthem followed by selections from *Grease*. The Flashes danced to "Georgia Peach" followed by the Jazz Band's rendition of "Groovin' Hard." Current and New Flash Officers took the floor with their "handy" routine to "Born to Hand Jive." Phillip Malone and the Concert Band performed "The Rose," followed by a special number played by Brian Stromberg and John Shasteen. The Sophomore and Junior Flashes upped the tempo with "Summer Nights," and the band echoed with "Hallelujah!" Senior Flashes then danced to their signature piece, "Hey, Look Me Over," which led to presentation of new members and their dance with their parents.

"Bohemian Rhapsody" opened the second half followed by the Flashes' disco dance to "Grease." After three band numbers, the Senior Flashes danced to "We Go Together," followed by the "Ashokan Farewell" by the Concert Band. Flash Officers continued with "You're the One That I Want," leading to "Gangnam Style" by the Concert Band. The last Flash routine was to "Wabash" and the finale by the entire cast to "Armed Forces on Parade."

Chaos continued in some areas on every continent. The media made sure the public was kept informed of every major disaster. On rare occasions, a glimmer of good news would be extended as a "treat" for watching television or checking the news on the Internet. 2013-2014 saw the first case of the Ebola virus in the United States, resulting in the patient's death, in Dallas, Texas. The virus spread to the patient's caretakers, and quarantines were issued...including one patient's dog!

Undaunted by illness, disease, or disasters, the Flashes were the best they could be and continued their tradition of providing outstanding halftime shows for 2013-2014.

Members of The Flaming Flashes were:

Colonel	Kacie Vance
Majors	Abbie Hooper, Nally Palomores, Emely Ramirez, Anna Satterwhite
Junior Flash	Jacie Dawson
Manager	Amanda Rodgers
Flash Guards	Tim Tooker, Chase Vance, Isaac Ramirez, Levi Foley, William Strickland, David Paulin, Erick Cozine (Jr. Guard)

Members of the 2013-2014 Flaming Flash Corps

Marissa Brown	Hailey Finley	Hailey Kizer	Delaney Steward
Shelby Clemments	Elle Grantham	Taylor Lowery	Lysette Vega
Floretta Davis	Ashley Hoskins	Crystal Rios	Infiniti Williams
Maria Alba	Ekera Hughes	Isamary Luveanos	Mimi Newsong
Cecilia Alba	Dalia Castillo	Lindsey McMurry	Alexis Perez
Stefany Anthony	Alondra Gonzales	Quyn Nash	
Rosa Darana	Lanie Harrington	Jazmine Neal	
Kari Brammer	Kelly Long	Yesenia Rodriguez	

Mr. Joel Weisberg, new GHS Director of Bands for GISD, put his shoulder to the wheel and got the GHS Band rolling in a forward direction. Drum Majors Ben Fawcett and John Shasteen were inspired by his contagious enthusiasm and energy.

Americans celebrated the opening of the new World Trade Center in New York...sending a message to the world...and creating a memorial for lives lost on September 11, 2001. Flash Colonel Kacie Vance was in awe of the tremendous effort taken to honor the fallen when she visited New York City during Spring Break. Facing challenges of her own, she felt energized to put more effort into the coming floorshow scheduled for May 2-3, 2014.

"Movie Night" opened with the National Anthem followed by the Flashes' opening routine to "Friday Night." Following a band selection, the Flashes

Kacie Vance

2013-2014 Flash Officers

danced to "Maniac" leading to "Pablo!" by the band and "Love Potion #9" by the Flashes. "Washington Heights March" by the band brought the traditional Senior Flashes' dance to "Hey, Look Me Over." Presentation of new members followed.

"Live and Let Die" rolled out the second half followed by "In the Mood" by the Flashes. "I've Had the Time of My Life" by the Senior Flashes brought "Captain America" into the program followed by "All That Jazz," a routine by Junior Flashes. Music from "The Incredibles" led to "Singing in the Rain" by Flash Officers and "Hogan's Heroes' March." The Flashes final dance to "Fame" led to the finale by the entire cast.

Most Americans were glad to see the price of crude oil falling in late 2014. Gasoline prices went down accordingly, making consumers happy. When the price of crude oil fell to less than $50 per barrel, concerns arose as to its impact on the economy.

Fall 2014 football season unveiled a series of events celebrating the Silver Anniversary of Flash Director Lori L. Butler. A pre-game presentation drew numerous members of Miss Butler's Flashes from the past twenty-five years to surprise their director and show their appreciation for her years of service. Members of the Flaming Flashes celebrating this 2014-2015 Silver Anniversary included:

              Colonel..Crystal Rios
              Majors...Lanie Herrington, Ashley Hoskins,
                                                                 Ekera Hughes, Taylor Lowery,
                                                                 Yesenia Rodriguez.
              Managers..Sharise Doty, Amanda Rodgers

Members

Cecilia Alba	Marissa Brown	Gabby Hernandez	Alexis Perez
Maria Alba	Maddie Burns	Julie Hollister	Anahi Savedo
Rosa Arana	Dalia Castillo	Raven Holmer	Lysette Vega
Dejah Ashford	Christiana Cuevas	Claire Hooper	Leona Traylor
Karissa Ballard	Florette Davis	Cynthia Hough	Jacey Wade
Dariana Becerra	Kia Denson	Wendy Lopez	Dashundra Wilson
Kari Brammer	Alondra Gonzales	Isamary Luevanos	Zikeyia Murphy

Author's Note: We look forward with great anticipation to the Annual Band and Flash Floorshow on May 2-3, 2015, and the induction of new members to the Band and Flash Hall of Fame. Best wishes to them all and congratulations to Miss Lori L. Butler on her Silver Anniversary as Director of the Award-Winning Flaming Flashes!

Greenville High School Band & Flash Hall of Fame

In Spring 2006, Band Director Tony Kullmer and Flash Director Lori L. Butler decided to initiate plans for a GHS Band and Flash Hall of Fame. Inductees named would have made significant contributions to the GHS Band and Flash program; must have served as Director of either the GHS Band or The Flaming Flashes; must have been away from GHS for at least twenty years; and/or, must have furthered education in either the area of dance or music.

Membership includes:

Year	Inductee(s)
2006	Miss Gussie Nell Davis
2007	Mrs. Julia Herlocker Gibson (Schwartz)
2008	Mr. Hal Wright and Mr. Weber Woodall
2009	Mr. James Coffman
2010	Miss Lori L. Butler
2011	Mr. Bob Cartwright and Mrs. Judy Routh Tarpley
2012	(No selection)
2013	Mr. Santos Garcia
2014	Dr. Mary Jane Vance
2015	Mr. Bill Goodson and Mrs. Mae Merrick Pickens

Flash Guards

A review of almost eighty GHS Yearbooks, *The Lion,* identified 1982 as the first year for Flash Guards to be selected for The Flaming Flashes. It is highly possible that in 1936, Miss Gussie Nell Davis, intended for her first Flash Managers, Leo Hackney and Joe Manning, to act as "guards" for the Flashes; however, this can only be assumed at this point.

Miss Butler, a Flash Officer in 1982, recalled a conversation with Choir Director Joan Graves, who convinced Mrs. Pam Clayton that having dependable male students as "guards" for the Flashes would be beneficial, especially at out-of-town games. Mrs. Clayton finally agreed and named these members of the GHS Choir as the first Flash Guards: Kevin Bost, Wayne Feezor, David Hunsucker, Jerry Weathers, and Tyler Veak.

Between 1982-2006, Flash Guards were not listed in a search of GHS Yearbooks. Miss Butler noted that in 2007, she and Mrs. Hoskins reinstated the "Flash Guards" with the following criteria:

1) A productive interview with Miss Butler;
2) Have and maintain grade average above eighty;
3) Good rapport with the Flashes; and,
4) Interviews with candidate(s) teachers.

Male students chosen as Flash Guards and their tenure were:

2007 – 2009	Spencer Hill
2009 – 2012	Cheston Henry
2012 – 2014	Levi Foley, William Strickland, Tim Tooker, and, Chase Vance
2014 – 2015	David Paulin (Head), Marcus Anderson, Maurico Becerra, Jacob Fort, Raul Osornio, Rene Osornio, DeMarcus Terry

Flash Guard Chase Vance

Four Generations of Flaming Flashes: Amy Tarpley (Wade), Jacey Wade, Judy Routh (Tarpley) holding portrait of Evelyn Moudy (Routh).

A Family Tradition

A prime example of the importance of The Flaming Flashes to families in Greenville, Texas, is the family of Mrs. Judy Routh Tarpley. Her mother, Evelyn Moudy Routh, was a First Generation Flash from 1936 to 1938 under the directorship of the famed Gussie Nell Davis, founder of The Flaming Flashes. Evelyn played the bass drum and shared many stories with her daughter, Judy, about marching to the Greenville High School Band as they played "Peruna" and perfoming during the Annual Band and Flash Floorshow.

Following in her mother's footsteps, Judy Routh (Tarpley), Second Generation Flash, became a member of The Flaming Flashes in 1964. She fell in love with Randy Tarpley when he escorted her onto the gym floor during the Floorshow to waltz to "Fascination." After graduation in 1966, this fascination continued for over 48 years since she became Mrs. Randy Tarpley. In 2011, she was inducted into the Band and Flash Hall of Fame...an honor she cherishes.

Tradition was continued when Judy's daughter, Amy Tarpley (Wade), Third Generation Flash, served in The Flaming Flashes from 1985 to 1988. At the young age of two, Amy became the Flash Mascot, with an identical uniform (made by her grandmother, Margaret Tarpley), when her aunt, Jamie Tarpley (Campbell) was a Flash. As Mascot, Amy presented roses to the new Flash Colonel, Carol Reynolds, during the 1971 Band and Flash Annual Floorshow.

The family tradition continued when Amy's daughter, Jacey Wade, Fourth Generation Flash) joined the Flashes in 2014. Jacey, a current member of The Flaming Flashes, hopes be named as an officer in her senior year. The Tarpley Family is so proud of her.

Other members of the Tarpley Family who served in The Flaming Flashes include: Judy's niece, Martha Grimes (New), 1988-1989; her two sisters-in-law, Jamie Tarpley (Campbell, 1970-1972 Banner Carrier, and Diana Tarpley (Mason), 1958-1960, American Flag Bearer.

* * *

An extensive review of GHS Yearbooks and interviews with former members of The Flaming Flashes gave evidence of multiple families with generations of Flash members. A few are included.

Mary Sue Williams (Alexander) was a Charter Member of The Flaming Flashes under Gussie Nell Davis in 1934. Her daughters, Patricia Alexander (DeVeny) and Sue Ann Alexander (Harting) were Flashes in 1954-56 and 1963-65, respectively. Patricia's daughter, Diane DeVeny, was a Flash in 1977-78. Rosabel Williams (Warren), sister of Mary Sue Williams (1934), was selected by Miss Davis in 1937 as a member, and served as Assistant Drum Major in 1939-1940. Rosabel Williams served as Flash Director from 1944-1946. Her daughter, Wynn Warren, was a member in 1965-66.

Dionne Moore (Wade), whose sister, Yvonne, was a Flash in 1947, joined the Flashes in 1948. She was Junior Majorette in 1948-49 and Head Majorette in 1949-50. Dionne's daughter, Valerie Wade, joined the Flashes in 1973 and was their Colonel during 1974-75.

Berniece Henson (Andrews) was a Charter Member of The Flaming Flashes in 1934, under Director Gussie Nell Davis. Multiple members of the Henson Family have served as Flaming Flashes and include: Patty Andrews; Judy Henson (Banner), 1958-60; Judy's daughter, Anne Banner, 1983-84; Judy's daughter, Ginny Banner, 1987-88 (Major '88-89); Frances Henson (Green), 1959-61; Elizabeth Henson (Green), 1962-64 (American Flag Bearer '63-64); and, Margaret Henson, 1965-67 (Flash Sergeant, '66-67) to name a few.

Dr. and Mrs. James Nicholson were kept very busy from 1969 through 1984 with their four daughters who were members and officers of The Flaming Flashes. Judy Nicholson served from 1970-1972 with her senior year as Lieutenant Colonel; Liz Nicholson was in the Flashes from 1974-1976, and carried the Texas Flag (Major) in 1976; Jennifer Nicholson served during 1977-1979, and wore the "red hat" as Colonel her senior year; and, Rebecca Nicholson was a Flash from 1982-1984, serving as Major her last year.

These listed are a very small part of the many who have honored the family tradition by being a member of The Flaming Flashes. Long live the Flashes and their traditions.

Reflections: Lori L. Butler

Thinking over my years as Director of The Flaming Flashes, I am amazed how my mind draws a complete blank. All those memories and special moments outweigh those that could have been difficult, but turned out well.

In July 1990, the Greenville *Herald Banner* released the news of my selection as the new director of The Flaming Flashes. I never dreamed I would still be their director all these years. I love my job, and not many will admit they do. I agree it is hard to wake up so early each morning, especially now after twenty-five years.

When I call the Flashes "my girls," I am often corrected. The simple fact is that I view each Flash, from 1990 to this date, as MINE. My Flashes all know I am there for them.

With each new group of Flashes, I write their names in my notebook, keep it with me, and read over their names until I have a mental picture of each of their sweet faces. From that point on, I care for them as if they were my own...something I learned at an early age from my parents.

I will always remember my first performance as a Flaming Flash and those "butterflies." They flew away when I became their Flash Director. I carry the responsibility for all the Flashes. Their performances are based upon how well I prepare them, and they have always made me proud.

The opening game in 1990 was a pom-pom routine and the band did not play the drum roll to begin. I was stunned. I closed my eyes, not wanting to watch, but, to my amazement, my girls began the routine and were amazing! One year, at Texas Stadium, I told Mr. Kullmer which song to play for their performance and walked away. As I returned to the stands, the Flashes marched onto the field, the band was set to play, and I realized my mistake. I had named the wrong song! I gasped! Erick Mack saved the day. He waved to Mr. Kullmer. He walked onto the field toward Erick, who explained to Mr. K that the song they were to play was the wrong one. The Flashes always wore capes when they performed to that particular song, and the Flashes were not wearing capes! Thankfully, Mr. K grabbed a drum, moved behind the Flashes, and played the correct beat to keep the Flashes performing. They had to hold a "stunt" in the air for three extra counts of eight due to my error, but they did it.

We prepared and transported oil derricks that were nine feet tall to use as props in a halftime routine when GHS played at Highland Park. Wind speeds that night were about 35 mph and I thought that plan would not work, and we could substitute "Hey, Look Me Over" instead. The Flashes would have none of that. They insisted that the team was playing and passing the ball with those winds, and they could stand on those oil derricks. Fourteen of the fifteen derricks were successfully climbed, with a Flash atop each. The one not completed was on the fifty-yard line, so it appeared to have been planned!

How can I forget "ROADKILL?" Only the Flashes will understand…then there was "HORSESHOES!" I still laugh over this one. Stacey Oliver and several other Flashes, along with some guys, helped us move the props from the school to the football field on Wednesday prior to the game. I was standing on the back of the truck and Stacey decided to crawl inside of the Horseshoe and roll it instead of waiting for someone to help carry it. She began rolling very fast onto the field. Coaches and the football team watched as I screamed. Stacey was ejected from the horseshoe, and I was not sure if she were dead or alive. The silence was broken by Stacey's laughter, and we all laughed.

My favorite memory is being able to share the Flashes with my niece, Jacey Lachelle Johnson. She has been their mascot and wore a Flash uniform from the time she could

Flaming Flash Sister Circle

Jacey Johnson

walk. She was my "shadow" until she became middle school cheerleader in Caddo Mills.

On a serious note, each Flaming Flash wears a golden angel on their hatband. These symbolic angels, given to the Flashes at the beginning of the year, represent Major Emily Johnson, my first Flash to leave for the "Drill Team in Heaven," and other Flashes, who have left Earth are now dancing with the angels. They are in our hearts.

So many great memories surface, as I recall the many people who have touched my life. Thank you, Larry Johnston, for believing in me the summer of 1990. You helped make all my dreams come true, and, perhaps, some day, I will gather them into a book.

As Director of The Flaming Flashes, I have been blessed more than I deserve. I have had the honor of seeing many weddings, births, and shared touching moments with families of Flashes. I have seen them through their losses and their triumphs. I have enjoyed each and every moment of my life as their director...every "Sister Circle"...being surprised for my 25th year...and Floorshow 2010, when I was inducted into the Band and Flash Hall of Fame and one officer from each of the past twenty years came forward to give me a single long-stemmed rose. The Flaming Flashes, the first high school precision dance and drill team in the world...are my life.

Jacey Johnson

walk. She was my "shadow" until she became middle school cheerleader in Caddo Mills.

On a serious note, each Flaming Flash wears a golden angel on their hatband. These symbolic angels, given to the Flashes at the beginning of the year, represent Major Emily Johnson, my first Flash to leave for the "Drill Team in Heaven," and other Flashes, who have left Earth are now dancing with the angels. They are in our hearts.

So many great memories surface, as I recall the many people who have touched my life. Thank you, Larry Johnston, for believing in me the summer of 1990. You helped make all my dreams come true, and, perhaps, some day, I will gather them into a book.

As Director of The Flaming Flashes, I have been blessed more than I deserve. I have had the honor of seeing many weddings, births, and shared touching moments with families of Flashes. I have seen them through their losses and their triumphs. I have enjoyed each and every moment of my life as their director...every "Sister Circle"...being surprised for my 25th year...and Floorshow 2010, when I was inducted into the Band and Flash Hall of Fame and one officer from each of the past twenty years came forward to give me a single long-stemmed rose. The Flaming Flashes, the first high school precision dance and drill team in the world...are my life.

Reflections from Friends and Family

Lori Butler, a very colorful and unique long-term Greenville resident, found her calling when she became Flash Director. As a Flash and Flash Officer, Lori's love for the Flashes came from the minute she became one and is still evident today. Lori cares for each and every Flash and dedicates countless hours to this amazing drill team. GISD is so lucky to have her.

—*Harry Gibson, Friend*

We were almost like sisters in the Flashes. I was a part of the 25th Anniversary celebration for Miss Butler in Fall 2014. Many of us, current and past members of the Flashes, had a wonderful reunion that brought back wonderful memories of our days as Flashes. The best memory was of our wonderful bond…our sisterhood of Flaming Flashes.

—*Heather Tresemer, 1997-98*

I smile every time I think about The Flaming Flashes, not only bcause it was a wonderful experience with my best friends, but because we had you as our leader. You made the experience incredible. I am the woman I am today because of your imipact on my life. You made me a strong, independent, and confident young lady. Your devotion, love, and selflessness has changed me, and I am forever thankful. I am here to say "thank you." Thank you for waking up at five every morning to push us, lead us, and shower us with blessings. Thank you for your devotion. Thank you for the endless amounts of laughter and crazy moments. Thank you for giving up your free time in order to make our years worth while. Thank you for being my second Mom during the years I needed you most. I only hope and pray I will impact as many people as you have! I love you and thank you for your endless support.

—*Allie Hansell,*
Flash Major, 2009-10

In the fall of 1970, my family moved to Greenville. I grew up in Farmersville and can't recall not knowing about The Flaming Flashes and the Kilgore Rangerettes. My parents and my mom's sister and her husband were good friends with Gussie Nell Davis. We always went to the Greenville Christmas Parade to watch The Flaming Flashes. I knew all about the story of how the Flashes began and the importance of female leadership. This led me to try out and become a Farmerette and Drum Major of the Farmersville Band.

A friend of mine told me about the Band and Flash Floorshow and thought my daughters, Lachelle and Lori, would enjoy attending. We have missed only one performance since then. Lachelle became a Flash in 1978 and was Flash Major in 1979-80. Lori followed in 1980 through 1982 and was Flash Major her senior year. She said she wanted to be a Flaming Flash Director throughout her college years, and, as she became a teacher, first with TEAMS math at GHS, then at Royse City. Larry Johnston, GHS Principal, called me and asked if Lori would be interested in being the Flash Director. I answered with an emphatic "Yes!!" She was hired and 25 years later, she is still their director.

—Mrs. Sandra Butler Marak,
Mother of Lori L. Butler

Author's Note: After "investing" over forty years in education and administration, one cherishes the "returns" from former students when they show their appreciation. Students do, indeed, become "ours," as one particular Bible verse declared:

"...I have called you by name, you are mine."
—Isaiah 43:1

Grun, Bernard. 2005. *The Timetables of History: A Horizontal Linkage of People and Events.* New York: Touchstone: Simon & Schuster, Inc.

Ann Faragher. "Flash Backs—Gussie Nell's 'Baby' Grew," *Greenville Herald Banner.* Sunday, 7 March 1971.

"'Peruna Strut' Helps Band and Flashes: Drums, Bugles and New Steps Add to Color of Two Units." *Greenville (Texas) Banner.* Thursday, 13 May 1937.

www.ingramcontent.com/pod-product-compliance
Lightning Source LLC
Chambersburg PA
CBHW080542170426
43195CB00016B/2646